The Courts of Genocide

The Courts of Genocide focuses on the judicial response to the genocide in Rwanda in order to address the search for justice following mass atrocities. The central concern of the book is how the politics of justice can get in the way of its administration. Considering both the ICTR (International Criminal Tribunal for Rwanda), and all of the politics surrounding its work, and the Rwandan approach (the Gacaca courts and the national judiciary) and the politics that surround it, *The Courts of Genocide* addresses the relationship between these three 'courts' which, whilst oriented by similar concerns, stand in stark opposition to each other. In this respect, the book addresses a series of questions, including: What aspects of the Rwandan genocide itself played a role in directing the judicial response that has been adopted? On what basis did the Government of Rwanda decide to address the genocide in a legalistic manner? Around what goals has each judicial response been organized? What are the specific procedures and processes of this response? And, finally, what challenges does its multifaceted character create for those involved in its operation, as well as for Rwandan society? Addressing conceptual issues of restorative and retributive justice, liberal-legalism and cosmopolitan law, *The Courts of Genocide* constitutes a substantially grounded reflection upon the problem of 'doing justice' after genocide.

Nicholas A. Jones is an Assistant Professor in the Department of Justice Studies at the University of Regina.

The Courts of Genocide

Politics and the Rule of Law in Rwanda
and Arusha

160201

Nicholas A. Jones

Routledge
Taylor & Francis Group

a GlassHouse book

First published 2010
by Routledge
2 Park Square, Milton Park, Abingdon, Oxon, OX14 4RN

Simultaneously published in the USA and Canada
by Routledge
270 Madison Avenue, New York, NY 10016

A GlassHouse book

Routledge is an imprint of the Taylor & Francis Group, an informa business

© 2010 Nicholas A. Jones

Typeset in Times New Roman by
Taylor & Francis Books
Printed and bound in Great Britain by
CPI Antony Rowe, Chippenham, Wiltshire

British Library Cataloguing in Publication Data
A catalogue record for this book is available from the British Library

Library of Congress Cataloguing in Publication Data
Jones, Nicholas A., 1968–
    The courts of genocide : politics and the rule of law in Rwanda and
Arusha / Nicholas A. Jones.
        p. cm.
    Includes bibliographical references.
    1. Criminal justice, Administration of–International cooperation. 2.
Political questions and judicial power. 3. International criminal courts. 4.
International Tribunal for Rwanda. 5. Gacaca justice system. 6. Genocide–
Rwanda 7. Criminal courts–Rwanda. 8. Restorative justice–Rwanda. 9.
Rwanda–History–Civil War, 1994–Atrocities. I. Title.
    K5001.J66 2009
    345.67571'0251–dc22

                                                                2009013257

ISBN10: 0-415-49070-7 (hbk)
ISBN10: 0-203-88080-3 (ebk)

ISBN13: 978-0-415-49070-2 (hbk)
ISBN13: 978-0-203-88080-7 (ebk)

This book is dedicated to the victims and survivors of the Rwandan Genocide in 1994 and to everyone, despite the tragedy of the past, working to achieve justice and reconciliation in a country demonstrating strength and determination as its people move forward.

Contents

x   *Contents*

List of tables and figures

Map

Tables

Figures

Acknowledgements

The Courts of Genocide: Politics and the Rule of Law in Rwanda and Arusha could not have been written without the assistance, insights, and contributions of a large number of people. To these people I owe a debt of gratitude and an apology if in my haste I have forgotten to mention you by name. First of all, I would like to thank the personnel in the Rwandan government, judiciary and National Service of Gacaca Jurisdictions who granted me interviews and facilitated a number of other aspects of the research. Specifically, Samuel Rugege, Martin Ngoga, John-Bosco Mutangana, Domitilla Mukantaganzwa, Laurent Nkusi, Edda Mukabagwiza, Charles Kayitana, Damien Mugabo, Christophe Bizimungu, Augustin Nkusi, and Innocent Musafili. Second, individuals in Rwanda working in a variety of other capacities essential for this research must be acknowledged: Fiacre Birsasa, Jean-Charles Paras, Dieter Magsam, Jean-Louis Kaliningondo, Anastase Shyaka, Philibert Kigabo, Immaculée Ingabire, Innocent Bizimana, and members of the Office of the Canadian Embassy including Jaques Lépine, Christian Pouyez, Marie Kagaju, and Tharcisse Urayeneza. Third, the various prosecutors, defence attorneys, and staff at the International Criminal Tribunal for Rwanda. The individuals that assisted with the research at the International Criminal Tribunal are too numerous to mention each individually. However, a few must be recognized for their contributions, Richard Renaud, Drew White, Alex Obote-Odora, Alloys Mutabingwa, Moustapha E. S. Hassouna, and Mame Mandiaye Niang.

I wish to express my gratitude to Dr Colin Perrin at Routledge-Cavendish for supporting the book from the start. Additionally, to Holly Davis for her patience and professionalism in moving the book forward to its completion.

I would also like to express my sincere gratitude to Dr Augustine Brannigan for his tireless efforts in supporting the research and the writing at every stage of the process. His contribution cannot be understated. Additionally, thanks go to Dr Al Patenaude for his valuable insights in the preparation of the manuscript.

My greatest debt of gratitude belongs to my family. The unwavering support and encouragement of my parents throughout my life has been instrumental in all of my work. I regret that my mom will not be able to share this book with me as she passed away before its completion. I would also like to thank my mother-in-law, Shirley McAuliffe, for all her work assisting in transcribing hours of interviews. Finally, I want to express my undying gratitude to my best friend and wife Kelly, and my children (Kael and Chloe). Without their support and understanding this book would not have been completed.

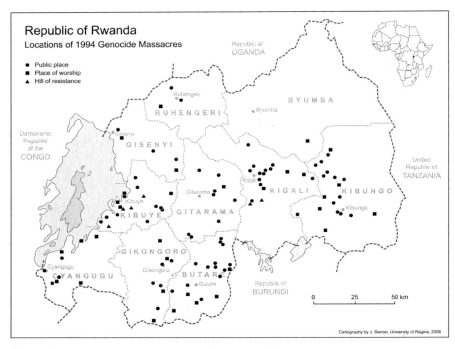

Map Republic of Rwanda: locations of 1994 genocide massacres.

1 The Rwandan genocide and the judicial response

> If you must remember, remember this ...
>   The Nazis did not kill six million Jews ...
>   Nor the Interahamwe kill a million Tutsis,
>   They killed one and then another, and then another ...
>   Genocide is not a single act of murder,
>   It is millions of acts of murder.

(Smith 2004)[1]

Erected at one end of the Kanombe District Office parking lot, the *Gacaca* (pronounced *ga-cha-cha*) court, literally translated as *justice on the grass* in Kinyarwanda, is a collection of crudely constructed benches under the shade of a semi-permanent tarp. A truck arrives in the compound with two men, dressed in neatly pressed pink prisoners' uniforms, sitting on the sides of the open box. The prisoners climb out of the back of the truck while the driver, who is also their armed police escort, gets out of the front. The crowd of approximately 100 people, who have been slowly gathering over the past hour, begin to find seats within the space delineated by the tarp. Once a week, members of the community descend upon *this court* to participate in this resurrected and modernized form of traditional Rwandan dispute-resolution mechanism.

This day, two men who have previously pled guilty to their crimes under the provisions outlined in the Gacaca Organic Law No 40 (2001) (later revised as Organic Law No 16; Government of Rwanda 2004a), will have their cases heard before the *Inyangamugayo* (literally translated as *persons of integrity*) who are community-elected judges in a process open to the entire community. The two accused prisoners take a seat in the front row, under the tarp, sitting beside and amongst other members of the community. Prior to the arrival of the judges, a brief exchange of greetings occurs between the accused and some members of the community. The formal arrival of the eight judges, each adorned with a sash in the blue and yellow colours of the Rwandan flag and inscribed with the word *Inyangamugayo*, take their seats behind a wooden table at the front of the court. In addition to the police escort, a red-uniformed individual representing the local defence force stands guard with an automatic weapon, under the shade of a nearby tree. The president of the court addresses the gathering and proceeds through a variety of formalities that signal the beginning of the court session.

The first defendant's case is called before the court. It is June 2005. The accused, who has been incarcerated since 1994, stands at the front of the court. He is facing a charge of manning a roadblock, while in possession of a firearm, in the district of Kanombe, in rural Kigali, during the 1994 genocide. Although many people were killed at or in the vicinity of this roadblock, no evidence is presented to suggest that he directly participated in any of the killings. However, as part of his confession, the law compels him to provide the court with any information that he has regarding the events that transpired during that time, regardless of whether he was personally involved or not. A judge presents him with the legislated guidelines regarding confessions and their ramifications to ensure that he understands them; he reads his written confession before all in attendance. Witnesses present at the court verify his confession. The Inyangamugayos then make a determination in accordance with the law as to whether the confession is sincere, truthful, and full. All persons in attendance are included in the process, and they are permitted to ask questions of the accused, through the judges, as well as also participate in the discussions that may inform the judges' eventual decision.

Approximately five and half hours after the start of the trial – without any breaks and continuing through a torrential downpour that lasted for almost an hour and a half – the judges leave the confines of the tarped area and move to a room in the District Office to discuss and render their decision on the case. Upon their return, 15 to 20 minutes later, they read their decision before the court. For his participation in the genocide, as outlined in his confession, the defendant receives a sentence of imprisonment for 12 years, plus 6 months of community service; the 12 years of imprisonment are imposed for manning the roadblock!

The defendant, who had been sitting with his head down and his hands covering his face during the pronouncement of the sentence, upon hearing the verdict lifts his head up with a decidedly relieved look on his face. With the time he has already served, his term of imprisonment is now finished. The local prison will hold one less detainee, at least for the time being, in the same overcrowded and arguably substandard conditions that exist throughout Rwanda.

Before finalizing the decision, a judge reads the entire hand-written transcript of the trial. The people in attendance openly discuss the transcripts for further clarification, amending them where required and, then, verify them one last time by signing the document. At the Kanombe District Gacaca, one trial was completed on that day and the other case held over to the following week. As the crowd disperses, his father among them, many address the defendant in what appears to be sentiments of congratulations.

According to Domitilla Mukantaganzwa, Executive Director of the Gacaca Jurisdiction in Kigali, throughout the country there are approximately

Figure 1.1 Gacaca in Kanombe.

760,000 outstanding cases that still require adjudication (Mukantaganzwa 2004). This single case may seem insignificant in the context of such numbers. However, given the circumstances that existed within Rwanda in the aftermath of the genocide – as part of a larger, multifaceted judicial process including the International Criminal Tribunal for Rwanda (hereafter referred to as ICTR), the Rwandan National Courts, and third-party trials adjudicated in foreign countries – each genocide case that is successfully completed demonstrates a culmination of extensive efforts to address the crimes of the genocide. As part of the Rwandan government's efforts to adjudicate individuals accused of genocide crimes, the proceedings in Kanombe during 2005 were part of a national pilot-project utilizing Gacaca.

What is genocide?

The recent Rwandan genocide that shocked the sensibilities of the 'civilized world' is not without historical precedent. Indeed, according to Chalk and Jonassohn, genocidal behaviour has occurred from the human atrocities observed in the destruction of the city-state Carthage by the Romans in 146 BC through the medieval Crusades, European expansion and colonization,[2] the civil wars in the former Yugoslavia, Rwanda and, arguably, in the ongoing situation in the Darfur region of Sudan (Chalk and Jonassohn 1990: 8).

Schabas also notes that 'the destruction of ethnic groups has marred the progress of human history almost from the beginning' (Schabas 1999: 1). That such examples of man's inhumanity to man are pervasive throughout the course of history presents a need for consideration of a statement, albeit an eerie one, made by Adolf Hitler that, 'natural instincts bid all living human beings not merely conquer their enemies but also destroy them. In the former days it was the victor's prerogative to destroy tribes, entire peoples' (as cited in Lemkin 1945).

In the aftermath of the Allied victory, despite the claim by Hitler and the actions taken by Germans during the course of the Second World War, perceived acceptance of such barbarity shifted. Through the elimination of what Chalk and Jonassohn refer to as a 'process of collective denial' (Chalk and Jonassohn 1990: 8), these atrocities would become recognized, defined, and collectively rebuked.[3] The specific circumstances of the Allied victory, the climate it created allowing victims to share their experiences, the conceptualization of human rights and the political climate both in Western and Eastern Europe, as well as the adherence to the ideology encapsulated within the rule of law and its resulting legalism, all played a part in the construction of a new era of international relations.

The atrocities that were part of the German war plan were recognized as the orchestrated destruction of entire groups of people based on an identifiable factor: race. According to Lemkin, '[R]eferring to the Nazi butchery in the present war, Winston Churchill said in his broadcast of August, 1941, "we are in the presence of a crime without a name"' (Lemkin 1946). Lemkin coined the term 'genocide' responding to a void in terminology for dealing with such events. Genocide, 'tragically enough must take its place in the dictionary beside other tragic words like homicide and infanticide' (Lemkin 1946).

By examining the root parts of 'genocide' (*genes*: Greek for tribe or race, and *cide*: Latin for killing) we get the literal meaning of the word, *the killing of a race or tribe*. According to Lemkin's initial conceptualization of the term, genocide 'refers to a coordinated plan aimed at the destruction of the essential foundations of the life of national groups so that these groups would wither and die like plants that have suffered a blight' (Lemkin 1946). He continues in his discussion by outlining the methods – political, social, cultural, religious, moral, economic, biological, and physical – by which the desired result can be achieved. Significantly, Lemkin further examines the elements that distinguish between genocide and individual killings: 'Genocide is directed against a national group as an entity and the attack on individuals is only secondary to the annihilation of the national groups to which they belong' (Lemkin 1946).

Lemkin's (1946) conceptualization of genocide includes a second defining aspect of the commission of genocide that addressed not the actions of the accused, but rather the level of intervention and/or response that such actions would suggest. Lemkin argued that 'by its very legal, moral, and humanitarian nature, [genocide] must be considered an international crime' (Lemkin 1946). The acts present an affront to all humanity and therefore concern the international community as a whole. Genocide, by virtue of its international consequences, therefore required a distinctly international means to address it. He further argues that '[t]he significant feature of international crime is a recognition that because of its international importance it must be punished and punishable through international cooperation. The establishment of international machinery for such a purpose is essential' (Lemkin 1946). The international and cooperative nature of such a response to genocide provides a level of condemnation that is unattainable at a national level. Lemkin referred to this reaction as the *Principle of Universal Repression*.

The United Nations discussed this principle and suggested the *machinery* that might accompany it. According to Chalk and Jonassohn (1990), the United Nations took its first step on the path towards addressing the crime of genocide in response to the urging of Lemkin. Incorporating much of the language found in Lemkin's work – although differences existed in defining potential victim groups – the idea of international condemnation for the crime of genocide was about to be realized in an international forum. According to Jacobs (2002), although the final definition of genocide incorporated into the Genocide Convention was not as broad as laid out originally by Lemkin, he is nevertheless considered to be the originator of the term and was instrumental in moving the United Nations on the path leading to the drafting of the Convention.

After 3 years of discussion, a final definition of genocide was reached. The draft UN Resolution of 9 December 1948 was ratified as unprecedented legislation on 12 December 1951. (The Convention on the Prevention and Punishment of the Crime of Genocide includes the following definition of genocide:)

> **Article 1:** The contracting parties confirm that genocide, whether committed in time of peace or in time of war, is a crime under international law which they undertake to prevent and punish.
> **Article 2:** In the present convention, genocide means any of the following acts committed with the intent to destroy, in whole or in part, a national, ethnical, racial, or religious group as such:
>   a) Killing members of the group;
>   b) Causing serious bodily or mental harm to members of the group;
>   c) Deliberately inflicting on the group conditions of life calculated to bring about its physical destruction in whole or in part;
>   d) Imposing measures intended to prevent births within the group;
>   e) Forcibly transferring children of the group to another group.
>
> (United Nations 1948)

The significance of the definition of what constitutes genocide is of great interest as the dual goals of prevention and punishment create a variety of obligations for the signatories in the event that genocidal behaviour occurs.

First, Article 1 recognizes genocide, as an international crime within the purview of international law. Second, the Convention also makes clear that no one is immune from accountability regarding acts of genocide regardless of the position he or she may hold within a given society. Additionally, as a signatory to the resolution, each individual State is required to fulfill three commitments: (1) to enact national legislation that would reflect the provisions of the Convention within their own territory wherein they would be required to put on trial and punish anyone suspected of genocide; (2) to agree to extradite any individual accused of the crimes to the originating jurisdiction; and (3) to engage in whatever is deemed necessary or appropriate action to prevent or put an end to acts of genocide (United Nations 1948).

In order to be ratified, the resolution required a minimum of 20 UN member states to affix their signatures to the document. According to Schabas, 'By contemporary standards, the work of preparing the legal instrument went rather quickly ... Within a few years it had been ratified by more than one-third of the United Nations membership, enough for it to enter into force' (Schabas 1999: 2). However, the initial speed with which the first one-third of the UN member countries became signatories to the resolution has not been matched in the years that have followed. 'As of 1998, it has been ratified by two-thirds of the member states, a relatively paltry number when compared with the number that have ratified the major human rights treaties' (Schabas 1999: 2). It is interesting that the United Kingdom and the United States, the two countries primarily responsible for the creation and operation of the Nuremburg trials, were relatively late in affixing their signatures to this Convention (1970 and 1988, respectively).[4] These two countries, among many others, voiced concerns regarding various issues either with the Convention itself or with how other countries have attempted to interpret the various articles.[5] Schabas discusses how the obligations for member states to prevent of genocide tend to be less clearly defined than the obligation to punish those who commit it. As put forward by Schabas, '[P]ut bluntly, are states required, as a legal obligation, to take action up to and including military intervention in order to prevent the crime from occurring?' (Schabas 1999: 6).

Whether this lack of clarity exists – which is suspect given the narrow definition of genocide outlined in the Convention – or that certain levels of intervention prove too costly and not in the self-interest of independent states (Bass 2000: 28), the responses that occurred in the face of the events that unfolded in the former Yugoslavia and Rwanda have been largely in the form of *after-the-fact* legal remedies. Despite the observation that, until the formation of the sister *ad hoc* tribunals for the former Yugoslavia and Rwanda, no charges had ever been laid for the crime of genocide, the judicial response to the Rwandan genocide has been influenced by the precedents of the past tribunals dealing with war crimes and crimes against humanity.

Under the cover of civil war, a premeditated and efficiently executed plan to exterminate the Tutsi (and politically moderate Hutu) was carried out with an efficiency never before seen. The killing began on 6 April 1994, merely hours after the plane carrying President Juvenal Habyarimana of Rwanda and President Cyprien Ntayamira of Burundi was shot down as it descended into Kigali. As part of the plan, the Hutu extremists mobilized mass participation among the civilian population creating a killing machine of the most rudimentary nature. Armed predominantly with machetes and other usually benign instruments, neighbours killed neighbours, Rwandans killed Rwandans. The killing continued until July 1994 when the Rwandan Patriotic Front (RPF) took control of the capital city Kigali and forced the Hutu army and militias west, past the French lines of Operation Turquoise and into the Democratic Republic of Congo. The civil war and the genocide were both brought to an end. Despite the warnings and reports of the genocide from the United Nations Assistance Mission for Rwanda (UNAMIR), the outside world stood by and did nothing to stop the carnage. The genocide in Rwanda left between an estimated 800,000 and 1,000,000 dead, and more than twice that either externally or internally displaced as refugees. The genocide left Rwanda in a state of ruin and much of the rest of the world in a state of shock.[6]

The adjudication of the Rwandan genocide

Regardless of the best intentions of the international community, genocidal massacres continue to plague humanity. However, the creation of the *ad hoc* international tribunals for both the former Yugoslavia and Rwanda, as well as increased international support for national judicial efforts, suggests an increased desire by members of the international community to hold those responsible accountable for their actions (Sriram 2002; Uvin 2003). The events that transpired in Rwanda from 1990 to 1994 were a blatant violation of the UN Genocide Convention. The Convention requires a measured response by its signatory states both internationally and, in the case of Rwanda, domestically. Given the lack of intervention on the part of the international community in preventing the genocide, holding those who participated in the atrocities accountable for their conduct, and punishing them in accordance with the law, became a means for states to partially fulfill their treaty-based obligations. The resulting judicial action is multifaceted, occurring both nationally and internationally.

The judicial response to the Rwandan genocide involves three central processes: (1) the ICTR; (2) the national courts in Rwanda (classic courtroom justice); and (3) the Gacaca. Further, two additional courses of action – beyond the scope of this book – operate in what can be described as a peripheral, yet significant, manner: (1) the trials adjudicated in the Rwandan military courts; and (2) international *third-party* trials taking place in foreign jurisdictions.

The use of legal proceedings as a means to achieve reconciliation across its territory is considered by the Rwandan government to be fundamentally instrumental. Despite recognition that 'genocide being a crime against humanity requires a collective response from the international community'

(Government of Rwanda 1995: 5), the Rwandan government sought to demonstrate its independence from the rest of the world as well as its ability to address matters internally.[7] It is certainly plausible that this decision was both a political and logistical reaction to the blatant non-response of the Western world during the civil war and genocide. It has also been argued that concerns over a number of issues relating to the configuration of the ICTR have also played a role (as discussed in later chapters).

The Gacaca courts

According to interviews with Philibert Kigabo (2005) of the Rwandan Human Rights Commission, a series of discussions – called the URUGWIRO meetings – followed an international conference that sought a Rwandan solution to a Rwandan problem. Karekezi, Nshimiyimana, and Mutamba write, '[T]he decision to develop Gacaca courts emerged from this series of "meetings of reflection" to discuss the country's future' (Karekezi, Nshimiyimana, and Mutamba 2004: 70). In 1999, continued meetings organized by Pasteur Bizimungu, then President of Rwanda, to address the issues and solutions regarding justice and reconciliation, resulted in a *re-birth* of a traditional Rwandan solution: the modernized Gacaca.

The Gacaca represents a uniquely Rwandan response to the genocide. It is a modernized version of a traditional dispute resolution mechanism wherein people of the community who had a grievance would present it before the Inyangamugayo, and it would be discussed and a decision reached (Mukantaganzwa 2004). After much preparation, 'in June 2002, the Republic of Rwanda embarked on an extraordinary experiment in transitional justice, inaugurating the pilot phase of a new participatory justice system called Inkiko-Gacaca' (Honeyman *et al* 2004: 1). The most current legislation providing for the operations of the Gacaca is the Organic Law No 10/2007 of 01/03/2007, which established the organization, competence, and functioning of the Gacaca courts charged with prosecuting and trying the perpetrators of the crime of genocide and other crimes against humanity committed between 1 October 1990 and 31 December 1994 as modified and complemented to date. This current legislation is a reflection of three previously enacted laws: the original legislation regarding the Rwandan adoption of the UN genocide conventions requirement for signatory states to adopt national legislation (Government of Rwanda 1996) and the first two 'Gacaca' laws (Government of Rwanda 2001a and 2004d).

Launched in 2002, the pilot-phase of the Gacaca operated in 12 sectors. Since its inception, it has been expanded to incorporate a total of 1,545 sectors, operating 751 jurisdictions, functioning at the cell, sector, and sector-appeal levels. The Gacaca experiment has received support and acceptance by those entrusted with the task of addressing this gigantic judicial undertaking. As the pilot-phase moved forward into the trial phase of the process, the National Service of Gacaca Jurisdictions began the national launch of the

Gacaca process across Rwanda. June 2005 marked the beginning of what is conceivably the largest-scale community-based justice initiative ever undertaken. According to Mukantaganzwa, the nationwide launch of the Gacaca involved the establishment of over 12,000 Gacaca courts and the election and training of approximately 108,000 individuals who, after being elected, voluntarily assume the role of judges (Mukantaganzwa 2004). It is the task of these courts to encourage reconciliation and national unity while also attending to the processing of the remaining 760,000 genocide cases.[8]

The Rwandan criminal courts

The Rwandan judiciary was created using the Belgian system as its model.[9] According to Vandeginste, the lower courts – the cantonal tribunals – did not play a role in criminal matters within the early Rwandan system. As a result, 'the tribunals of first instance – twelve in numbers – are now the key level for the trials of genocide suspects' (Vandeginste 1997: 5). The passing of Organic Law No 8/96 in 1996 created Specialized Chambers that existed within the tribunals of first instance to exclusively preside over the genocide trials; unfortunately, these chambers have since been dismantled. Vandeginste detailed a few other notable characteristics of this judicial system which include, but are not limited to: (1) the ability of the judiciary to detain an accused individual while evidence is being gathered; (2) the burden of proof resides with the prosecutor; and (3) the defendants' guarantee of the right to counsel although not at the government's expense (Vandeginste 1997: 5).

The International Criminal Tribunal for Rwanda (ICTR)

At the same time as the aforementioned discussions were taking place, the international community was embarking on its measured response to the atrocities committed in Rwanda. Discussions surrounding an international response began before the end of the military conflict. As noted by Des Forges and Longman, '[Even] during the genocide, international actors began to talk of the need for justice, an idea that was fed by their guilt' (Des Forges and Longman 2004: 51). A multitude of factors, both political and legal, greatly influenced the decision by the United Nations to create the *ad hoc* tribunal for Rwanda: (1) the enormity of the crimes committed in Rwanda; (2) the recent creation of the *ad hoc* tribunal for the former Yugoslavia; and (3) the collective guilt resulting from non-recognition of, and non-intervention during, the genocide as it transpired.

According to Bass, '[T]here was a distinct tokenism to this legalism' (Bass 2000: 281). The Rwandan government, which originally supporting the tribunal's creation, was the only country to vote against the resolution to invoke its mandate. Indeed, the Rwandan objections to the ICTR were three-fold: (1) no application of the death penalty; (2) that it is located outside of Rwandan territory in Arusha, Tanzania; and (3) they did not agree with the method used to appoint the ICTR judges (International Crisis Group 1999: 27). The ICTR, 'is the product of the international community; it is fully managed and funded by it and exists to no small extent over the objections of the government of Rwanda' (Uvin and Mironko 2003: 219).

Other relevant jurisdictions

This research is focused on the three judicial responses outlined above. In addition to these foci, the following jurisdictions present additional judicial responses to the events that took place in Rwanda in 1994. To date, there is very little information available regarding these additional sources of adjudication. However, in order to appreciate and understand the previous legal actions more completely, it is important to briefly introduce these other relevant jurisdictions: (1) trials that have been undertaken by the Rwandan military; (2) national transfers and transmissions; and (3) genocide trials occurring in third-party states.

Military trials

The *repatriation* of Rwanda by the Rwandan Patriotic Army – the military branch of the RPF – which brought an end to both the civil war and the genocide, also brought accusations of reprisal massacres attributed to the victors. The Rwandan government does not deny that some members of the RPF did commit human rights violations. However, they stress that 'the individuals concerned have committed these crimes in their personal capacity and not as a pattern of government-sanctioned violence against the public' (Government of Rwanda 2005). By virtue of this position, according to Ngoga (2005), the government has made a claim for a lack of *moral equivalence* as to nature of these crimes. As such, they claim that these trials do not belong in the same judicial venues as those who perpetrated the genocide. Furthermore, according to Kagame:

> The army courts are working and have already prosecuted some cases. The fact that these people are being brought to justice should reassure people that it is not the system carrying out revenge. Its individuals, and the individuals are being dealt with.
>
> (Gourevitch 1996: 175)

Nevertheless, the seriousness of these accusations cannot be understated as they constituted the commission of war crimes and/or crimes against humanity. Des Forges describes numerous human rights violations ranging from pillaging property to abducting civilians and summarily executing individuals known to be members of the former government or those accused of genocide crimes (Des Forges 1999: np). Moghalu notes that these trials are 'reminiscent of the domestic trial of German war criminals in Leipzig following World

War I' (Moghalu 2005: 143). Other observers, representing non-governmental organizations working in the area, substantiate his claim by providing evidence of the paucity of trials as well as the light sentences to those who are tried (International Crisis Group 1999: 18).[10]

The concept of *victor's justice*, applied negatively to the ICTR, the Rwandan criminal courts, and to some degree the Gacaca, is most evident within the military trials.[11] That the 'extremely serious allegations of war crimes by Rwandan troops ... have not seriously been investigated far less prosecuted by Rwandan authorities' (Human Rights Watch 2001: 10) demonstrates a politicization of the judicial process as a whole. The inseparable relationship that exists between the military (RPA) and political (RPF) branches of the Rwandan Patriotic Front may result in the government becoming inseparably tied to factions involved in the commission of human atrocities.

The accusation of unjust treatment towards the Hutu offenders accused of crimes calls into question the legitimacy of the entire judicial structure, thereby undermining attempts to reconcile the nation. A fundamental condition necessary for the establishment of a just system is its independence from political interference. The truism, that for justice to be done, justice must be seen to be done, demonstrates the importance that the perception of impartiality plays in eyes of the citizenry. Within the context of a country undergoing a process of rebuilding that requires reconciliation and the unification of fractured parties, the readily apparent presence of substantive justice is crucial. 'The way things stand, punishment is meted out for past genocide crimes, but justice is not being served, and with it, the chances for reconciliation decline' (Uvin 2001: 184).

The respect that is given to the system by the people may be conceived of as relative or proportionate to the sense of justice that the system displays. Des Forges observes that 'the proper prosecution of the genocide could permit the Rwandan state both to end impunity and to lay the foundation for the rule of law' (Des Forges 1999: np). Therefore, the assertion by Rwandan authorities that the path to reconciliation and peace in Rwanda is based upon the application of justice does have a possible foundation upon which to build. However, for this to be realized, the observed miscarriages of justice must be rectified with the same attention and zeal as the genocide crimes. While it may be argued that there does not exist a sense of moral equivalence between the acts of the perpetrators of genocide and those engaged in reprisal killings, both crimes must be treated without prejudice with respect to the law since 'the struggle against impunity must ensure that no group is favoured above another or the credibility of the justice system will be at risk' (International Crisis Group 1999: 18).

Genocide trials in foreign jurisdictions

In accordance with the responsibilities outlined in Article 5 of the Convention for the Punishment and Prevention of the Crime of Genocide, all signatory states have a duty to enact national legislation 'to provide effective penalties for persons guilty of genocide' (United Nations 1948). Accompanying that provision is the duty either to extradite the accused to an accepted jurisdiction (as long as it does not contradict national legislation) or to engage in prosecuting the accused within his/her national jurisdiction. Additionally, the ICTR Statute also invokes obligations. In accordance with Article 28, 'States shall cooperate with the International Criminal Tribunal for Rwanda in the investigation and prosecution of persons accused of committing serious violations of international humanitarian law' (ICTR 2007: 63).[12]

The nature of the criminal acts described in the Convention suggest acts deserving of universal contempt and therefore:

> [i]nvolve a reliance on the principle of universal jurisdiction, the right to prosecute certain crimes recognized by international law as so heinous as to require prosecution without regard to the site of the crime, when it took place, or the nationality of the accused or victim.
>
> (Des Forges 1999: np)

The legal arguments that are involved in the determination of universal jurisdiction, and the relative competence of individual jurisdictions that is required in order to proceed in trying these cases are beyond the scope of this book.[13] As Schabas noted, the debate around the exercise of universal jurisdiction over genocide crimes has focused on the permissive versus prohibitive *intent* of Article VI of the Genocide Convention: 'The drafters of the Convention meant to exclude universal jurisdiction, although courts have tended to interpret Article VI of the Convention as being merely permissive, and in no way a prohibition of universal jurisdiction' (Schabas 2003: 39). The third-party prosecutions of genocide crimes, and the implications that these trials may hold for the judicial enterprise in Rwanda and the ICTR, remain unclear.

Nevertheless, what is clear, is that a number of countries – the United States (a civil matter), Canada (one a criminal trial; a second a matter of extradition), France, Belgium, and Switzerland – have all engaged in the legal processing of individuals accused of genocide crimes in Rwanda.[14] Each successive case tried by a third-party State presents additional international recognition that the crimes that occurred in Rwanda in 1994 are unacceptable and deserve a measured response that vilifies them. Further, each case adjudicated by a third-party State also reduces the burden on both the ICTR and the Rwandan courts. The involvement of these countries in the process of dealing with one aspect of the judicial response in the aftermath of the Rwandan genocide presents an example of international cooperation. When addressing mass atrocities, international cooperation requires the full cooperation of UN member states to achieve success. While the positive effects of these countries' involvement are yet to become evident, the negative effect of countries that do not cooperate is readily apparent, as seen in the harbouring fugitives of the Rwandan genocide.

Looking forward

When visiting the multitude of genocide memorials throughout the country in Rwanda, one can readily observe the realities underlying the quotation that opened this chapter. The widespread participation of the general populace in the massacre of both Tutsi and moderate Hutu Rwandans resulted in mass graves that literally overflow with human remains. This presents a visually horrific demonstration illustrating a statement made by Lemkin nearly 50 years before that '[t]he disease of criminality, if left unchecked, is contagious' (Lemkin 1945). In the aftermath of the Rwandan genocide, there have been, and continue to be, a variety of judicial responses that attempt to address the crimes that took place during what has been referred to as 'one of the fastest, most efficient, most evident genocides in recent history' (Dallaire 2003: xvii).

This book is an investigation of the multifaceted judicial response to genocide located within three *spheres* of Rwandan society, namely: (1) the community sphere (Gacaca); (2) the national sphere (Rwandan National courts); and (3) the international sphere (ICTR). By engaging in what Mills (1959) referred to as the *sociological imagination* – locating the judicial response, its requisite institutions, as well as the goals, procedures, practices, and outcomes within the historical and cultural context in which it evolved to its current operational state – I provide an understanding of the cultural, political, and legal forces involved in their creation and potential impact. The effect of the events that transpired during the 1994 genocide and the ongoing judicial response cannot be understood without regard to its magnitude. Together they continue to affect every aspect of Rwandan society from its societal institutions to each community, family, and individual citizen.

The examination of antecedents to the judicial responses will provide insight into a number of questions that arise regarding the decisions made as well as the potential impacts that may come as a result. Throughout history, the world has witnessed an unfortunate and ongoing occurrence of genocide and human rights violations. Included within the global history of genocidal events have been a number of methods used in attempts to resolve these events. In light of this history, a number of questions central to this investigation emerge:

- What aspects of the Rwandan genocide itself – located within the context of both the global history of genocide and the specific Rwandan historical context – played a role in directing those involved in the decision-making process to arrive at the judicial response that has been adopted?
- What political and cultural factors provide a framework for understanding the manner in which both the international community, as well as the newly established Rwandan government approached the crimes committed during the genocide?
- What theoretical explanations in the field of justice can provide insights into the choices made and their potential results?

- Around what goals is the specific judicial response organized, and what are the specific procedures and processes of the judicial response that will allow for the attainment of the stated goals?
- What challenges does this multifaceted judicial response create for those involved in its day-to-day operations?
- What are the possible impacts for the citizens of Rwanda and Rwandan society as a whole?

With a basic understanding of the judicial processes central to the situation in Rwanda (the ICTR, Rwandan criminal courts, and the Gacaca), this study examines a variety of issues that are instrumental in attempting to determine the likelihood of each process' success in achieving both its stated goals and justice for the victims of the 1994 genocide. The process of individualizing the guilt and calling to account the perpetrators also serves to identify the individualized nature of the crimes against the victims that the genocide was a million acts of murder. This investigation also addresses an underlying theoretical query that involves sensitizing concepts incorporated within restorative and retributive conceptualizations of justice, within the framework of legal-realism and its antithesis, summary justice, in order to assess their impact on societal conditions in the aftermath of genocide in the Rwandan context.

Notes

1 This inscription is written on a plaque inside the Genocide Memorial at Gisosyi in Kigali, Rwanda.
2 According to Kaplan, '[E]very single European power in Africa was guilty of crimes against humanity. The kind of crimes routinely perpetrated on Africans were never considered legitimate when practiced against other whites. The rationalization that permitted such behavior was the same in every case: deep-seated racism' (Kaplan 2008: 24).
3 One must note, however, as mentioned by Bass (2000) in his discussion of 'victor's justice', that had the outcome of the Second World War been different (ie a German victory), the German military officials would likely not have been held to account for their actions and, in fact, it may have been Allied Commanders on trial after the war (assuming the creation of a tribunal). Furthermore, the fact that Germans were unsuccessful also differentiates this scenario from past examples presented by Chalk and Jonassohn (1990) wherein the victims in this instance were effectively liberated by the Allied forces and therefore not subjected to German rule, free to tell the story of the events of the holocaust and its horrors rather than accepting their fate, whilst the victor's wrote the history of the events.
4 It should be noted that the Nuremburg trials were not, by definition, 'genocide' trials, but rather 'war crimes' trials. This point is made quite evident by Bass (2000) who notes that, on many occasions, many people have come to associate Nuremburg with an international response to the holocaust, when, in fact, the holocaust was a secondary concern to the war crimes that the Germans had committed. Support for the inclusion of the atrocities committed against the Jews did not become apparent until the realities of the concentration camps became evident, which was after the idea and formulation of Nuremburg had occurred.

5 For a complete listing of the comments made by both the United Kingdom and the United States see Prevent Genocide International at, www.preventgenocide.org/law/convention/UNTreatyCollection-GenocideConventionStatusReport.htm (accessed 22 February 2009).

6 For an in-depth discussion of the events that transpired in Rwanda in the 100 days of genocide see Prunier (1995), Des Forges (1999), Caplan *et al* (2000), Mamdani (2001), Dallaire (2003), and Melvern (2004).

7 The introduction to Organic Law No 16 states, 'Considering the necessity for the Rwandan society to find by itself, solutions to the genocide problems and its consequences' (United Nations 2004).

8 Estimates are the result of extrapolation by the National Service for Gacaca Jurisdiction from the results of the 'pilot-phase' (Magsam 2004).

9 Sarkin discusses the original Rwandan Penal Law as 'originally a replica of Belgian law. However, in 1940 the Congo Penal System was extended in Rwanda, and a specifically Rwandan penal code was adopted in 1977' (Sarkin 1999: 793).

10 Additional evidence for this claim is presented by Human Rights Watch. *Rwanda: observing the rules of war?* In their report, they state that:

> [t]he Rwandan military justice system has prosecuted a number of cases of grave human rights violations. But most convictions have been of ordinary soldiers or low-ranking officers. Senior officers have rarely been tried on such charges and if tried and convicted have generally received light sentences.
>
> (Human Rights Watch 2001: 10)

11 Failure to hold accountable members of the Rwandan Patriotic Army (RPA) demonstrates a politicization of the judiciary wherein only the vanquished Hutu offenders will be tried for their crimes.

12 For a link to the full ICTR Statute, please see the References.

13 For a more complete discussion of the legal issues underlying the notions of 'universal jurisdiction' and 'competence,' see Bassiouni (2001) and Sriram (2002).

14 United States: Civil case: defendant John-Bosco Barayagwiza; Canada: *Regina v Leon Mugesera* and *Regina v Desire Munyaneza*; France: Wenceslas Munyeshyaka; Belgium: four charged, three transferred to ICTR, final individual charged; and Switzerland: Alfred Musema.

2 A historical and conceptual framework for understanding justice in the aftermath of the Rwandan genocide

> Only through a process of making individuals accountable for their crimes can we hope to banish the poison of collective guilt and unite communities against violence. We cannot talk of reconciliation without justice in the context of Rwanda.
>
> (Kagame 2004)

The context of the Rwandan genocide itself, as well as the policies and practices that have evolved to address the crimes committed, presents a unique case in comparison to other occurrences of genocide. According to Drumbl, the uniqueness of each genocide 'manifests itself in the differences of experiences of genocide survivors, the level of social mobilization of aggressors, the public or secretive nature of the aggression, and the historical context from which the violence emerged' (Drumbl 2000: 1224). The challenges facing a country in the aftermath of an event of this enormity are extremely varied and complex. Kagame has called the genocide 'the defining event in Rwandan history' (in Gourevitch 1996: 167). The importance of how Rwanda addresses such a significant aspect in its history cannot be overstated. Sarkin states that 'in all probability, how a society deals with its past has a major determining influence on whether that society will achieve long term peace and stability' (Sarkin 2000: 112). The impact of the events leading up to and during the genocide affects the decisions made with respect to how survivors cope with it.

Given the potential ramifications of the legal and political processes utilized in addressing the genocide, it is paramount to understand the complex and intertwined actions of the various institutions engaged in a combined, albeit sometimes conflicting, response to an event of such magnitude. An attempt to provide such an understanding of the current judicial response in Rwanda, therefore, must involve locating the response within the unique context in which it developed. The critical aspects of Rwanda's historical ethno-political relations, the genocide, and the demands of social reconstruction in the aftermath of such horrors are key elements of the contextual framework for this book. Restorative and retributive justice, liberal-legalism, cosmopolitan law, and the rule of law comprise elements of the theoretical foundation used to examine the judicial responses.

A brief history of ethnicity and politics in Rwanda

Although the Rwandan genocide was the result of an intricately interwoven ethno-political struggle, the influence of forces both inside and outside of Rwanda is crucial in understanding the situation that occurred within its borders. These forces were instrumental in shaping Hutu and Tutsi relations. A brief overview of the history of these relations is presented to provide a context in which the genocide occurred, as well as implications that they may have for the decisions made in the search for justice.

It is important to note that there are contentious accounts of the events in Rwanda and that they vary in accordance with the group in power at a given time. As is often the case, especially in societies that transmit history through oral traditions, the group in power determines the version of history transmitted to future generations:

> History in Rwanda has always been malleable, growing out of story lines of one's own choosing. If one was Hutu, then heroes were Hutu. If one was Tutsi, the opposite was true. In that story-telling, that exaggeration and embellishment, came the seeds of conflict.
>
> (Temple-Raston 2005: 17)

Despite the creation of a dominant historical perspective within a given era, an alternative interpretation of events continues to exist. Although it may do so, arguably, to a greater or lesser degree at the fringes of society, it is there and may rise to a more prominent existence as power structures and politics change.

Pre-colonial ethnic relations and political organization

There is much debate among scholars (Newbury 1998; Magnarella 2000; Melvern 2004) about the nature of relations that existed between the Hutu and Tutsi in Rwanda prior to the arrival of the European colonialists in Rwanda.[1] Reconciling this debate is crucial in the present circumstances of seeking a post-conflict reconciliation. Newbury has argued that 'the post-genocide government in Kigali has not only to deal with the trauma of a whole people and society, but it also has to consider how its policies will be interpreted within the various contexts of Rwanda's past' (Newbury 1998: 7).

The geographic origin of Rwanda's three ethnic groups, together comprising the *Banyarwandan* people – the Bahutu (Hutu), Batutsi (Tutsi), and Batwa (Twa) – as well as their settlement patterns in Rwanda is also contested. Further, these factors have played a significant role in the polarization of the groups. According to Magnarella, a generally accepted premise amongst historians is that the first inhabitants of the territory were the ancestors of the Twa, followed by the Hutu, and finally the Tutsi (Magnarella 2000).

Some anthropologists, [however], contest the idea that Hutu and Tutsi are distinct groups. Others maintain that the Tutsi came to Rwanda from elsewhere, originating in the Horn of Africa and migrating south where they eventually achieved dominance over the other two groups, the majority Hutu and the small number of Twa.

(Melvern 2004: 4)[2]

A part of the Rwandan history that people do not contend is that some time in the fifteenth century, a monarchy was established led by a Tutsi king – *Mwami*. The structure of the Tutsi-led kingdom was highly organized, resembling a 'centralized state ruled by a king' (Taylor 1999: 37). According to Melvern, '[I]t was organized on four levels: province, district, hill and neighborhood' (Melvern 2004: 5). Each level fell under the administrative control of the Mwami and his court, with court-appointed chiefs operating at each successive level of Rwandan society.[3] The hierarchy of administrative control originated within the royal court of the Tutsi monarchy. Individual Hutu, nevertheless, did find themselves in positions of power, albeit lower ones, within this administrative structure: 'The Hutu, the most populous group of society, generally ran the neighbourhoods in Rwanda's highly controlled hierarchy; they obeyed the orders of those from above, most of whom were Tutsi' (Melvern 2004: 5). The degree of subjugation and oppression of Hutus at the hands of the Tutsi in this era varies with the version of history that one accepts.

There are two competing narratives with respect to pre-colonial relations between the Tutsi and Hutu. According to Corey and Joireman, one historical account – representing the Hutu perspective – 'insists that ethnic discord is rooted in pre-colonial history, and that these previously existing divisions were merely exacerbated by changes wrought by colonial domination' (Corey and Joireman 2004: 74). The other, an arguably Tutsi outlook on the past, claims a state of peaceful co-existence between the Hutu and Tutsi prior to colonization. These critical divergences of historical interpretations are relevant to the discussion about moving forward after mass atrocities because 'the distortions inscribed in the cognitive maps of both victims and perpetrators, i.e. memory, in response to the exigencies of the moment, in turn [provided] justification for further killings' (Lemarchand 1998: 5). In order to move towards reconciliation between the Hutu and the Tutsi, there needs to be a reconciliation of history. According to Mamdani, '[H]istory teaching in schools has stopped … [b]ecause there is no agreement on what should be taught as history' (Mamdani 2001b: 267).

The politicization of history may have significant effects with respect to perceptions of accountability for the genocide and, by extension, appropriate responses to it. As stated by Mamdani, '[N]either the identification of the perpetrator nor that of the survivor is transparent in Rwanda … [it] is contingent on one's historical perspective' (Mamdani 2001b: 267). Rwandan historical accounts of the relations between Hutu and Tutsi are not immune to this process of politicization. The current government in Rwanda is embarking on a process of truth-telling as a major component of its judicial response. The intent is to provide an accurate historical account of the genocide and its antecedents, which are crucial to the promotion of a foreign cause for the ethnic tensions. According to Cory and Joireman, '[T]he government would like to emphasize the peaceful cohabitation that once existed, and to minimize talk of "natural" or "ancient" antagonisms between ethnic groups' (Corey and Joireman 2004: 75). In asserting this version of Rwanda's history, the path towards reconciliation would appear to be much smoother if much of the blame for the antecedent factors fell outside of their borders.

This perspective claims that the establishment of the Tutsi kingdom led to a reduction in the previous autonomy of the predominantly agricultural Hutu. According to Moghalu, the appropriation of Hutu-held land for the purpose of creating pastoral areas for cattle created tensions between the two groups in the pre-colonial era (Moghalu 2005).[4] Regarding the state of ethnic divisions during this era, Moghalu wrote that:

> [t]he dividing line between the two groups was not as rigid as is commonly presumed by non-Rwandans – they both spoke (and still speak) the same language, Kinyarwanda; intermarriage was common, and, with the performance of certain sociocultural rites, a successful Hutu could 'become' a Tutsi.
>
> (Moghalu 2005: 10)

In what Magnarella refers to as a *process of ennoblement*, members of the Tutsi royalty could elevate the status of a Hutu to that of a Tutsi (Magnarella 2000). The reverse was also possible: Tutsi nobles or royalty could essentially demote another Tutsi to the social rank of Hutu based primarily on economic failure or marrying into a Hutu family. Despite this observed malleability in the social structure and the potential it may have provided for upward mobility, what remains clear is that there was a hierarchical society with the Tutsi at its top echelons.

The positioning of the Tutsi at the centre of power resulted in a number of policies being brought forth that reflected Tutsi dominance and Hutu inferiority. Magnarella discusses how many laws favoured Tutsi and reflected their ethnocentrism:

> Although cattle theft was generally prohibited, a Tutsi could steal cattle from a Hutu with impunity so long as the Hutu had no Tutsi lord or patron to protect him. Murder was also generally prohibited, but the penalty for it varied with the classes of the parties.
>
> (Magnarella 2000: 7)

The inequity of social stratification was most evident in the creation of the feudal-like relations between Tutsi lords and Hutu residing in their fiefdoms.

In what Magnarella likens to a caste system, the Tutsi subjugated the Hutu through two primary methods, *uburetwa* and *ubuhake*: 'Uburetwa (*corvée* labor service and offerings of beer in return for access to land) became a principal means of Hutu subjugation' (Magnarella 2000: 5). With respect to ubuhake, wherein poor men became clients or *children* of a Tutsi lord, they then are obliged to 'provide a variety of services to his patron or lord, including cultivating his fields, repairing his huts, and possibly giving him wives or daughters as concubines' (Magnarella 2000). This regimen of forced labour was the source of much discontent and anger directed towards the Tutsi by the Hutu. Additionally, in the colonial period that followed, the colonial powers opportunistically incorporated the practice of indentured labour into their practice.

The colonial era: the institutionalization of ethnicity and Tutsi political dominance

The politics of colonialism in the entire Great Lakes region of East Africa played a significant role in shaping the conditions that set the stage for the genocide of 1994. The European colonial practice of *divide and rule* created states in which, 'for many Africans, identifying with their new artificial colonial construct made little sense … instead [serving] to reinforce original ties of ethnicity or clan' (Schabas 2005: 25). The impact of German and – to a much greater degree – Belgian rule in Rwanda precipitated the ethnic violence by creating a divisive environment conducive to fostering ethno-political struggles between the Hutu and Tutsi during the colonial and post-colonial eras. According to Newbury, '[T]he horrors can be traced to intense struggles over power carried out by leaders – struggles involving the politicization of ethnicity as a pervasive dynamic of violence and fear' (Newbury 1998: 7).

European colonization of Rwanda began with the arrival of Germans in 1884. According to Moghalu, 'Europe's "scramble for Africa" in the late nineteenth century made Rwanda a German protectorate as a result of the Anglo-German treaty of 1880 by which much of East Africa became German colonies' (Moghalu 2005: 10). The German presence and control over Rwanda was cut short due to the terms of surrender following the Allied victory in the First World War: 'After the First World War the western provinces of German East Africa, Ruanda (Rwanda) and neighbouring Urundi (Burundi) were given to Belgium under a League of Nations' mandate' (Melvern 2004: 5). However short-lived the German rule, the policy of indirect rule that was utilized in Rwanda, 'established a pattern that would come to characterize the relations between Europeans and Africans and between Rwanda's two most numerous groups, Tutsi and Hutu' (Taylor 1999: 41). The Germans controlled the Tutsi who, in turn, controlled the rest of the population. According to Magnarella, '[T]he principal means by which the Germans maintained authority was often the brutal punitive expedition' (Magnarella 2000: 9).

Another key aspect of the German rule was the solidification of the pre-colonial attempts by the Tutsi monarch to gain more centralized control over the entire country. German rule enabled the Tutsi kingdom to expand its control over resistant territories within Rwanda's boundaries. As Prunier notes, the result of this mutually beneficial relationship was the continuation of the 'pre-colonial transformation towards more centralisation, annexation of the Hutu principalities and increase in Tutsi chiefly power' (Prunier 1995: 25).

A continuation and further exploitation of the contentious relationship between the Hutu and Tutsi was part of the Belgian strategy in Rwanda. Moghalu explains: 'To sustain and strengthen its hold over the country, the Belgian colonizers used a classic divide-and-conquer method, first among the Tutsi to select those most willing to advance Belgium's agenda, and then between Tutsis and Hutus' (Moghalu 2005: 10). The Belgians, like the Germans, were impressed with the Tutsis' ruling monarchy and viewed it as evidence of their superior nature. Their policies demonstrated an even greater affinity with the Tutsi than had been present under German rule. The Belgian colonial rule was responsible for the institutionalization of the concept of ethnicity that intensified the contentious divide between the Hutus and Tutsis.

The Hamitic Hypothesis[5] formed the basis for the Belgian use of the Tutsi as their administrative arm in Rwanda. Colonial ideas of racial superiority and inferiority provided the foundation for this hypothesis.[6] According to Prunier, '[T]here are probably few instances, in Africa or elsewhere, of a country that became the subject of myth to the extent that Rwanda was in the late nineteenth and early twentieth century' (Prunier 1995: 346). The incorporation of the Hamitic Hypothesis[7] and the accompanying idea of racial superiority of the Tutsi within Rwanda were instituted in the work of the early Belgian colonialists during the 1933 census:

> The divisions in society were enforced ... Teams of Belgian bureaucrats arbitrarily classified the whole population as Hutu, Tutsi or Twa, giving everyone an identity card with the ethnic grouping clearly marked. Every Rwandan was counted and measured: the height, the length of their noses, the shape of their eyes ... Some people were given a Tutsi identity card because they had more money or cows.
>
> (Melvern 2004: 6)

This ethnic division of Rwanda had important consequences in all aspects of social and political life. 'Racialization was also an institutional construct. Racial ideology was embedded in institutions, which in turn undergirded racial privilege and reproduced racial ideology' (Mamdani 2001b: 87).

The institutionalization of this privilege became apparent in all aspects of Rwandan society. Although everyone spoke Kinyarwanda, the Belgians granted Rwandan-Tutsis access to a superior Western education (taught in

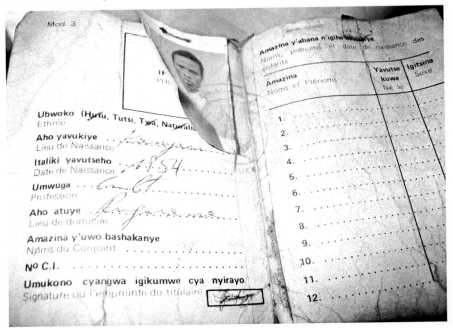

Figure 2.1 Pre-genocide Rwandan identity card.

French), while the Hutu children continued a basic education taught in Kinyarwanda or Swahili (the common language of labour). At the local level of politics, the Belgians recruited and placed Tutsi in positions of power and control, answering only to the Belgians at the national level. As noted by Magnarella, 'Belgian administrators replaced Hutu chiefs with Tutsi. The replacement was so extensive that by 1959, 43 out of 45 chiefs, and 549 of 559 sub-chiefs were Tutsi' (Magnarella 2000: 10). The colonial system in Rwanda enshrined the supremacy of the Tutsi minority, institutionalizing them as a superior, but alien, race.

The institutionalization of ethnicity was also prevalent within the Catholic Church. Early on in the process of colonization, the Belgians sought out the Catholic missionaries as a source of information regarding the inhabitants of Rwanda: 'Soon after colonization, the Belgian state ordered a reflection on Rwanda from the White Fathers. The purpose was to elaborate and implement "race policies"' (Mamdani 2001b: 88). The information provided in anthropological treatises constructed by various missionaries became critical sources of support for the racialized policies that were to follow.[8] A close-knit relationship between the Church and the State was developed with 'the Church [becoming] integral to the workings of the state' (Mamdani 2001b: 88). This relationship would appear with significance once again during the Hutu social revolution in 1959.

The Hutu social revolution in 1959: the reversal of ethnic politics

The Hutu social revolution of the late 1950s was a demonstration of the majority Hutu revolt from both the Belgian colonizers and the Tutsi oppression in both the pre-colonial and colonial periods of Rwandan history. The late 1950s witnessed a movement towards decolonization throughout Africa, and Rwanda was no exception to this trend.[9] Accompanying decolonization in Rwanda was the first wave of ethnic violence. According to Moghalu, there are three factors identified as the underlying causes of this initial violence:

> The first factor was the increasing agitation by Tutsis for independence from Belgium in the mid-1950s. The second (and most important) was the arrival of mostly Flemish Belgians as missionaries in Rwanda in the 1940s, in contrast to the predominantly French Belgians who preceded their compatriots at the turn of the century. ... The third factor that triggered the violence during the colonial era was the Belgian colonizer's resistance to the scenario of an independent Rwanda led by Tutsi, who now enjoyed the support of elements of the international communist movement.
>
> (Moghalu 2005: 11)

These antecedents to the violence that occurred during the genocide set a precedent in Rwanda for violence as a means for settling disputes within the political arena.

In 1957, a UN decolonization mission arrived in Rwanda. Both Tutsi and Hutu factions approached the mission, each with their own agenda, attempting to secure their political dominance in the anticipated independent Republic. 'Anticipating the Mission's visit, the Mwami's High Council proclaimed an all – Rwandan emancipation program ... [which] called for a rapid transfer of power to the king and his council' (Mamdani 2001b: 116). The Hutu contingent, one month later, presented the Mission with their response to the Tutsi claim: 'Signed by Kayibanda and eight other Hutu, and originally titled *Notes on the Social Aspect of the Racial Native Problem in Rwanda*, the Bahutu Manifesto maintained that the heart of the problem in Rwanda was "the conflict between Hutu and Hamitic – i.e. foreign – Tutsi"' (Mamdani 2001b: 114).[10] The politicization of ethnicity based on diverse interpretations of Rwanda's history was instrumental in this divisive position. The Hutu, claiming the Tutsi to be *aliens* to Rwanda, and, as such, having no inherent right to rule, was at the very heart of their argument to the UN mission for *democratic*, essentially Hutu, rule.

In 1959, based on the Mission's conclusions and strong Belgian support, the creation and proliferation of multiple political parties occurred. According to Moghalu, the Catholic Church, now comprised mainly of Flemish Belgians – as a reflection of their own political struggles in their home country against the ruling French Belgian minority – supported the movement toward democracy and its majority-rule philosophical foundation (Moghalu 2005: 12). Twagilimana states that 'on the Catholic Church's side, the period after 1945 saw the replacement of Walloon priests with Flemish priests from the working class and lower middle class, who easily projected their plight of oppressed majority in Belgium to that of the Hutu in Rwanda' (Twagilimana 2003: 60). Additionally, the Hutu more readily received the missionaries than the Tutsi. The Christian message contradicted the 'indigenous belief in the Tutsi king's divine nature; it also prohibited polygyny, a practice common among rich Tutsi and Hutu. By contrast, poor and marginal Hutu regarded the European churches as their new, protective patrons' (Magnarella 2000: 10). The Catholic Church was instrumental in emancipating disillusioned and disenfranchised Hutu from the domination of the Tutsi monarchy that had been enshrined in indigenous religious beliefs. With the previously held ideology of the inherent right to rule of the Tutsi king no longer entrenched, the door was opened through which the concept of democratic parties emerged.

These parties, from moderates seeking political power-sharing and inclusive politics to extremists seeking political dominance on the part of either Hutu or Tutsi, were largely divided along ethnic lines. 'Violence between Hutu and Tutsi political groups broke out in 1959, when U.N.A.R. supporters attacked a group of Hutu who belonged to the Association pour la Promotion Sociale de la Masse (APROSOMA) in Gitarama' (Taylor 1999: 44).[11] This action provoked a series of reprisal attacks initially focused on members of UNAR: 'Soon, generalized attacks against Tutsi civilians spread to other parts of the country, particularly to northern Rwanda, where Tutsi domination was relatively recent, brutal, and resented' (Taylor 1999). Accompanying these attacks was the rise in prominence of the Hutu social revolution. 'This new movement of extremist Hutu politicians and peasants announced that it had cast off the yolk of centuries of domination by the Tutsi minority' (Moghalu 2005: 12). The racist underpinnings of the Hutu social revolution became the moniker for the future ethnic divide in Rwanda. 'Thus a racist ideology sealed the end of the Hutu revolution, and the years that followed it became the foundation of political policies, statements, and practices that set the country on the wrong course' (Twagilimana 2003: 72).

The rampant violence resulted in the United Nations stepping in to oversee the election process in 1961. The landslide victory established the Parmehutu as the ruling party, under the leadership of Rwanda's first President, Gregoire Kayibanda. It also witnessed the final step in the abolition of the monarchy. A second election, in 1962, reconfirmed the extremist Hutu dominance of the political arena in Rwanda, the independence of Rwanda from Belgium, and the beginning of total disenfranchisement of Tutsi in all aspects of social and political life:

> Ushered in by political violence, [the election] led to the routing and dis-
> mantling of Tutsi power at the local administration level. It also triggered

broader constitutional and political developments that led to a transfer of governmental power from a Tutsi to a Hutu elite.

(Mamdani 2001b: 104)

Post-colonial Rwandan political structure: the first and second republics 1959–92

Politics within the newly established Republic of Rwanda 'not only left standing, but reinforced, the political identities created by colonialism' (Mamdani 2001b: 104). For example, Kayibanda formulated a policy referred to as the *équilibre ethnique*, ethnic redistribution, as a result of the 'rationale that there were too many Tutsi in high schools and in institutions of higher education' (Twagilimana 2003: 76). The policies and practices of the Kayibanda regime were easily implemented because of the many raids by armed Tutsi refugees into Rwanda from neighbouring countries enabling Kayibanda to 'exploit lingering fear of Tutsi for his own political ends' (Taylor 1999: 45). Mamdani describes the first Republic of Rwanda as an exclusively Hutu State (Mamdani 2001b: 131).

Despite the policies implemented by Kayibanda aimed at keeping the Tutsi in check, discord between rival regional factions of the Hutu elite began to surface in Rwanda. 'Although fewer Tutsi died in comparison with the 1959–64 period, enough were killed to provoke generalized panic among them, and once again thousands streamed across the borders' (Taylor 1999: 45). Under the cover of the violence perpetrated against Tutsi, which ensued in Rwanda following the massacres of Hutu in Burundi during 1972, Juvénal Habyarimana ousted President Kayibanda from power in a military coup: 'Seizing the opportunity to establish himself as Rwanda's "saviour" while re-establishing order, Kayibanda's Defence Minister, Juvenal Habyarimana, an army officer from Northern Rwanda, took control of the country in a "bloodless" coup d'état' (Taylor 1999). Thus began the Second Republic in Rwanda.

According to Mamdani, the newly established government sought a balance between two areas of persistent tension: (1) reconciling Tutsi political participation to reflect their minority status; and (2) justice as redress in Tutsi-dominated institutions (Mamdani 2001b: 138). In what might be described as 'affirmative action', a state-based quota system was set in motion based on equality, ethnicity, and regional notions of representation. An immediate consequence of the actions taken by the new government was the virtual end to the violence in Rwanda. However, one area that remained outstanding was the plight of the Tutsi refugees living in the neighbouring countries who had fled the anti-Tutsi violence of the previous decades.

Like Kayibanda before him, Habyarimana refused the return of these refugees as Rwandan citizens. According to Prunier, two factors premised the blatant disregard for the return of the Tutsi refugees: (1) a shortage of useable land due to the overpopulation of the country; and (2) the continued and pervasive racist ideology that labelled the Tutsi as a political threat (Prunier 1995). This refusal, combined with the political situation in neighbouring

Uganda that denied the Tutsi refugees Ugandan or Rwandan citizenship, prompted the formation of the Rwandan Patriotic Front (RPF) and its military wing, the Rwandan Patriotic Army (RPA). This group, initially led by Fred Rwigyema, comprised well-trained soldiers who had been in the service in the National Resistance Army in Uganda. The RPF set out to secure the return of all Tutsi refugees by force, and ordered the RPA to invade Rwanda.[12] The ensuing civil war in Rwanda, which provided the violent backdrop to the genocide, began with the first attack on 1 October 1990. This initiated what became a low-level civil war.

This initial invasion attempt by the RPA had a very deleterious effect on both the political situation, as well as the very existence of Tutsi living within Rwanda. The Tutsi had enjoyed a much improved existence under the Habyarimana regime than that during Kayibanda's presidency: 'Branded an *alien* minority under the First Republic, the Tutsi were redefined, even rehabilitated, as a *Rwandese* minority under the Second Republic' (Mamdani 2001b: 189). The RPA invasion returned to the foreground the racial politics of Hutu power, which had come to hold less and less significance under the Second Republic.

Having suffered great losses in this initial invasion attempt, General Paul Kagame reconstructed and revitalized a nearly defeated, and severely handicapped, rebel army.[13] By the end of 1991, Kagame had amassed a sizeable force by recruiting displaced Tutsi from Ugandan refugee camps. They were successful in securing a hold on a relatively large geographical area in Rwanda. 'Hitherto, the demand that power must remain Hutu [that] had been the rallying cry of those opposed to President Juvénal Habyarimana's line of "ethnic reconciliation" between Hutu and Tutsi' (Mamdani 2001b: 189), became a commonplace sentiment among a sizeable portion of the Hutu population in Rwanda. At the centre of the propaganda put forth by Hutu power was the non-indigenous status of the Tutsi in Rwanda and, therefore, the lack of legitimacy of any claim put forward by the Tutsi of a right to Rwandan citizenship. Another wave of massacres of Rwandan Tutsi ensued because of these rallying cries. An extremist-constructed culture of fear and hatred of the Tutsi invaders by Hutu extremists seeking the eradication of all Tutsi on Rwandan soil destroyed the integrative policies put forth by the Habyarimana government.

Hence, the civil war may have been the catalyst for the genocide, but the ideological foundations for excluding the Tutsi from national political life have much deeper roots in the colonial re-fashioning of identities and the rigid juxtaposition of social differences in the Belgian-colonial Rwanda and in the post-Belgian government of democracy that superseded it.

The Arusha Accords of 1992

In an effort to resolve the ongoing conflict, instability, and bloodshed in Rwanda, the international community organized peace negotiations in the town of Arusha in neighbouring Tanzania. Under the terms of the Arusha Peace Agreement,[14] the Rwandan government agreed to govern within a framework that called for political power-sharing between Hutu opposition parties and the Tutsi minority. The hope among moderate Rwandans and foreign diplomats was that Hutu and Tutsi would at last be able to co-exist in harmony (Power 2002: 336).

Despite the occurrence of these talks, it appears that neither side had any real intention of completing this negotiation. On the part of the Habyarimana regime, Moghalu reported that, 'the Rwandan despot made reluctant, half-hearted gestures in that direction but had no real intention of ceding real power' (Moghalu 2005: 14). Melvern stated that Lieutenant-Colonel Nsengiyumana, head of military intelligence in Rwanda, told the president that 'the real intentions of the enemy were to take Kigali. The RPF was only pretending to negotiate' (Melvern 2004: 34–5). Indeed, on a number of occasions, the talks broke down and had to be re-started.

According to Mamdani, four elements of the Arusha Accord were instrumental in the Hutu extremists moving forward with their claim for a return to the Tutsi domination of the past (Mamdani 2001b). First, the two armies merged into one Rwandan force, presenting the current Rwandan Army with a great dilemma as the RPF was to supply 40 percent of the soldiers and 50 percent of the officers. This would have led to massive unemployment among young Hutu recruits. Second, the appointment of a Tutsi to the cabinet position of Minister of the Interior within the newly-mediated agreement was another source of displeasure. The extremists argued that this arrangement positioned the Tutsi to control both local administration and the coercive force of the army. The third objection by the Hutu extremist faction was that although the RPF was limited in the number of positions granted in the political sphere, there was no representation of the extremist faction itself. Additionally, according to Taylor:

> Although the President's political party was to be guaranteed a substantial number of seats in the legislature and several key ministerial portfolios, the powers of the presidency were considerably diminished under the Arusha accords. Habyarimana was destined to become a figurehead president rather than an absolute dictator.
>
> (Taylor 1999: 50)

Finally, the Hutu faction considered the granting to all Rwandan refugees the right of return to Rwanda to be unacceptable because of the anticipated political and economic impact brought about by their sheer number.

With pressure from Western countries, particularly France, Habyarimana and the representatives from the other factions involved in the talks signed the Arusha accords in August 1993. 'In the months that followed, Habyarimana and his coterie, including many who were more extreme than him, did everything possible to subvert the accords' (Taylor 1999). The Hutu extremists deemed the power-sharing arrangement unacceptable, thus setting the stage for their assertion of power and control over the Rwandan political landscape, and the perpetration of the genocide in 1994.

Critical contextual aspects of the genocide

Each occurrence of genocide happens within a context that is, to some degree, unique. The Rwandan genocide is no exception:

> The Rwandan genocide stands out from other atrocities in a number of ways: It was astounding in the number and concentration of the killing, the extensive use of rape as a form of ethnic violence, and the massive involvement of the Rwandan population.
>
> (Daly 2001–2: 355)

A key distinguishing feature of the Rwandan genocide is the mass participation and resulting complicity of the Rwandan civilian Hutu population. The extremist Hutu leaders enlisted the participation of as many Rwandan Hutu civilians as possible in the planning, organizing, and carrying out the atrocities and genocide (Gourevitch 1998; Dallaire 2003; Mamdani 2001b; Drumbl 2000).

Evidence corroborates this mass participation. Recent estimates of those alleged to have participated in the genocide suggest that projections place the number between 760,000 and one million (Mutangana 2005). Based on the general population of Rwanda at the time of the genocide, this number indicates that one-tenth of the Rwandese people were *actively involved* in the slaughter. Additionally, participation in the genocide included participation at all levels of Rwandan society, 'at the behest of the government, with the agreement of the local authorities, and by the hands of the ordinary Rwandan men and women. Responsibility for the repression is thus shared by the individual, the collectivity, and the state' (Drumbl 1999: 28).[15] The mass involvement of the general populace in carrying out the atrocities also presented the newly established, post-conflict Rwandan government with a distinctive challenge: the victims and perpetrators had no other option than continued co-existence:

> Never before in modern memory had a people who slaughtered another people, or in whose name a slaughter had been carried out, been expected to live with the remainder of the people that was slaughtered, completely intermingled, in the same communities, as one cohesive national society.
>
> (Gourevitch 1998: 302)

The international community perceived the signing of the Arusha Peace Agreement by the disputing parties as a potential indication for a desire to return to the pre-colonial environment of peaceful cooperation. The shooting down of the plane transporting President Juvenal Habyarimana and the president of neighbouring Burundi obliterated any hopes associated with the Accords.[16] The climate that was potentially conducive to peace and cooperation was promptly destroyed after the downing. In the words of Kagame, '[T]he twist was abrupt, and the magnitude of the *problems* that arose afterwards were immense. People had prepared to live together because of the negotiated settlement. Then suddenly they were made more apprehensive than ever before' (cited in Gourevitch 1996: 175). The required necessity for continued co-existence of the two groups following a rapid course of events, highlighted by extreme atrocities, resulted in an environment that was highly volatile, and presented Rwanda with an ever-present threat of continued violence and instability.[17]

The policy of *maximal accountability* in and of itself presented the post-conflict Rwandan community with a nearly insurmountable task. This process, when combined with the necessity to rebuild completely not only the judicial system, but also the entirety of Rwanda's social institutions, presented a complex and daunting challenge. According to Gourevitch, '[T]he demand of national reunification, of national security, and of justice presented the new leaders with an extremely difficult balancing act' (Gourevitch 1996: 167). The demand of national reunification is highly dependent on the achievement of both personal security and the development of an identity based on a sense of nationalism as opposed to ethnicity.[18]

The aftermath of the genocide left Rwanda, a country among the poorest in the world, in a state of ruin and turmoil that was highlighted by insecurity. The necessity for the maintenance of peace and the establishment of personal security – to an acceptable level, allowing for the advancement of policies and programmes designed to seek justice and hence reconciliation – was of the utmost concern. A further issue for the fledgling government was achieving a stable environment within which the policies of the Government of National Unity could be addressed.[19] Of primary importance to this process was achieving an end to the ongoing attacks from across the border in the Democratic Republic of Congo (DRC) and, to a lesser extent, Burundi, attacks that were organized by Hutu rebel extremists fleeing to both countries. This threatened the lives of not only those who had remained in Rwanda after the RPF victory, but also those Rwandans living in refugee camps located in the DRC and Burundi.[20] Indeed, many of these refugees were forced to return, while others sought to return to Rwanda on their own accord. Beyond the deaths, according to Mamdani, 'the war also displaced a substantial minority, so large that it came to include *one out of every seven Rwandans*' (Mamdani 2001b: 203). Relocation camps for returning externally, as well as internally, displaced Rwandans, constructed within the borders of Rwanda, were additional sources of concern based on allegations of inhumane treatment and indiscriminate killings of suspected collaborators of the Hutu extremist rebels (Human Rights Watch 2001). The rampant fear among both returning refugees,[21] and survivors still living in Rwanda created a situation of great tension and anxiety.[22]

Manby and Odinklalu argue that under these conditions of instability, 'the easiest way to guarantee a repeat of war is to fail to invest in rebuilding the institutions that prevent impunity in peace time' (Manby and Odinklalu 2004: 154). Sarkin observed fear, based on membership in an ethnic group, existing on the part of both Hutus and Tutsis in the months and years following the genocide (Sarkin 1999: 782). The culture of impunity, a pervasive condition within Rwanda, was another source that attributed to observed fear.

Issues of personal security increase significantly in an atmosphere in which there has been no accountability for those who perpetrate crimes. An environment in which there exists a belief in one's status of exemption from punishment enhances the likelihood of becoming involved in criminal activity. Hatzfeld explains that:

> [c]rimes against the Tutsi usually went unpunished. Two members of the gang from Kibungo, for example, killed a Tutsi before the genocide without ever being convicted by the judicial system: Élie Mizinge, the former soldier, admits to the murder of a social worker during a demonstration in 1992; another youth protests his innocence but is implicated in a murder by all the evidence, including testimony from his friends.
>
> (Hatzfeld 2005: 55)

The importance of establishing the rule of law by the judiciary is of even greater significance to the Rwandan situation given the deplorable historical record of that judiciary.

A culture of impunity existed in Rwanda from the Hutu revolution of 1959 to the proliferation of the genocide in 1994. This was particularly evident with the questioning and conviction of those involved in crimes against Tutsis. Martin Ngoga, Deputy Prosecutor of Rwanda, reported that:

> [i]n the pre-1994 era, the people of Rwanda endured human rights violations on a massive scale over a period spanning more than those decades. Beginning in 1959, State inspired violence was directed against innocent citizens in form of persecution, loss, or destruction of property, torture, imprisonment, death, and banishment to exile. Unfortunately the culture of impunity prevailed for all that long. No attempts were ever made to bring the perpetrators of this violence to justice, and as a result, a culture of impunity took root in Rwandese society.
>
> (Ngoga 2005: np)

Behind a social understanding, in which the idea of exemption may be thought to have existed, lay an institutionally-created environment that shaped such a condition. This period of unchecked violence, which began with the Hutu revolution of 1959 and continued through the genocide of 1994, set a precedent of impunity that created this social mindset within Rwandese society. It established the belief that the judicial system was unsympathetic towards the plight of its citizens who suffered from violence perpetrated within its own borders by other Rwandans.[23]

An institutional component of major significance – with regard to not only the creation and establishment of a culture of impunity, but also concerning the decision-making process undertaken by the Rwandan government following the genocide – was the codification of the culture of impunity in the form of Amnesty laws. In accordance with the first Law of General Amnesty of 1963, the government provided for amnesty as follows:

> 1. Unconditional general amnesty is given for all offences, committed during the Social Revolution between 1959 October 1 and 1962 July 1, that, due to their nature, their motives, their circumstances or to what inspired them, are part of the fight for national liberation, and take on a political character even though these offences are an infringement to the common law.
> 2. Offences committed during this period by people opposing the liberation of the oppressed mass from feudal colonial domination are not benefiting from the amnesty given in the first article of this present law.
> (Government of Rwanda 1963: 431)[24]

Section 1 represents the Law on General Amnesty for political offences committed between 1 October 1959 and 1 July 1962. The Hutu government in power at the time created a publicly-recognizable and politically-defended culture of impunity for those who engaged in violence against their fellow citizens at the behest of the State. This apparent abuse of law, as a means for political ends, can be argued to have set the stage for the violent bloodshed of the 1994 genocide. Additionally, the second section of the law may be interpreted as specifically denying amnesty to the Tutsi population who committed crimes against the masses of people struggling for national liberation – or alternatively, Tutsis who committed crimes in self-defence. Liberation from feudal colonial domination represents the majority Hutu struggle against both the colonial rule of the Belgians, and the monarchist rule of the Mwami, a position in Rwandan pre-colonial history held by a Tutsi.[25] The institutionalized nature of the government's approach to violent crimes became more evident and further entrenched in Rwandan society when the second amnesty decree, in 1974, conferred immunity for violent crimes that, 'due to their nature, their motives, their circumstance as to what have inspired them, have a political character' (Government of Rwanda 1974: 626). According to Caplan *et al*:

> Violence and extremism swiftly burgeoned in the hothouse atmosphere that soon prevailed throughout Rwanda. Old patterns re-emerged. There had been no punishment for those Hutu who had led the massacres of the Tutsi in the early 1960s and 1972–73, and the careers flourished of those who organized cruel repression of opponents throughout the first decade and a

half of the Habyarimana regime. Now, in the wake of the October 1, 1990, invasion, impunity flourished for the demagogues who were deliberately fuelling the latent animosity toward those they considered perfidious outsiders, a category including not just the Tutsi refugee-warriors of the RPF but every Tutsi still in Rwanda, as well as any Hutu alleged to be their sympathizer.

(Caplan et al 2000: 39)

As noted, the culture of impunity observed in Rwanda is a historically key component in the process of arriving at a judicial form for dealing with the genocide in post-conflict Rwanda. As such, the Rwandan government made 'justice one of the cornerstones of its policy. It argued that unless the "culture of impunity" was once and for all ended in Rwanda, the vicious cycle of violence would never end' (Uvin 2001: 181).

The international context

One must consider the contexts that framed the role of the international community before, during, and after the genocide. Dallaire, Manocha, and Degnarain state that 'the Hutu génocidaires were able to realize their murderous plans because three major powers [France, United States, and the United Kingdom] helped create and maintain the necessary conditions – a context of impunity – that made it effortlessly easy' (Dallaire, Manocha, and Degnarain 2005: 862). The factors that were crucial in determining the intervention, or lack thereof, by these major powers are three-fold: (1) failure to intercede in Rwanda to prevent the genocide before it actually occurred; (2) ending it after its onslaught had begun;[26] and (3) the decision to adjudicate the perpetrators in an international court. Beyond the arguable complicity of the international community in allowing the genocide to occur,[27] two specific elements are of contextual importance. First, the previously-discussed historical response to mass atrocities originating in the Nuremburg Trials, and, second, the parallel creation and operation of the International Criminal Tribunal for Yugoslavia (ICTY). These factors have played a significant role in the search for justice and the path taken by the international community.

Des Forges and Longman state that there was 'international refusal to recognize [that] the genocide was wrong, both morally and legally. When the killing began, evidence of preparations for mass slaughter had been available to the UN, the United States, France, and Belgium for several months' (Des Forges and Longman 2004: 51).[28] They further argue that the failure of the international community to take actions, based on the information that was presented, produced a sense of guilt that was a significant contributing factor in the development of the ICTR (Des Forges and Longman 2004: 52).

According to Uvin and Mironko, as a result of the inaction by the international community during the genocide, despite information of its occurrence, the International Criminal Tribunal for Rwanda (ICTR) was not created as assistance to Rwanda: 'rather, it is about symbolic politics: we, the international community, do care about Rwanda, are outraged by it, and solemnly pledge to show our disapproval' (Uvin and Mironko 2003: 220). This statement can be observed to reflect an attempt to reduce the international community's feelings of guilt rather than an altruistic attempt at assistance.[29] The United Nations's response to the situation in the Balkans, including military action to address the conflict as it was occurring, followed by the creation and operation of the ICTY, set a precedent for action under such circumstances. Having failed the Rwandan people by their inaction in preventing or stopping the genocide, it is therefore not surprising that the United Nations would feel compelled to embark on a judicial process similar to that in the Balkans.

A final contextual element that played a role in the involvement of the international community was the creation and operation of a parallel *ad hoc* tribunal addressing crimes committed during the conflict in the former Yugoslavia. Referred by Bass (2000) as the *twin tribunal*, the establishment and development of the ICTY provided a template for an *ad hoc* international tribunal for Rwanda.

Conceptual framework

Within a process of restructuring a stable and functioning government to meet domestic and international concerns, it can be argued that 'justice becomes the causality of a political calculation' (Allen 2001: 315). Given the crucial contextual elements presented here, the first concept that needs addressing is justice and how this concept was understood and operationalized by the various actors involved in this judicial process at the time. A consideration of how justice was actually implemented will follow in later chapters.

The concept of justice is broad and wide-ranging in scope. For the purposes of this discussion, the central theoretical focus is provided by the related, yet distinct, concepts of restorative and retributive justice. Both forms of justice are relevant to the Rwandan context since they provide a theoretical basis for understanding the methods through which justice will be achieved. The various methods of adjudication, and the forums in which they occur, involve a further theoretical line of inquiry: the distinction between what Bass refers to as liberal-legalism and its antithesis, totalitarian show trials (Bass 2000: 26). The relationship that the search for justice for Rwanda has within the framework of *cosmopolitan law*, as put forth by Hirsch (2003), is also germane and will be addressed here. Finally, the creation and establishment of the rule of law as a permanent fixture in the newly-constructed socio-political landscape of Rwanda will be examined.

Restorative and retributive justice

Justice, broadly defined, 'is a response to a powerful moral intuition that "something must be done," that something (someone) has disturbed the way things out to be and something must be done to right the wrong, to make things right' (Llewellyn and Howse 1998: 13). The conceptualization of justice within the Rwandan context focuses primarily on criminal justice responses to address the crimes that took place during the genocide. For that reason, this theoretical framework will focus on this narrower realm of justice. Although there are additional theories of justice that fall within this narrower conceptualization, such as procedural justice, distributive justice, and others,[30] the two justice paradigms that will applied here are restorative and retributive justice. Scholars argue that these two paradigms offer competing conceptualizations of justice, utilize different processes, and seek to achieve different results.

Restorative justice, including its composite set of theories and practices, is a relatively recent development that has received increasing attention, interest, and support.[31] Johnstone argues that, until recently, 'in public discourse it [was] commonly taken for granted that the usual response to the commission of crime should, when possible, be a court trial followed by judicial punishment for the perpetrator' (Johnstone 2002: 1). The underlying philosophy and associated practices of restorative justice have gained in both popularity and relative use over the traditional criminal justice system that focuses on a retributive justice philosophy and practices.[32] More than 30 years following its modern-day inception, Miller and Schacter argue that 'restorative justice has assumed a legitimate place in criminal justice discourse' (Miller and Schacter 2000: 405). Restorative justice theory, policy, and practice have garnered attention worldwide, and have resulted in the development and implementation of restorative justice processes throughout the world.

Broadly speaking, restorative and retributive theories of justice share an overarching sense of the desired outcome when confronted with an injustice: 'their commitment to establishing/re-establishing social equality between the wrongdoer and the sufferer of the wrong' (Llewellyn and Howse 1998: 21). Additionally, they both seek to censure wrongdoing as part of the process of seeking justice. Although both perspectives engage in the clarification of what is considered normal or deviant, and thereby permissible or non-permissible, within a given society, they radically differ from each other with respect to how to attain that goal. Daly presents a succinct overview of the sharp distinction that critics make about these so-called competing paradigms:

(1) restorative justice focuses on *repairing the harm* caused by crime, whereas retributive justice focuses on *punishing and offence*;
(2) restorative justice is characterized by *dialogue and negotiation* among the parties, whereas retributive justice is characterized by *adversarial relations* among the parties; and
(3) restorative justice assumes that community members or organizations take a more active role, whereas for retributive justice, 'the community' is represented by the state.

(Daly 2002: 58–9)

Braithwaite notes that restorative justice has typically been defined with respect to what it is not, retributive justice (Braithwaite 1999).[33] Defining a paradigm of justice through a process that considers what it is not, as opposed to what it is, has led to much confusion and debate within the scholarly work surrounding restorative justice.[34] Nevertheless, there have been significant efforts undertaken to provide a set of foundational criteria that represent restorative justice. According to Galaway and Hudson, restorative justice is characterized by three central components:

> First, crime is viewed primarily as a conflict between individuals that results in injuries to victims, communities and the offenders themselves, and only secondarily as a violation against the state. Second, the aim of the criminal justice process should be to create peace in communities by reconciling the parties and repairing the injuries caused by the dispute. Third, the criminal justice process should facilitate active participation by victims, offenders, and their communities in order to find solutions to the conflict.
>
> (Galaway and Hudson 1996: 2)

Proponents of restorative justice argue that these underlying components provide the fundamental point of departure from a retributive justice approach.

The development of a polemic definition of restorative justice opposing retributive justice is the direct result of the social context in which it developed, namely to address the perceived inadequacies and failures of the criminal justice system.[35] Approaching crime from a different perspective, proponents of restorative justice began by asking different questions about the causes of crime and, by extension, how to address them. According to Zehr:

> Restorative justice sees things differently ... Crime is a violation of people and relationships ... it creates obligations to make things right. Justice involves the victim, the offender, and the community in a search for solutions which promote repair, reconciliation, and reassurance.
>
> (Zehr 1990: 181)

It has been argued that this conceptualization of crime is in stark contrast to the definition of crime within a retributive paradigm wherein crime is conceived as a wilful violation of the law that is punishable by the State: 'We can respond to behaviour that breaks law by focusing exclusively on the rule that was broken [retributive response] or by looking first at the harm it causes to people and relationships [restorative justice]' (Van Ness *et al* 2001: 3). The way in which one defines crime has implications with regard to the appropriate response to crime. As a theory of justice, restorative justice:

> provides a new vision for a future community justice response to crime based on a different set of values and principles, focused on the needs of a

different set of clients, and involved as participants in a range of decisions about the most appropriate response to crime.

(Bazemore 1998: 777)

This perspective considers restorative justice to be a relational process involving all those affected by crime: the victim, the offender, and the community. The inclusion of all the stakeholders in a dialogical response to crime is a central tenet of the paradigm. Unlike the retributive justice approach, which focuses on violations of law and punishment of the offender using a 'just deserts' philosophy, the primary focus of the process is to address and repair the harm that has resulted from the violation of the law.

As an alternative to what are viewed as the ineffective, undesirable, and counter-productive responses to crime found within the traditional court system, the restorative justice philosophy manifests itself in a variety of processes (McCold 1998: 5). These include victim–offender mediation, sentencing circles, healing circles, restitution programmes, and family group conferences.

The judicial responses to the crimes committed in Rwanda in 1994 involve a number of processes to achieve justice. Explicit within all of their mandates is both a restorative aspect contributing to reconciliation, as well as a retributive element that seeks to eradicate the culture of impunity through punishing individual offenders. Former Registrar of the ICTR, Agwu Ukiwe Okali, addressing the concerns of witnesses and victims at the tribunal, 'laid out his conceptual argument for a victim-oriented restorative justice for Rwanda, to be undertaken, not by the tribunal's judges, who in the context needed to focus on trials, but by the office of the registrar' (cited in Moghalu 2005: 68). The capacity for achieving reconciliation will be argued to be associated with the type of justice incorporated into the judicial response. The ICTR and the Rwandan national judiciary have incorporated the traditional trial method, while the Gacaca employs a more community-based approach to dealing with the offences. Despite this initial distinction, each response contains elements from both perspectives. Therefore, they need to be assessed as to whether a retributive, restorative, or mixed approach to justice has provided the underlying philosophy behind each of their processes. Additionally, more depth that is theoretical is provided in the course of the analyses as conclusions are drawn with respect to each response's perceived ability to address the crimes and the extended issues associated with them.

Responsive regulation

Ayres and Braithwaite developed the idea of *responsive regulation* in response to 'the need to transcend the intellectual stalemate between those who favor strong state regulation of business and those who advocate deregulation' (Ayres and Braithwaite 1992: 3). Braithwaite extends this idea to a more broadly-defined notion of social control by including a discussion of the relative positioning of restorative methods of justice and the traditional retributive methods of justice: 'The basic idea of responsive regulation is that governments should be responsive to the conduct of those they seek to regulate in deciding whether a more or less interventionist approach is needed' (Ayres and Braithwaite 1992: 29). The State's response to unwanted social conduct should be responsive, that is altering its response to the way that people regulate their own conduct outside of the confines of State intervention. Braithwaite continues by sharply contrasting responsive regulation with its antithesis, regulatory formalism: 'The formalist says to define in advance which problems require which response and write rules to mandate those responses ... Responsive regulation requires us to challenge such a presumption' (Ayres and Braithwaite 1992).

The *regulatory pyramid* provides a model of responding to crime that 'attempt[s] to solve the puzzle of when to punish and when to persuade' (Ayres and Braithwaite 1992: 30). In response to both the character of the individual actor, and their response to attempts to regulate their behaviour, the pyramid provides a fluid process that suggests the appropriate degree of intervention required:

> The crucial point is that this is a dynamic model. It is not about suggesting in advance which are the types of matters that should be dealt with at the base of the pyramid, which are the more serious ones that should be in the middle, and which are the most egregious ones for the peak of the model.
>
> (Ayres and Braithwaite 1992)

Beginning at the bottom of the pyramid with a restorative justice dialogue-based response, seeking to persuade, the escalation of responses finishes at the top with a retributive response, incapacitation. 'The idea of the pyramid is that our presumption should always be to start at the base of the pyramid then escalate to somewhat more punitive approaches only when the more moderate forms of punishment fail' (Ayres and Braithwaite 1992: 30). Braithwaite qualifies the base presumption of the model stating that circumstances will confront those addressing crime that do not permit for a strict adherence to the model. Nevertheless, Braithwaite suggests that wherever possible, the model will lead to positive results.

The suggested success of the model is premised on the observation that the various methods of seeking justice are all destined to fail under some circumstances: 'This design responds to the fact that restorative justice, deterrence, and incapacitation are all limited and flawed theories of compliance' (Ayres and Braithwaite 1992: 32). The model of responsive regulation proposes to address the weaknesses of each type of intervention through a process that allows the utilization of other intervention strategies in a complimentary way. When one intervention fails, another is utilized to address the failure. Furthermore, Ayres and Braithwaite state:

The ordering of the strategies in the pyramid is not just about putting the less costly, less coercive, more respectful options lower down in order to save money and preserve freedom as non-domination. It is also that by resorting to more dominating, less respectful forms of social control only when more dialogic forms have been tried first, coercive control comes to be seen as more legitimate.

(Ayres and Braithwaite 1992)

Finally, they suggest a rational choice account for the proposed success of the model. Resulting from the escalatory nature of the pyramid, that depends on the individual's response to the selected intervention strategy in which 'non-compliance comes to be seen (accurately) as a slippery slope that will inexorably lead to a sticky end' (Ayres and Braithwaite 1992: 33). The potential and real threat of increasingly punitive measures at the disposal of those responding to crime will eventually lead to compliance, or alternatively, incapacitation.

Liberal-legalism: the use of trials within the context of mass atrocity

The notion of holding those who have committed large-scale acts of atrocity accountable before an international court of law originated with the trials that took place following the Second World War at Nuremburg. Bass states that the elevation of Nuremburg War Crimes Tribunal as *the* distinctive event in dealing with mass atrocities in an international arena is misleading due in large part to both its recent occurrence and its perceived success (Bass 2000: 5). He demonstrates this by presenting seven historical and judicial precursors to Nuremburg that facilitated the debates surrounding the formation of the Nuremburg trials.[36] Despite this contested status, the impact of the Nuremburg trials was of great significance in providing a legacy whereby the legalistic model became the accepted method for dealing with the perpetrators of mass atrocities. It reflected what has been referred to as a post-Cold War move towards liberal-internationalism, which 'sees the relevant political community as nothing less than body of humanity ... and, [employs] the tools of liberal legalism to legitimize the overwhelming preponderant place that the institutions of liberal societies have come to play' (Chibundu 2008: 2).

As the means to address the atrocities committed by the Germans during the Second World War, the decision to embark upon the formation of an international tribunal was not an easy process. According to Kochavi:

A joint allied policy was reached only after the end of the war; the issue of punishing war criminals was widely discussed throughout most of the war years and entailed a host of diplomatic, military, legal, and moral considerations and the interplay of domestic and world political factors.

(Kochavi 1998: 1)

Amidst the numerous factors that were involved in the decision-making process, the decision of how this process was to occur was one of the most central aspects of the discussions. The nations involved in the pursuit of justice – by holding those responsible for the crimes accountable and punishing them for said crimes – each brought to the debate their own domestic policies regarding the resolution of crime and punishment, as well as the experiences that their soldiers and civilians had endured during the war. According to Bass, this debate centred on concepts of idealism placed in an international forum, and the struggle between those who on the one side were realists (or pragmatists) and those on the other side who were liberal-legalists (Bass 2000). The debate between realism and liberal-legalism as the foundation for Nuremburg can be observed in the policies of the nations involved. It was also readily evident in the internal debate that occurred in the United States concerning the type of solution that it would endorse.

Bass argues that a nation's domestic policy will affect its decisions concerning foreign and international policies as well (Bass 2000: 17). The legalistic model used in the creation of the Tribunal was but one available option debated.[37] The range of options considered were vastly different, ranging from the totalitarian show-trials endorsed by the Soviets with the potential summary executions of an estimated 50,000 German officers and some civilian leaders, to the resulting highly-legalistic military trial of the major war criminals that was greatly endorsed by the United States.

Bass described the philosophical underpinnings of both sides of the debate. The realist argument was 'that international relations differ from domestic politics in the lack of a common ruler among self-interested states ... In the dangerous brawl of international anarchy ... idealistic and legalistic policies are a luxury that states can ill afford' (Bass 2000: 9). The realists' solution to these issues was that the victorious states, acting in their own self-interest, would impose whatever sanctions they desire upon their defeated enemy and determine justice as they see fit. They will engage in 'an amoral struggle for security – regardless of their domestic ideals' (Bass 2000: 16). According to the realists, therefore, the concept of engaging in international moralizing (itself a non-issue) in the form of a tribunal is an enigmatic farce. Morgenthau readily demonstrated the expedient solution, according to this position within the internal debates that occurred in the United States: 'What in my opinion they should have done is set up summary courts-martial. Then they should have placed these criminals on trial before them within 24 hours after they were caught, sentenced them to death, and shot them in the morning' (Bass 2000: 10). The expedient realist solution was not to be realized.[38]

The liberal-legalistic model provided the structural foundations for Nuremburg. In the internal debate within the United States, Stimson successfully championed the liberal-legalist approach. Stimson argued that Nuremburg should necessarily proceed through a process of fair trials, seeking to hold individuals accountable for their war crimes, in an effort to demonstrate clearly the wrongs done, and effectively punish them as a deterrent of any such future actions. These standards associated with a liberal-legalistic approach, 'clearly grew out of Stimson's respect for basic American legal rights, with explicit reference to the Bill of Rights' (Bass 2000: 156). The procedural justice of due process was another element of Stimson's rhetoric: 'I do not mean to favor the institution of state trials or to introduce any cumbersome machinery but the very punishment of these men in a dignified manner consistent with the advance of civilization, will have a greater effect upon posterity' (Bass 2000: 165).

As was previously noted, the incorporation of the liberal-legalistic model was not the sole option available. Bass, therefore, argued that the domestic policy employed by a nation would play a significant role in how the State engages in international affairs (Bass 2000: 14). In a fashion similar to that observed in the development of US policy, other countries also arrived at similar policy implications resulting from their domestic policies. The resulting legalistic model was, according to Tutorow, almost a natural occurrence: 'It is inevitable the formulation of rules of warfare should lead to increasing concern with the issues of legality and illegality, since rules are inevitably violated and violations imply some sort of responsibility and accountability' (Tutorow 1986: 4). This statement echoes the idealistic view of liberal-legalism, which, at its core, claims that it represents 'the ethical attitude that holds moral conduct to be a matter of rule following, and moral relationships to consist of duties and rights determined by rules' (Shklar 1964: 1).

On 8 August 1945, representatives from Great Britain, France, the United States and the Soviet Union signed the London Charter for the International Military Tribunal.[39] In Accordance with Article 1, the Tribunal was created for the purpose of 'the just and prompt trial and punishment of the major war criminals of the European Axis' (London Charter 1945). In what may be described as a resounding recognition of the defeat of a realist approach in favour of the liberal-legalistic approach, the opening statement at Nuremburg by Justice Jackson began a process that would, in spite of continuing questions and criticisms, become a recognized standard framework for dealing with mass atrocities in an international forum: 'THAT FOUR GREAT NATIONS, flushed with victory and stung with injury, stay the hand of vengeance and voluntarily submit their captive enemies to the judgment of law is one of the most significant tributes that Power has ever paid to Reason' (cited in Bass 2000: 147). The significance of the Nuremburg Tribunal can be observed in the establishment of additional international tribunals that have been constructed on the legalistic foundation that it firmly established.[40]

The precedent set by the Nuremburg Tribunal, itself a result of other evolutionary, albeit unsuccessful, attempts at establishing law within the international arena, has resulted in legislation that transcends the boundaries of national sovereignty. The underlying belief in the universality of basic human rights associated with the liberal-legalistic tradition permits the ideological crossing of national boundaries by definition. As stated by Bass, '[U]niversal human rights do not respect "geographical morality" or sovereignty' (Bass 2000: 22). The extension of the legalistic model, with its focus on a fair trial resulting from a deeply-held respect for due process – beyond national borders to address cases where the universal rights ascribed to all human beings have been violated – is seemingly apparent in its justification and not, in theory at least, an unthinkable step. The establishment of the liberal-legalistic model, utilizing the trial method as the pre-eminent means of dealing with violations of human rights regardless of national borders, is of monumental significance.

In contrast to what many have come to remember Nuremburg – such as the Allies dealing with the unthinkable offences of the Holocaust – for its primary aim was to address the *crimes against peace* and additional war crimes. According to Meltzer, '[T]he paramount role accorded by the Tribunal to crimes against peace was in sharp contrast to the extremely limited scope it gave to crimes against humanity' (Meltzer 2002: 563). Despite what may be referred to as a self-interested focus by the United States on crimes against peace, the inclusion of crimes against humanity in the Tribunal's Charter along with the record that it created in the process of the trials, set the groundwork for the UN Genocide Convention (Meltzer 2002: 564).

The historical record of international responses to the gravest of human actions provides an account of the ideological struggle that resulted in the establishment of liberal-legalism as the accepted model, or *modus operandi*, for international criminal proceedings. Propelling the model into the international arena is the recognition of the universality of human rights and a belief that national borders and contentions of sovereignty do not insulate one from accountability. It further established the trial method, and its unwavering dedication to due process and individual rights, as the appropriate method for dealing with those who choose to violate the legislated rules. This historical process represents, as a cumulative end, the extension of the rule of law from its previously held position of respect at the national level, and establishes itself as a presence in international concerns and conflicts.

Cosmopolitan law

Before embarking on the initial analysis of the three judicial responses, it is important to first address the method through which the attempt to achieve a sense of justice was made. One of the central features of the adjudication of the perpetrators involved in the Rwandan genocide is that the overall process encompasses three distinct, albeit intertwined, realms of the Rwandan context: (1) the *international* as represented by the ICTR; (2) the *national* represented by the Rwandan formal judiciary; and (3) the *community* where the Gacaca operates. The interconnectedness of these responses, combined with their independence, provides a complexity of their structuring and functioning in producing the goals they seek. The Gacaca courts address the lower-level offenders, the national courts deal with the most serious offenders within the national jurisdiction, and the ICTR addresses the criminals who have escaped prosecution within Rwanda. The net impact of this approach is the widening of the net of accountability for the crimes.

The judicial activity at the ICTR can be argued to be an inchoate step in the direction of what Hirsch refers to as *cosmopolitan law*: 'the emerging body of law that aims to protect the human rights of individuals and groups, primarily from serious threats that may be posed to them by their "own" states, by invading states, or by other state-like social formations' (Hirsch 2003: vi). The focus of cosmopolitan law becomes the individual rights of all human beings. As an extension of international humanitarian law, it goes further in addressing the issue of human rights since its treatment of the issues begins with the premise that the 'outdated categories of sovereignty, national interest and international law do not provide an adequate framework to make sense of current conflicts or to challenge their worst excesses' (Hirsch 2003: iii). This new form of law challenges the unilateral supremacy of national sovereignty through the incorporation of a Kantian conceptualization of a global community of humanity, or universalism, which overrides the concerns and authority of any individual nation-state. 'The logic of cosmopolitan law is to tie the idea of universal human rights to a legal structure that can give those rights some concrete reality independently of the state' (Hirsch 2003: 11).

The realization of cosmopolitan law in actual practice, according to Hirsch, remains somewhat illusive, in a state of developmental infancy, and accompanied by a record that included a few instances demonstrating modest examples of limited success (Hirsch 2003: xiv). Additionally, cosmopolitan law is merely one complimentary tool in a toolbox of activities employed to establish an overall cosmopolitan ideal: 'Law is just one weapon. It is a compliment to, not a substitute for, political action, education, and organization against those social foundations that seek to commit genocide or ethnic cleansing' (Hirsch 2003).

Nuremburg is cited by Hirsch as 'the beginning of the process of the actualization of cosmopolitan law' (Hirsch 2003: 38). He further notes a number of significant legal precedents that have resulted from the various international trials and tribunals that have prosecuted gross violations of fundamental human rights and the issues surrounding them. With regard to specific accomplishments, Hirsch recognizes the following:

> A state may no longer argue that the principle of national sovereignty disbars foreign courts from trying its nationals for such crimes or trying those suspected of committing such crimes within its territory. The right of sovereignty is not absolute, but is related to other rights. Crimes against humanity are the concern of humanity as a whole, irrespective of where and under what jurisdiction they were committed. The principle of individual behest of states, by the leaders of states, or with the blessing of the legal system of states, is also clearly established.
>
> (Hirsch 2003: xiv)

The importance of these trials – in their potential for establishing concrete applications of the principle of universalism and cosmopolitan law –

additionally established the use of the trial method as the accepted vehicle whereby international, and arguably national, responses to the violation of fundamental human rights became institutionalized.

The rule of law

Within Rwandan society, there is an evident need for the establishment of a concept of justice that permeates all aspects of the society. The idea that justice involves a societal approach suggests that all structural elements of society incorporate the concept of justice. The observation that justice must extend throughout society demonstrates the interplay between the individuals that make up a given society and the institutions in which they operate on a daily basis.[41] Thompson states that 'the notion of the regulation and reconciliation of conflicts through the rule of law – and the elaboration of rule and procedures which, on occasion, made some approximate approach towards the ideal – seems to me a cultural achievement of significance' (Thompson 1975: 266).

In the study of British society from historical, cultural, and Marxist perspectives, Thompson attested to the significance of the role of law in the process of societal evolution and relations (Thompson 1975). From his investigations into the creation and results of the Black Act of 1723 in England, he theorized about the familiar notion of the rule of law.[42] At that period in history, he notes that 'what is remarkable (we are reminded) is not that the laws were bent but the fact that there was, anywhere in the eighteenth century, a rule of law at all' (Thompson 1975: 261). The importance of law is premised, to some degree, by what Thompson believed to be missing in earlier Marxist explanations: 'I am insisting only upon the obvious point, which some modern Marxists have overlooked, that there is a difference between arbitrary power and the rule of law' (Thompson 1975: 265). His definition of the rule of law states that 'the rule of law itself, the imposed inhibitions upon power and the defence of the citizen from power's all-intrusive claim, seems to me to be an unqualified human good' (Thompson 1975: 266).

Thompson stresses the importance of law within a given society, and the impact that it has on determining the structural arrangements that underlie the functioning of other social institutions and social relationships in society (Thompson 1975: 260). Despite his observation that law serves an ideological function-lending support to the hegemony of the ruling class in a given society – that nevertheless results in creating boundaries for the ruling class themselves. While the law may be observed as providing legitimization for the structuring of ruling class position and power, it nevertheless also presents them with boundaries regarding their own actions and, by extension, provides the lower class with a means of redress against actions by the ruling class that do not comply with the ideological structure of the law:

> The rulers were, in serious senses, whether willingly or unwillingly, the prisoners of their own rhetoric; they played the games of power according

to rules which suited them, but they could not break those rules or the whole game would be thrown away.

(Thompson 1975: 263)

Thompson, it appears, remained optimistic that the rule of law demonstrates the potential for emancipation of the oppressed class in society. As a check on intrusions of power, governed by strict regulations, the law can provide all citizens with the potential for redress of wrongs done to them.

According to Cosgrove (1980), Venn Dicey's writings focused on the British Constitutional arrangements, presents a conceptualization of the rule of law and its function in society that is congruent with, and to some degree extends, beyond that of Thompson's. Cosgrove states that:

> In the first sense, Dicey believed in the 'absolute supremacy or pre-dominance of regular law as opposed to the influence of arbitrary power, and excludes the existence of arbitrariness, of prerogative, or even of wide discretionary authority on the part of government. Englishmen are ruled by the law, and by the law alone; a man may be punished for a breach of law, but he can be punished for nothing else'.
>
> (Cosgrove 1980: 78)

Evident in Dicey's qualification of the rule of law is the idea that law is applicable to all. That is, no one is above the law, and all are equal under the law. Furthermore, the rule of law reflects the principles of *crimen sine lege* (no crime without law) and *poena sine lege* (no punishment except as a consequence for violating law).

The following chapters explore each *level* of the judicial response in the post-conflict Rwanda. It provides a discussion of their history, creation, and proposed method of responding to the genocide, as well as how these aspects operate within the theoretical framework described above.

Notes

1 See Newbury (1998), Taylor (1999), Melvern (2004), and Moghalu (2005) for a more detailed discussion of this debate.
2 According to Mamdani, the importance of the latter point of view was significant in the production of the anti-Tutsi sentiment and propaganda that was critical in the promulgation of the genocide in 1994 (Mamdani 2001). The 'Hamitic Hypothesis', both created and supported that idea that the Tutsi were an 'alien' race to Rwanda and therefore, did not have a legitimate claim to engage in political life in Rwanda:

> The Tutsi may have emigrated from elsewhere, but they did not see this as a politically relevant fact. It is worth noting that while royal myths claimed a sacred origin of the *mwami* (king), they never claimed a foreign origin.
>
> (Mamdani 2001: 79)

3 This historical structure of Rwandan society continues to exist in current-day Rwanda. The country remains a highly organized state with centralized control emanating from the government located in Kigali, Rwanda's capital city. The political structure remains consistent with the noted historical four-tiered divisions of the country: province, district, sector, and cell.

4 It is important to note that this appropriation of land did not solely target Hutu lands, but also the land of 'lower-ranking' Tutsi. Additionally, accompanying this land appropriation was 'the institution of payment of dues – commodities or service – by the Hutus and socially lower ranked Tutsi' (Moghalu 2005: 10).

5 According to Mamdani, '[T]he idea that the Tutsi were superior because they came from elsewhere, and that the difference between them and the local population was a *racial* difference, was an idea of colonial origin' (Mamdani 2001: 80). The construction of the Tutsi identity as an *alien race* was incorporated into Rwandan society and became fixed as a *natural occurrence*. For a more detailed explanation of the Hamitic Hypothesis see Mamdani (2001).

6 Argued to be among the first to explore racial superiority based on biological characteristics, Speke published *Journal of the discovery of the source of the Nile* in 1864. The notion that racial superiority based on the successful subjugation of one race over another via military conquest formed the basis of his work.

7 The Hamitic Hypothesis was 'constructed' during the colonial period in Africa. It is not unique to the Rwandan context, but it was incorporated into Rwandan society in a manner not observed elsewhere. It became an accepted explanation of the ethnic differences and division between Hutu and Tutsi, not only from the colonial powers, but also the Rwandan people themselves. The basic idea behind the hypothesis is that the Tutsi, the observed dominant group in pre-colonial society, were descendants of Ham, the son of Noah who had been sent away by his family in disgrace, and, therefore, were not actually Negroid in its background, but a dark-skinned white race. The Hamitic Hypothesis was constructed in order to make sense of the existence of a highly organized and structured society that was not conceivably possible to have been created by a savage, backwards, Negroid race.

8 According to Mamdani, this work was completed by 'Fathers Arnoux, Hurel, Pagés, and Schumacher – Church fathers with expertise' (Mamdani 2001: 88).

9 According to Mamdani:

> [D]ecolonization in Africa unfolded along two different trajectories, setting apart the process of decolonization in settler colonies from that in colonies without settler minorities … the two trajectories – one armed, the other non-violent – were at the same time testimony to different modes of colonization in these places.
>
> (Mamdani 2001: 103)

The situation in Rwanda, however, did not fall into either of these two modes as a result of its unique colonial background which was 'more of a halfway house between a direct rule and indirect-rule colony' (Mamdani 2001: 103).

10 According to Newbury:

> [I]n May 1958, a group of conservatives at the royal court responded to the Hutu Manifesto in arrogant, dismissive language. In a public statement, these notables wrote that there was no basis for brotherhood and cooperation between Hutu and Tutsi, since many years ago Tutsi had subjugated Hutu by force.
>
> (Newbury 1998: 10)

11 UNAR stands for Union Nationale Rwandaise, a political party organized by members of the Tutsi elite (Mamdani 2001: 119).

12 See Des Forges (1999), Taylor (1999), Mamdani (2001), and Twagilimana (2003) for a more in-depth exploration and analysis of the activities of the Rwandan Patriotic Front.

13 According to Moghalu, Paul Kagame was, in fact, 'an infant survivor of the massacres of Rwandan Tutsis in 1959 who had been taken into exile in Uganda by refugee parents' (Moghalu 2005: 14).

14 The Peace Agreement, signed at Arusha, Tanzania, between the Government of Rwanda and the Rwandese Patriotic Front was negotiated over a period of time extending from October 1990 to August 1993. (This is commonly referred to as the Arusha Accords.)

15 In his book *Shake hands with the devil: the failure of humanity in Rwanda* (2003), Dallaire further outlines how the international community should also share in the burden of responsibility for the genocide.

16 The historical record of a peaceful co-existence between the Hutus and Tutsis in Rwanda's pre-colonial history is not fully known and has been debated by a number of scholars including Des Forges (1999), Prunier (1995), Gourevitch (1998), and Sarkin (1999). There is, however, little debate over the existence of institutionalized divisions and social inequality between the two groups following the entrenched ethnic divisions initiated by the Germans, followed by the implementation of 'ethnic identity cards' during the course of the Belgian colonial rule in Rwanda.

17 Sarkin discusses the violence that continued long after the civil war had ended. He states that 'consequentially, Rwandans are "living in a state of fear, knowing that whatever their ethnic origin or perceived affiliation, they may become targets of arbitrary violence by one side or the other"' (Sarkin 1999: 782).

18 See Mamdani (2001) for a detailed discussion of the issues surrounding the concept of citizenship and the importance that it played in both the creation of conditions conducive to the genocide, as well as the necessity that he claims for national identity and citizenship in the effort to address the genocide and establish Rwanda anew.

19 Sarkin (1999) argues that the process of establishing a truth and reconciliation commission in Rwanda required such a stable environment. Despite the observation that the Rwandan government had rejected such a policy (which will be discussed later), Sarkin's conceptualization that requires a stable situation in which a process seeking justice can be advanced remains relevant. He states that:

> it could be argued that with the violence in Rwanda, Burundi, and Congo, the time is not ripe to undertake such an exercise. However, if one followed this line of thinking it may be that the time is never ripe, or when it is so, much more damage has been done so that the task will be even more difficult.
>
> (Sarkin 1999: 768)

Sarkin also discusses additional issues that arose as a result of the mass repatriation efforts including such things such as disputes over land, arrests, and prison conditions, as well as, the economic struggles that accompanied the situation.

20 Gourevitch discusses the return of the refugees and some of the struggles and concerns that emerged form this effort in repatriation:

> As the return got underway, it was widely reported that the ex-FAR and the interahamwe had retreated deeper into Zaire with the remnants of Mobutu's army, allowing the so-called ordinary refugees to head home. The reality was not so perfect: among those who fled west into Zaire's jungles – perhaps a

hundred and fifty thousand people, perhaps twice as many; nobody knows – there were many noncombatants; and inside Rwanda, it quickly became clear that a great number of people with crimes to answer for had melted into the flood of returnees.

(Gourevitch 1998: 300)

See also Prunier (1995) and Des Forges (1999) for additional commentary of the refugee crisis and process of repatriation. In order to appreciate the massive scale of the project of repatriation, Gourevitch states that the process of repatriation 'culminat[ed] in the return of nearly 1.5 million Hutus from self-imposed exile' (Gourevitch 1996: 167).

21 See United Nations (1996a), Gourevitch (1998), and Alison Des Forges (1999) for a discussion of the realistic basis upon which these fears were created. There are documented occurrences of reprisal attacks on the refugees by members of the Rwandese Patriotic Front in the process of closing the refugee camps and forcing repatriation on the Hutu refugees that have themselves been classified by some as crimes against humanity.

22 Even in the present situation within Rwanda, where there has been comparatively very little violence perpetrated against Tutsis as solely a result of their ethnicity, great fear and anxiety has accompanied the release of prisoners from prison to await their trials in an effort by the government to reduce the observed overcrowded and 'inhumane' conditions of the prisons.

23 Des Forges (1999) also mentions the existence of this historical violence perpetrated in the same time period. She states that 'during the 1960s and again in 1973, Gikongoro was the scene of serious violence against Tutsi' (Des Forges 1999: 2).

24 Translation of the 'Codes et Lois du Rwanda' from French to English was performed by Lucy Pratt. Additionally, for a more complete discussion of the Amnesty Laws, see Brannigan and Jones (2008).

25 See Mamdani (2001) for an insightful discussion into the process undertaken by the two political 'camps' in Rwanda during the process of seeking national sovereignty for the United Nations: the predominantly Tutsi contingent claiming rightful leadership based on the historical rule of the Tutsi Mwami, and the Hutu contingent arguing for leadership based on the concept of 'majority rule'. The decade of the 1950s was one in which a general trend of de-colonization occurred throughout Africa as a result of post-war politics. Rwanda was among the countries that petitioned the United Nations for their independence. The push for independence was supported by both the Hutu and Tutsi in Rwanda. However, they did not agree on the vision that a post-colonial Rwanda would embrace. The Tutsi, while supporting the idea of independence from Belgium, were claiming political control of Rwanda based on historical traditions in the country that placed them in control of the political appointments. The Hutu, by way of contrast, were seeking a democracy, majority rule, as laid out in the Bahutu Manifesto written and signed by Kayibanda and eight other prominent Hutu intellectuals. This manifesto outlined a 'double liberation', first from the colonialist rule of the Belgians, but also from the oppression at the hands of the Tutsi minority.

26 See Dallaire (2003) for a detailed explanation of the international community and especially the United Nations (specifically the Security Council) non-intervention.

27 See Des Forges (1999), Dallaire (2003), Dallaire, Manocha, and Degnarain (2005), LeBor (2006), and Kaplan (2008) for a more detailed discussion of the international factors that contributed to the genocide.

28 Additionally, Hirsch addresses the politics of such a decision-making process. He states that:

the US Government instructed its officials to refuse to call this genocide. This was because, even though a legal duty to act in defense of those being killed does not flow directly from such a characterization, a refusal to use the term makes it easier not to act.

(Hirsch 2003: v)

29 This criticism of the United Nations's involvement and the ICTR in general will be addressed later. At this time, however, the idea of the possibility of the self-serving and inappropriate nature of the United Nations's response is reflected in a statement made by Paul Kagame in which he says, 'In our situation, it's primarily up to the Rwandese. If the international community is going to become involved, there's no way to stop it, given a situation like genocide. But they may provide the wrong remedies to our problems' (Gourevitch 1996: 175).

30 Llewellyn and Howse (1998) discuss the relationship between restorative justice and corrective justice, justice as restitution, and retributive justice.

31 Although discussed as a new paradigm of justice, the ideas behind the restorative justice movement are not *new*. Bianchi (1994), in writing *Justice as sanctuary*, which is in conjunction with the abolitionist movement at the time (see also Cayley 1998, *The expanding prison*), points out that alternative means for achieving justice, such as his focus on the idea of sanctuary, existed prior to the legalistic model that we now refer to as the tradition of the criminal justice system. This is additionally exemplified in the practices of many indigenous cultures prior to the creation of modern criminal justice systems, usually as a result of Western influence in a variety of forms.

32 It should be noted that the use of the term 'traditional' when describing the current criminal justice system is somewhat deceptive as the principles that are associated with the restorative justice movement are said to pre-date the current justice system.

33 According to Daly, 'The oppositional contrast between retributive and restorative justice has become a permanent fixture in the field' (Daly 2000: 34).

34 There has been additional criticism of referring to restorative justice as a paradigm. According to London (2006), the terminological use of 'paradigm', in a Kuhnian sense, locates restorative justice within a closed system, suggesting complete incompatibility with the traditional system and thereby reducing its effectiveness in achieving its goals. Additionally, there are many scholars that argue that retributive and restorative justice are not completely opposite in their conceptualization, sharing some facets in common (see Llewellyn and Howse 1998 and Daly 2002).

35 Llewellyn and Howse (1998) provide a discussion of the social context that the modern restorative justice movement took place within. They identify the following social elements as instrumental in the movement progressing: the informal justice movement, restitution as a response to crime, the victim's rights movement, and the reconciliation/conferencing movement.

36 The list includes the:

abortive treason trials of Bonaparte ... German war criminals after WWI; abortive prosecution of some of the Young Turk perpetrators of the Armenian genocide ... Nuremburg ...; a parallel but less successful process for major Japanese war criminals at the Tokyo international military tribunal; the current ex-Yugoslavia tribunal; and a twin tribunal for Rwanda.

(Bass 2000: 5)

37 For an in-depth discussion on the various options and their specifics, see Kochavi (1998) *Prelude to Nuremburg: allied war crimes policy and the question of punishment.*

38 Bass (2000) recognizes that liberal states, when presented with sufficient concerns regarding their own self-interest, may become tempted to abandon the legalistic ideal in favour of non-legalistic solutions. He notes that issues, such as the safety for their own soldiers and the protection of their citizens, combined with their awareness of the potential risks of carrying out a legalistic approach (such as the acquittal of an accused individual for example, a underlying assumption of a 'fair trial' and the guarantees associated with due process) as possible, may make a legalistic model more difficult to endorse: 'The war crimes policy of liberal states is a push-and-pull of idealism and selfishness' (Bass 2000: 8).

39 According to Meltzer (2002), although all four countries are signatories to the London Charter for the International Military Tribunal the United States, particularly Justice Joe Jackson, was the major contributor to the document's construction. This had an effect on the way that the trial was to move forward, particularly the focus of the trial, which has been observed to be crimes against peace and war crimes, and not, as some people have come to believe, the holocaust, which fell under the limitedly constructed 'crimes against humanity' article.

40 Since Nuremburg, there has been the creation of the International Military Tribunal for the Far East (the Tokyo Trial), the two *ad hoc* tribunals for the former Yugoslavia and Rwanda, an international court erected in Sierra Leone, and discussions of a further court to address the Cambodian atrocities.

41 The Marxist tradition is formulated in a 'dialectical mode of logic [adopted from] Hegel' (Ritzer 1992: 152). 'It argues that society has a definite structure and organization, as well as a central dynamic, which pattern social practices in specific, describable ways, and connect together areas of social life' (Garland 1990: 85). The use of a dialectical framework implies two important factors in its analysis of social phenomena:

> First, the dialectical method of analysis does not see a simple one-way, cause and effect relationship among the various parts of the social world. ... [Secondly], in dialectical analysis, especially as Marx developed it, social values are not separable from social facts.
>
> (Ritzer 1992: 152)

Additionally, this notion of justice may be argued to take the form of what Marxists refers to as an 'ideology.' Marx claims that:

> the ideas of the ruling class are in every epoch the ruling ideas: i.e., the class which is the ruling *material* force of society is at the same time its ruling *intellectual force*. The class which has the means of material production at its disposal, consequently also control the means of mental production, so that the ideas of those who lack the means of mental production are on the whole subject to it.
>
> (cited in Cain and Hunt 1979: 116)

Whether the conceptualization of justice is illusory in its nature, as Marxists may claim, it is nevertheless vital in the Rwandan context.

42 According to Garland, Thompson was one of many writers who undertook the study of law, 'within a Marxist historiography which had moved far away from the rigours of classical orthodoxy towards a more humanist, more culturally oriented understanding of social life' (Garland 1990: 88). Thompson, in his historical analysis of the origins of the Black Act (1723) in England, presents an historical account of the process involved in the construction of law. The culturalist perspective calls into question the rigid 'economic reductionism' often cited as a limitation of the traditional Marxist perspective with regard to the study of law

(Spitzer 1983). Additionally, as suggested by Cole, 'Thompson's conception of the Rule of Law, ... points the way towards a possible reconciliation of liberal and radical approaches to law' (Cole 2001: 178). The cultural analysis of law calls this previously held Marxist tenet into question on the basis of three aspects of the law: law as an institution, law as an ideology, and law as a cultural or ideological system with its own logic (Thompson 1975: 266–7).

3   The Gacaca courts

I think that the Gacaca can bring people together because once you bring people together to dialogue, to discuss the issues that affect them directly, to discuss about whether they took part – one accused of murdering another, the other saying 'you did this,' 'I didn't do this,' 'I did this, I'm sorry, can you forgive me?' That's a very important dialogue, and finally, starting from the hard facts is difficult, but finally you reach a consensus, whatever the case. Once people come together, you will definitely come up with a changed attitude. Previously people didn't want to even look at one another, but now they can hope to, they can hope to sit down and they can discuss issues.

(Kayitana 2006 [2005])

The Hutu extremist government planned, organized, and ordered the genocide in Rwanda. However, the killings and other crimes that accompanied the slaughter were, in the majority of cases, perpetrated by average citizens.[1] The entrenched and institutionalized culture of impunity in Rwanda's recent past led to the Government of National Unity to establish a policy of maximal accountability. The massive arrests and subsequent detention of suspected genocidaires – has been described as both arbitrary and unlawful[2] – and has propelled international human rights groups to call for immediate remedial action.

From 1–5 November 1995, the Office of the President Pasteur Bizimungu convened an international conference to open a dialogue to address the impact of the genocide. In arranging the conference, 'the Government of Rwanda wanted to associate the international community to its genuine search for a viable and coherent solution to the problems faced by Rwanda in the aftermath of [the 1994] genocide' (Government of Rwanda 1995: 5).The perceived culture of impunity existing in Rwanda's history greatly influenced the debate. The conference concluded by putting forth a number of recommendations regarding the best way to address the crimes allegedly committed during the genocide.

In consideration of other models, specifically that of a Truth Commission similar to that employed in South Africa, the recommendation of the conference was that it 'rejects any consideration of a blanket amnesty which would imply continued tolerance of impunity' (Government of Rwanda 1995: 16). Further-more, Vandeginste observes that 'fighting impunity is seen as the key instru-ment of rendering justice and justice is considered an essential pre-condition for reconciliation in Rwanda' (Vandeginste 1999: 7). As stated by Mamdani, when comparing the South African model with that of Rwanda's, South Africa 'exemplifies the dilemma involved in the pursuit of reconciliation without justice, whereas Rwanda exemplifies the opposite: the pursuit of jus-tice without reconciliation' (Mamdani 2001a: 383). In recognition of the need to address historical impunity for such crimes:

> [the] new government, inclusive of Hutus but dominated by Tutsis, made justice a cornerstone of its policy. It argued that unless there was an elimination of the culture of impunity in Rwanda through full retributive justice, the vicious cycle of violence would never cease.
>
> (Uvin and Mironko 2003: 222)

Cognizant of the culture of impunity and as a result of the deliberations, 'the current Rwandese government decided on a policy of maximal accountability for the crime of genocide and crimes committed against humanity from the outset of the armed conflict' (Amnesty International 2002: 1). The govern-ment's application of the policy, seeking maximal accountability, sought a trial method framework in its initial formulation. The government considered classical and non-classical judicial processes for prosecuting and punishing the perpetrators of the genocide. To achieve this goal, a debate concerning the most appropriate means of addressing the crimes 'involved discussions about the appropriate level of judicial intervention' (Drumbl 1999: 25). The November 1995 conference suggested that one of two avenues for the adjudi-cation of accused genocidaires should occur: (1) an independent Specialized Tribunal or (2) a Specialized Chamber within the normal judiciary. Based on the recommendations, the decision was to pursue a Specialized Chamber for the genocide trials.

The argument supporting this choice claims that it presents the government with an opportunity to establish a foundation upon which the rule of law – as a fixture on the Rwandan social landscape – could be (re-)established. According to the Office of the President, '[A] new culture emphasizing respect for the rights of all individuals must be actively promoted' within Rwanda to move it for-ward (Government of Rwanda 1995: 7). Drumbl asserts, '[T]rials offer a transi-tional mechanism … to express public condemnation of aspects of the past, as well as public legitimation of the new rule of law' (Drumbl 1999: 32). The achievement of justice, through the prosecution and punishment of the per-petrators of the genocide within the framework of the rule of law, demonstrates the first step in the attempt to reconcile a previously bitterly-divided country.

However, given the deplorable conditions in which the national judiciary existed in the immediate aftermath of the genocide, and the massive numbers of accused, the Rwandan government realized that reliance on the formal judiciary to address those crimes was not realistic. Combined with the internal need to begin the process of rebuilding a highly ethnically-polarized nation, the government undertook a search for alternative mechanisms to address the judicial issues facing them.

The Gacaca entails a community-based approach to justice and reconciliation in Rwanda. These courts, uniquely applied within the Rwandan context, represent a modernized version of a Rwandan method for resolving disputes that was present in traditional pre-colonialist society. In addressing the crimes committed in Rwanda during the 1994 genocide, the Gacaca further represents the largest attempt, in recent times, at a community-based system of justice to deal with both the magnitude and severity of horrific crimes. The re-emergence of the Gacaca onto the social landscape of modern Rwandan society involved an in-depth process of re-conceptualization. A tradition that had all but disappeared underwent a process of transformation and revitalization into a widely-accepted method to address the small country's darkest hours of violent upheaval.

In attempting to gain an understanding of the Gacaca, it is important to trace its history, including some aspects of its traditional form as well as its development and adaptation into the *initial* modernized form. The legislation enacted to govern the Gacaca, as well as the changes to the legislation – as a result of what was observed during the pilot project of the Gacaca – provides insight into both the structure and process that guides the Gacaca in its current conceptualization. Following a pilot-phase, nation-wide implementation of the Gacaca occurred in the summer of 2005. Understanding of the process leading to its implementation allows for an analysis of the Gacaca within the conceptual framework.

The history and development of the Gacaca

On 17 October 1998, on the occasion of one of the weekly consultation meetings between Rwandan President Pasteur Bizimungu and some political leaders and civil society representatives, it was decided to establish a Commission to look into mechanisms that might increase popular involvement in the ongoing judicial proceedings against suspected perpetrators of the genocide and other crimes against humanity committed in Rwanda between 1 October 1990 and 31 December 1994.

(Vandeginste 1999: 1)

The creation of the commission and its resulting investigatory mandate emerged out of a series of meetings known as the Urugwiro Meetings.[3] Philibert Kigabo,[4] a member of the Rwandan Human Rights Commission, provides a description of the commission's process:

Every Saturday, around four hundred people would gather around the president. Those people included politicians, religious or church people.

All political parties were represented, ministries, professors, university teachers, youth, all those people would meet together in the presidential residence, the Village Urugwiro.

(Kigabo 2005)

The meetings also involved discussions of the potential for implementation of the Gacaca as a judicial tool in dealing with genocide. A three-pronged investigation followed which included anthropological, legal, and religious components in the framework for their investigation (Kigabo 2005).

Anthropological considerations

The anthropological aspect of the investigation involves an attempt to gain a better cultural understanding of the operation of the traditional Gacaca. The commission believed that, to assess the Gacaca's potential application in the current Rwandan context, there was a need to understand what had occurred in the past. Creating a link to their past also provided the Rwandan government with an opportunity to present to the people a uniquely Rwandan solution to its present circumstance, one they already understood, and, possibly therefore, one they were more likely to accept:

At that time, the idea was of going back to the culture to see how, in the past, Rwandans would resolve their conflict, and to see if we could use that system to solve problems now. That is how the idea was born.

(Kigabo 2005)

The investigation revealed that 'the Gacaca did not disappear completely; but with the influence of the churches and after colonization, the Gacaca was no longer considered as something that could help settle conflicts; it had lost its influence, but it still existed' (Kigabo 2005).[5] The Gacaca emerged spontaneously in the northern province of Ruhengeri in 1995, functioning before the President Bizimungu's November conference had taken place or the regular judiciary was re-established. In fact, this spontaneous societal response re-incorporated the Gacaca as a means of addressing community conflict in the wake of the genocide and was the catalyst in garnering the government's attention to the possibilities that Gacaca presents (Kigabo 2005). The role that the Gacaca embraced was to assist the regular courts in dealing with the vast number of detainees accused of both minor and serious offences; it was progressing and would eventually evolve fully into this mould. The mould for a uniquely Rwandan response to its own recent tragic history was carved out of a metal forged by both the traditions of the past and a concern for establishing a sound legal system for the future.

The traditional, pre-colonial Gacaca was truly a community-based system for resolving disputes among individuals within a community or among family and/or clan members. According to Amnesty International, '[T]he primary goal [of the traditional Gacaca] was to restore social order, after sanctioning the violation of shared values, through the re-integration of the offender(s) into the community' (Amnesty International 2002: 20). In any given situation in which individuals involved in a dispute were not able to resolve it by themselves, outside intervention was sought in the form of the Gacaca on a voluntary basis.[6] The process of the traditional Gacaca was an *ad hoc* system of dispute resolution that operated within a flexible and adaptive framework and was convened by local residents responding to a pressing need within their community. Although a culturally-common practice in traditional Rwandan society, its procedures and structure were informal. Although an option for those unable to resolve their own disputes, the traditional Gacaca was not a 'permanent judicial or administrative institution ... There [were] no generally applied rules or criteria to determine the number of participants in the discussion' (Vandeginste 1999: 16). If the Gacaca were to become a legislated national institution, there was a need to address the commission's observations that the Gacaca had historically operated with some degree of regional variation (Vandeginste 1999). As illustrated later in this chapter, the commission made a decision to formalize this process within a legislative framework that provided some degree of a consistent application of procedures.[7]

When asked to describe the traditional Gacaca, Kigabo gave the following response:

> When there was a conflict between two people, suppose that one had come and hit the person, beat the person, and each of them has a family, so the two families would gather and meet and hear the point of views of each of you and then see how to resolve the conflict. One of you would have to ask for forgiveness and then be punished, meaning that you could give some beers, and then the whole matter would be settled.
>
> (Kigabo 2005)

This example involved a dispute over a physical attack on an individual and was most likely the most serious type of crime dealt with by the traditional Gacaca. Additionally, the example provides insight into the types of penalty observed in the Gacaca in that period. Following the dialogue between the parties, there would be a discussion regarding the appropriate means for resolution and, quite often, the agreed upon sanction took the form of restitution.[8] It is conceivable that the use of restitution was predominant as 'generally, the types of conflict dealt with by the Gacaca are related to land use and land rights, cattle, marriage, inheritance rights, loans, damage to properties caused by one of the parties animals, et cetera' (Vandeginste 1999: 17). The application of the Gacaca to more serious crimes, especially murder, needed addressing for it to function in the post-conflict context.

As the genocide of 1994 involved the killing of nearly 1,000,000 people, it is interesting to note that the traditional system of Gacaca did not involve reconciling cases of murder:

In the case of murder, if someone killed someone from a different family, the practice was that that family would come to the family of the killer and kill someone from that family; and then it would go on and on. That is why the officials, including the Mwami had to intervene because otherwise it would be endless. So, if you kill someone from that family, then all of the relationships are stopped. You cannot marry someone from that family; you cannot go and have a glass of beer or water from that family. So, to stop all of this, the Mwami, or king, or his authorities would have to intervene to stop that process of hatred between families.

(Kigabo 2005)

The one offence that most succinctly captures the essence of genocide, murder, remained outside the jurisdictional realm of the traditional Gacaca. According to Vandeginste, the Gacaca addressed the less serious crimes and the Mwami, the highest authority in the land, addressed the crime of murder in traditional Rwandan society (Vandeginste 1999: 17). There were many who felt that a similar scenario should exist in the current context: the State and its representative judiciary should process murder cases, with the Gacaca should concern itself with less serious crimes.

Another feature of the traditional Gacaca was that is was exclusively a phallocentric activity within the traditional patriarchal Rwandan society. In virtually all instances, men controlled the proceedings and the decisions of the Gacaca. 'Respected male elders in the community would be entrusted with the task of pronouncing judgments or solutions fairly, sincerely, wisely and honestly in the presence of all those affected by the conflict or crime' (Lambourne 2005: 2). The proceedings excluded women unless they were a direct participant in the act, directly affected by the act themselves, or a spectator:

Only male adults take part in the proceedings, which are chaired by family elders, supposedly wise old men, who seek to restore social order by leading the group discussions which, in the end, should result in an arrangement that is acceptable to all participants in the Gacaca.

(Vandeginste 1999: 16)

The modern version of the Gacaca appears incongruent with the traditional model. However, according to Amnesty International, '[T]he officials in the Rwandese government emphasize that the GACACA Jurisdictions are not intended to duplicate the customary gacaca procedures though they anticipate the same results' (Amnesty International 2002: 21). Thus, although based on the traditional model, there are some significant differences between the traditional and modernized Gacaca courts.[9] Ntampaka (2001) states that the new Gacaca is also inconsistent with traditional Rwandan law:

When we talk of gacaca, two main characteristics can be pointed out: the active role played by the population in determining the laws and the conciliatory nature of the decisions taken. The custom is that it is pre-ferable to come to an agreement than go to court. Taking someone to court is an act of enmity and should only be a last resort.

(cited in Penal Reform International 2003: 3)

The concept and role of Gacaca, in settling disputes within communities that incorporate participation at the local level, remained a foundation upon which the government moved ahead with the modernized Gacaca.

Legal considerations

In keeping with the United Nations conventions,[10] the Republic of Rwanda recognized that the crimes committed were also in violation of the Rwandan Penal Code. The first law enacted in Rwanda to address the crimes of genocide passed through the stages of the Rwandan Parliament and Senate in 1996 as the Organic Law No 8/96 of 30 August 1996, On the Organization of Prosecution for Offences Constituting the Crime of Genocide or Crimes Against Humanity Committed since 1 October 1990. This law established the criteria for all future prosecutions of the individuals involved in the 1994 genocide. The preamble to this law presents further specific considerations given the events that transpired in 1994, but also recognizes the history of Rwanda prior to those events:

Given that, in order to achieve reconciliation and justice in Rwanda, it is essential that the culture of impunity be eradicated forever;

Given the exceptional situation in the country requires the adoption of specially adapted measures to satisfy the need for justice of the people of Rwanda.

(Government of Rwanda 1996)

The letter of the law specifically links the concept of reconciliation with the need for justice within the Rwandan context. It also reflected the policy of maximal accountability and its association with the desire to eradicate the culture of impunity evident in Rwanda's history.

This law served as the enabling legislation for the establishment of all future Gacaca jurisdictions. The establishment of this law is notable for a number of reasons, including:

(1) The categorization of criminal offences into four categories (Articles 2 and 3);[11]
(2) The creation of a range of sentences that offenders placed in these categories would receive if convicted of their crimes (Articles 14–18);
(3) The formalization of plea bargaining with its procedural process and method for determining its acceptability;
(4) The creation of a judicial framework which jurisdiction would adjudicate the various offences; and

(5) Specialized Chambers and the Office of the Prosecutor were created in accordance with Articles 19–21 and Articles 22–26, respectfully, to prosecute those crimes.

Following its inception, an attempt was made to implement this law. During the course of this process, those involved drew the conclusion that the law, for the most part a result of practicality, could not succeed in achieving its goals:

> The law failed if you consider the organizational matters. It didn't achieve results ... The modern legal system could not settle all the cases. It was not possible. That's why they decided to resort to a system that is very close to the population to see how it could help ... So practically it was not possible to find judges, prosecutors, all those people. It was not practically possible.
>
> (Kigabo 2005)

Nevertheless, following the discussion in the Urugwiro meetings and the research compiled by the Justice Commission,[12] the implementation of the Gacaca system of justice, to assist the prosecutor's office in addressing the crimes outlined in the 1996 law, presented as a both a workable and widely-accepted solution.

The first law to address the inclusion of the Gacaca in the judicial process passed parliament in 2001. The Gacaca fell under the jurisdiction of the newly-reorganized Supreme Court in accordance with Organic Law No 40 (Government of Rwanda 2000). The introduction to the law states consideration of the following factors:

> a. That prosecution must be based on the penal code;
> b.   The necessity, in order to achieve reconciliation and justice in Rwanda, to eradicate for good the culture of impunity and to adopt provisions enabling to ensure prosecutions and trials for perpetrators and accomplices without aiming for simple punishment, but also for the reconstitution of the Rwandese society made decaying by bad leaders who prompted the population to exterminate one part of society;
> c.   That it is important to provide penalties allowing convicted persons to amend themselves and to favour their reintegration into Rwandese society without hindrance to the people's normal life ...
>
> The parliament creates the Gacaca jurisdictions.
>
> (Government of Rwanda 2000)

According to Mukantaganzwa, the pilot phase of the Gacaca consisted of '751 Gacaca courts of the cell within 118 sectors countrywide' (Mukantaganzwa 2004). The achievements during the pilot phase include 2,883 confessions before the courts, 606 preventive detentions, 555 individuals released, and 63,447 persons added to the list of suspects (Mukantaganzwa 2004). Based on the findings, the government demonstrated a great deal of flexibility and political agency in its approach, revising the first law in 2004. The new law, Organic Law No 16/2004, in accordance with Article 15, resulted in the creation of the National Service of Gacaca Jurisdictions as an independent government agency. The new law does not reflect ideological or philosophical changes, but rather structural and logistical changes. These changes maintain the integrity of the purpose for, and reasons behind, its creation, while adapting its everyday functioning in a manner more conducive to its success-ful operations. Despite the legislation, the Gacaca as a nation-wide judicial process, a connection to the flexibility of the traditional model exists as there remains a degree of openness for regional variation. According to Law No 08/2004 of 28/04/2004, Article 3:

> In the fulfillment of its mission, the Service shall neither enjoin nor forbid any GACACA jurisdiction to try in its own determined way.
>
> It shall not interfere with the Gacaca Jurisdictions in a way that may endanger their independence.

(Government of Rwanda 2004b)

The government recognizes the importance of different regional Gacaca jur-isdictions, incorporating the Gacaca into their communities in a manner that reflects traditional practice.

As stated previously, Rwandan is a highly structured society, organized at five levels of governance: national, provincial, district, sector, and cell (cel-lule).[13] Under the first Gacaca law, the Gacaca was organized nationally, and functionally operated across the other four levels of governance. Given the burden that holding Gacaca at the provincial and district levels placed on citizens, with respect to time and travel, the government restructured the Gacaca operations to reflect the local governance structures, a step considered to be crucial in the Gacaca's success. Under the revised law, the Gacaca structurally operates at two levels in Rwanda, in the cell and the sector, and within the sector, in which there is also a Sector Appeal Gacaca. These pro-cesses significantly reduce the travel and time of citizens incurred because of their participation in Gacaca proceedings.

All members of a community over the age of 18[14] come together to form the general assembly which, in turn, elects nine judges (Inyangamugayos) to serve on an individual Gacaca. They also elect an additional five individuals to serve as deputies, in the event that a judge is unable to perform his/her duties or is replaced for any number of reasons. Additionally, within the Seat (a term used to refer to the collective of nine judges), five individuals are elected amongst the judges themselves to serve as the coordination committee. They are required to read and write Kinyarwanda. Additionally, they will serve specified roles, such as president of the court and secretary, that involve a few additional duties.

In defining what constitutes a person of integrity (an Inyangamugayo or judge), Organic Law Article 14 (Government of Rwanda 2004d) states a number of conditions that must be met to be considered for the position of judge. In trying to determine how that definition would be interpreted by members of the community, I asked the question 'What kind of qualities are considered when deciding to call someone a person of integrity?':

> It is difficult to explain, but people inside the community would know who is a person of integrity, because of his behaviour, because of his honesty. These people would be wise people, known to be wise people, with usefulness if you like. People would know exactly if that person has integrity. There are no standards, but people would know that.
>
> (Kigabo 2005)

According to one Gacaca judge, the process of becoming a volunteer judge occurred through a meeting of the general assembly in their cellule:

> We were called, and then we went. We were advertised to the people and we went to see them. The people of the community already knew that they had good character and behaviour in the community; they cannot find anything negative and they cannot have been involved in the genocide, or have the spirit of genocide. The whole community agrees. If someone knows something, at anytime, wrong with someone they can say so and the community talks about it.
>
> (MM 2005)[15]

The people who serve as judges offer a fairly good representation of the spectrum of Rwandan society. According to Article 14:

> Any person of integrity who is at least 21 years old and meeting all the conditions required by the organic law, can be elected a member of the organ for a Gacaca Court without any discrimination, such as that based on sex, origin, religion, opinion or social position.
>
> (Government of Rwanda 2004d)

When asked about the positions that the judges in their cellule held in the community prior to being elected to their posts, another judge stated that 'some work; some don't work. They may be students, civil servants. Their position doesn't matter' (NN 2005). Each individual accepting the position is required by law to take an oath of voluntary service for a period of one year.

The law provides specific reasons for the exclusion of an individual from participating as a judge; according to Article 15:

> Cannot be elected member of the Seat for a Gacaca Court:
> 1° the person exercising political activity;

2° the person in charge of centralized or decentralized Government administration

3° the soldier or policeman who is still in active service

4° the career magistrate

5° the member of the leadership for a political party.

(Government of Rwanda 2004d: 6)

Article 14 of the Gacaca law reflects the constitutional mandate of a legislated sexual equality within the society. As such, there has been a rather dramatic increase in the status of women in various aspects of Rwandan society.[16] The Gacaca is no exception. Unlike the traditional Gacaca in which the role of women was peripheral at best, in the new Gacaca many women hold the position of judges.[17]

According to the report from the National Service of Gacaca Jurisdictions, the nationwide launching of the Gacaca resulted in 12,103 jurisdictions (Mukantaganzwa 2004). Under the guidelines of the original law, the number of volunteer judges that this massive judicial experiment would require was unrealistic. Once again, changes to the legislation occurred because of observations made during the pilot-phase of the Gacaca with respect to the number of judges required. These changes are substantively logistic in their nature and seek to improve the overall functioning of, and participation in, these courts. The number of judges required under the old law by each Gacaca court was considerable – 19. It would have required the recruitment of 19 judges in addition to the five deputies to serve in the estimate 12,139 Gacaca courts, requiring over 290,000 volunteers. Given the considerable demands placed upon the volunteers, the 2004 legislation reduced the number from 19 to nine (still maintaining the additional five deputies). This represents a deduction of almost 50 percent in personnel required to operate the courts, over 100,000 fewer volunteers.

A report developed by the National Service of Gacaca Jurisdictions outlines the specific goals and duties of the Gacaca:

> To reveal the truth on the genocide events;
> To speed up genocide trials;
> To eradicate the culture of impunity;
> To reconcile and strengthen unity among Rwandans;
> To prove the Rwandan's Society's capacity to solve its own problems.
> Nowadays, we notice that Gacaca Jurisdictions can achieve its duties as long as each and every one supports them and plays his role as required.

(Mukantaganzwa 2004)

The first phase of each Gacaca is to reveal the truth about what transpired within its specific geographical location during the genocide: 'Finding out what happened during the genocide, and establishing the truth is an integral part of the gacaca process. It is also considered to be a paramount element of moving towards reconciliation' (Wolters 2005: 8). Considered to be their duty as Rwandans, participation in this truth-telling and information-gathering phase of the Gacaca is mandatory.[18] This involves the gathering of information and the creation of a number of lists including: (1) Who lived within the jurisdiction at the time? (2) Who was killed within the jurisdiction? (3) Who participated in the killing? (4) Who perpetrated crimes other than killing? (5) Who was killed in other jurisdictions? (6) Who formerly resided within the jurisdiction? and (7) Who was killed in the jurisdiction that was not originally residing within it? Kayitana states:

> Then, after that, they have that information through the consensus. They are agreed that those are the crimes, those telling lies, what is true, this and that, and they also confirmed those people already detained in the prisons to give evidences. Now that is the information that is collected and then members of the bench, the Gacaca judges, will sit in closed session after that, after gathering and cross-checking that information while still in closed session, [to] verify that information.
>
> (Kayitana 2006 [2005])

Based on the information gathered in the first phase, the categorization phase follows. In this phase, categorization into one of the three categories outlined in Article 11 of Organic Law No 10, 2007 occurs for all those who accused of involvement in any criminal activity.[19]

First Category:
    1. The person whose criminal acts or criminal participation place among planners, organisers, incitators, supervisors and ringleaders of the crime of genocide or crimes against humanity, together with their accomplices;
    1° the person who, at any time, was in the organs of leadership, at national, prefecture, sub-prefecture, and commune levels, leaders of political parties, members of high command of the army and gendarmerie, of communal police, leaders of religious denominations, or illegal militia groups who committed those offences or encouraged others to commit them, together with his or her accomplices;
    2° the person who committed acts of rape or sexual torture, together with his or her accomplices;
    The Prosecutor General of the Republic shall publish, at least twice a year, the list of persons classified in the first category, forwarded to him or her by Gacaca courts of the Cell.
Second Category:
    1° the well known murderer who distinguished himself or herself in the area where he or she lived or wherever he or she passed, because of the zeal which characterized him or her in the killings or excessive wickedness with which they carried out, together with their accomplices;

2° the person who committed acts of torture against others, even though they did not result in death, together with his or her accomplices;

3° the person who committed dehumanising acts on the dead body, together with his or her accomplices;

4° the person whose criminal acts or criminal participation place them among the killers or authors of serious attacks against others, causing death, together with his or her accomplices;

5° the person who injured or committed other acts of serious attacks, with intention to kill them, but who did not attain his or her objective, together with his or her accomplices;

6° the person who committed or participated in criminal acts against persons, without any intention of killing them, together with his or her accomplices.

Third Category:

The person who only committed offences against property. However, if the author of the offence and the victim have agreed on an amicable settlement on their own initiative, or before the public authority or witnesses, before this organic law came into force, he or she cannot be prosecuted.

(Government of Rwanda 2007a)

These different categories represent the Rwandan understanding of various degrees of complicity with regard to the crimes:

People in Rwandan society did not all have the same responsibility for the crime of genocide. We needed to establish differences between masterminds, people like Bagasora for instance, and small people from the villages, even though they may have killed someone. They don't have the same responsibility, even if the crimes are the same.

(Kigabo 2005)

The next phase of the Gacaca is distribution to the appropriate jurisdiction for trial. The Gacaca transfers all first category files and information to the criminal court prosecutor's office. It is the responsibility of the Gacaca courts to adjudicate the second and third category offenders.[20] In what appears to be the results of the nation-wide categorization process in the Gacaca, the most recent information available from the National Service of Gacaca Jurisdictions states that in total 818,564 individuals are accused of genocide crimes: Category 1 (77,269), Category 2 (432,557), and Category 3 (308,738) (nd).

Confession and plea bargaining procedures

The Gacaca law incorporates an intricate policy and set of procedures for confessions and guilty pleas. It is interesting to note that in opposition to previous Rwandan judicial structure, which was based on the Belgian civil law model, the use of confessions and plea bargaining has greater affinity with the

Anglo-Saxon common law judicial system. Additionally, there is a distinct affinity with Protestantism in these procedures. For those who confess, plead guilty, apologize, repent, and seek forgiveness before the proceedings of the Gacaca begin, this policy provides for a significant reduction in sentence, providing the offender with the possibility of serving half of the sentence in the community.[21] Given the large number of accused already imprisoned for many years awaiting their day in court, the guilty plea arrangement may facilitate a reduction of prisoners, easing the burden on the overcrowded prisons, while a sentence reduction may result in a sentence equivalent to time already served. This process has provided great incentive for many of the accused to take advantage of the plea bargaining process. However, despite the stated benefits, there are many criticisms that accompany the perceived benefits of these procedures.[22]

The requirement under the modernized version for a public confession is incongruent with the traditional model, and can exacerbate an already emotionally-charged and tense situation. Rwandan tradition holds that 'confessing in front of victims is considered an insult and an aggravating circumstance as it is considered a show of force' (Penal Reform International 2003: 3). This problem in the Gacaca process is due in part to the lack of understanding that the public has with respect to the new Gacaca. The government's attempts to sensitize and educate the population about the new Gacaca have 'focused more on rallying support behind, rather than provide information about, gacaca ... The result is a considerable lack of information regarding both the operation and ethical rationale underlying gacaca' (Amnesty International 2002: 22). The result of the lack of clarity has manifested itself in situations in which prisoners perceive that the community grant them forgiveness in addition to the reduced sentence and appear to demand forgiveness. This causes an imposition on the survivors and other community members that does not resonate positively as it undermines the expected sincerity of a confession and apology. The incongruence between these two groups' experiences in the plea bargaining process may not only foster resentment and tension, but undermine the goal of reconciliation.

According to Penal Reform International (2003), other concerns also arise from the confession and plea bargaining procedure with innocent prisoners pleading guilty to crimes that they did not commit because of the lure of a reduced sentence and uncertainty about their success in the court. Additionally, the potential exists for the accused to confess to lesser crimes than he or she actually committed and thus undermine the goal of accessing the *truth*: 'There is no doubt that the rewards of the confession procedure also encourage false and partial confessions ... In some instances, prisoners or accused also attempt to shift the blame, accusing people who are dead or in exile' (Wolters 2005: 10). Given the traumatic nature of the events and the contents of the confessions, it is questionable whether the community, particularly the judges, have the capability to assess the sincerity and veracity of the confessions. This is a crucial element since the judges must agree that the confession is both complete, and the apology sincere, for it to be accepted. Finally, and, perhaps more outrageous are reports that wealthy prisoners are attempting to pay others to plead guilty, a process known as *Kugura umusozi*, or 'buying a cell' (Wolters 2005: 10). Despite these concerns, it is interesting to note that a common theme expressed by many of the people interviewed in Rwanda was that although some of the perpetrators may attempt such methods of deceit, there is always someone who knows the truth in every community. It was felt that the truth would eventually surface and people would know it.

Schabas provides a brief overview of the results of the plea bargaining process. Although initially slow, with respect to the numbers of prisoners using the process, 'by the end of 1999, there were 15,000 confessions and by early 2000, more than 20,000' (Schabas 2005: 887). However, he notes that the logistical issues of dealing promptly with these cases of confession and the inability to keep those prisoners who confessed separate from those who had not (assuring their safety from reprisals), undermine the process. Had the government been able to address these issues, the idea 'might well provide a useful model to other post-conflict societies where there are very large numbers of accused' (Schabas 2005: 887).

The trial process

The trials represent the next phase of the Gacaca. The Gacaca trial process itself is simple in terms of its procedures. Although there is some variation depending on the presence or absence of a confession for crimes categorized in the second category and for property crimes in the third category, the process is fairly standardized. In accordance with the Organic Law No 16, 2004, the process begins with the general assembly convened according to a pre-arranged time. The president of the Gacaca calls the case, identifies the defendant, reveals the charges to the general assembly, reads the relevant sections of the Organic Law – the information regarding the evidence – and provides the defendant with the opportunity to plead guilty. Defendants who do not plead guilty have the opportunity to present their recollections of the events and make their case. There is no provision for a defence counsel; the accused represent themselves.

The court proceeds to hear witnesses in the case. The court grants permission to any interested member of the general assembly to ask questions of the defendant. The court secretary constructs a list of those identified as victims in the case. The president of the court reads the trial transcript to all. Barring any further discussion or necessary clarification, each person who participates in the process signs and fingerprints the statement and the president declares the hearing closed. The court notifies the defendant of the date for pronouncement of the judgment. In the event that the judgment immediately follows the hearing of the case, the nine judges deliberate in private and reach a decision. The judges return to the court and inform the defendant of the decision and the parties present at the trial sign and fingerprint the judgment.

The sentences delivered to those convicted of genocide crimes may vary considerably within the legislation in two central aspects: (1) the category of the offence; and (2) whether or not the accused participated in the confession and plea bargaining process.[23] Although the Gacaca courts do not directly adjudicate the category one offences, they are nevertheless included in the process that may result in the application of these sentences within the national judiciary. Regardless of what jurisdiction actually hears the cases, the information and categorization phase occurs in the Gacaca. For example, Section III, Chapter IV, Article 72 states:

> Defendants, falling within the first category, who refused to have recourse to confess, plead guilty, repent and apologize, as stipulated in article 54 of this organic law, or whose confessions, guilty plea, repentance and apologies have been rejected, incur a death penalty or life imprisonment.[24]
>
> Defendants falling within the first category who confessed, pleaded guilty, repented and apologized as stipulated in article 54 of this organic law, incur a prison sentence ranging from 25 years to 30 years imprisonment.[25]
>
> (Government of Rwanda 2004d: 21)

For those who are placed in the second category,[26] the sentence range is set from 7 to 12 years, incarceration for those who confess before the information gathering process of the Gacaca has been completed, and half of the sentence may be served in the community performing voluntary community service. Those who confess after the information gathering is complete may receive 12 to 15 years, incarceration of which half may also be served in the community. Those in category three are required to make civil reparations for their crimes. Persons who do not confess and are found guilty tend to attract the maximum sentence without early release.

There is an additional aspect of sentencing that outlines the loss of civil rights to any offender convicted of the crime of genocide or crimes against humanity. In accordance with Article 76:

> 1° perpetual loss of civil rights, in conformity with the penal Code, for persons classified in the first category 2° persons falling within the second category as prescribed in points 1° and of article 51 of this organic law, are liable to permanent deprivation of the right:
>   a. to vote;
>   b.   to eligibility;
>   c.   to be an expert witness in rulings and trials, except in case of giving mere investigations;
>   d.   to possess and carry firearms;
>   e.   to serve in the armed forces;
>   f.   to serve in the police;
>   g.   to be in the public sector;

h.   to be a teacher or a medical staff in public or private service.

(Government of Rwanda 2004d: 22–3)

If a situation arises after the categorization of an offender, or if the offender does not accept a sentence that the court renders, there is an avenue for appeal. The appeal process in the Gacaca jurisdictions is limited to the Gacaca itself. There is no means of appealing to the regular judiciary, a decision made in the Gacaca. An offender may appeal judgments from the cell level to the sector level, and those at the sector level may further appeal to the Sector Appeal Court. However, the possibility does exist that an individual acquitted in the national courts may find himself or herself brought before the Gacaca (Ngoga 2005).

Religious considerations

The final approach used in the research and discussions that took place within the Urugwiro meetings considered the religious aspect of Rwandan culture. Rwanda is predominantly Catholic with upwards of 70 percent of the general population following the Catholic faith (Kigabo 2005). Within Rwandan culture, members of the community consider the leaders of the church to be highly-respected members of the community. From the period of colonization, when missionaries and the colonial powers worked hand-in-hand through the decolonization of Rwanda to the present day, there has been a close relationship between the Church and State: 'Since 1959, the Catholic Church has sided with the leadership in place' (Kigabo 2005).[27]

The massacres that took place in Rwanda between 1959 and 1994 presented the Church with a dilemma between continued support for the leadership and meeting a moral obligation to protect people. According to Kayitana, 'I can tell you that in 1959 it was like a pilot phase of genocide. They did a pilot and it worked, and the ones, the outsiders, they were aloof, 1959, '60, '61, '62, '63, '67, '73, '82, '90, and then in 1994; all those things were like stages' (Kayitana 2006 [2005]). In these early trial runs of genocide, people fleeing the killing sought and received refuge provided by the church. In 1994, this was not the case. Kigabo claims, 'Before, when people sought refuge in churches, they were protected, and that's why in 1994 they also went to churches. But in 1994, even those who had sought refuge in churches were killed' (Kigabo 2005). In fact, African Rights states that 'more Rwandese citizens died in churches and parishes than anywhere else' (African Rights 1995: 865). Because of the intertwined relationship previously forged between the Church and local political leadership, religious officials were powerless in the face of political pressure:

The Catholic Church, sided with the leadership in place; and in 1994, when the government, the leadership, the power, decided to kill people in the churches, the Catholic Church was not strong enough to prevent those people from going to kill those people because basically they had become one body.

(Kigabo 2005)[28]

There remains a continued sense of connection between Church and State in Rwandan society. The Catholic Church now represents a potential vehicle in support of peace and reconciliation, a positive tool, as opposed to its questionably complicit functioning of the past.

The consideration of religious aspects within the Rwandan context resulted in the development of an interesting link between the Church and the Gacaca process. The confession and guilty plea procedures within the legal framework of the Gacaca are an outgrowth of the observation of Protestant church officials' activities within the prisons in Rwanda:

> The Protestant churches ... started asking for prisoners in prison to ask for forgiveness to God, to confess their crimes and ask for forgiveness. As a result, those people confessed their crimes and said what they had done, and this gave a key to the Gacaca to see where to go, which way to go, to know what happened, because these people who actually participated in the killings, and they knew what they had done and with whom, and when.
>
> (Kigabo 2005)

Unlike the Catholic confession, which is a private matter between the priest and the individual making the confession, 'the Protestants, when they accept to confess what they have done to God, they do it in public, in churches, so that everybody can hear what they have done' (Kigabo 2005). The public confessions as outlined in the Gacaca law had their foundation in this process of public confession in church.

Gacaca courts and the search for justice

Given its prominence in the current context in Rwanda, the Gacaca is an institution of critical significance in the attempt to develop an environment conducive to justice and as a measure of that progress. The opportunity exists for the Gacaca to fill the need for justice as a precondition for reconciliation. According to Kayitana, it is of vital importance to the success of the Gacaca process that the leadership at all levels of the country must be supportive of the process and lead by example (Kayitana 2006 [2005]). The Gacaca allows the leadership of Rwanda to disseminate, to the population, the foundational principles upon which they are seeking justice.

Restorative and retributive justice?

The Gacaca combines elements of both restorative and retributive justice. According to Llewellyn and Howse (1998), both restorative and retributive justice perspectives seek to attain the final goal of social equality. Where they differ is in their focus and means for achieving that goal through the often-stated intermediate goals of punishment and repairing harm, respectively. On the one hand, within retributive justice, the focus remains on individual findings of guilt and the method for achieving social equality is through a set of state-imposed, coercive, and, arguably, arbitrarily-determined punishments. Restorative justice, on the other hand, although seeking the same result, does so through a dialogical process involving all stakeholders – victim, offender, and community – in the event. Rather than punishment as an end, the goal is to find an appropriate set of practices that considers the concrete needs of all those affected by the event. Consideration of these various needs reflects the three central elements of a restorative justice approach as presented in the previous chapter.

The Gacaca legislation clearly contains elements that are distinctly retributive in nature. The determination of individual guilt and imposition on the offender of a pre-ordained range of punishments is certainly retributive. However, the process of plea bargaining may demonstrate the government's attempt to legislate a restorative element into the process. An offender who willingly accepts responsibility, takes ownership of his or her actions, and demonstrates his or her contriteness and willingness to tell the truth about the events that occurred, may receive a reduced sentence and an earlier return to the community through the application of the community service aspect of the plea. The legislation provides the accused with an avenue through which they may attempt to make amends for the harm they have caused. Additionally, this may present offenders with an opportunity to increase their likelihood for re-integration into the community, because other members of the community witness these attempts at restitution.[29]

In terms of aligning with restorative justice practices, the Gacaca courts differ from trials in the Rwandan criminal justice system and the ICTR since they actively provide all stakeholders – the victims, the offenders, and the community – with the opportunity to share their stories, engage in dialogue, and contribute to the decision-making process. Bazemore asserts that:

> [t]o move beyond punishing and treating offenders toward outcomes focused on repairing harm and building community capacity, proponents of community and restorative justice suggest the need for a new criminal justice process based on maximizing involvement of victims, offenders, and their supporters and communities.
>
> (Bazemore 2001: 226)

Despite the observation that the Gacaca judges make their final decisions in seclusion, the process of the community electing those same judges, and the Gacaca process itself, ensure that all members of the community are entitled to give their input into each case that comes before the court because the entire transcript of the proceedings is read out loud. Additionally, Gacaca judges may seek consensus about events from all those in attendance as to what transpired during the court proceedings, and those persons in attendance can openly discuss and challenge any discrepancies that arise and suggest amendments when the necessity arises.[30] Structuring processes in which each participant has an equal opportunity to engage in the decision-making can increase the likelihood of achieving justice. It does so as the system, from the perception of the participants, reflects fairness in the process and, hence, the outcome.

Within the Gacaca process, the process of engaging in a dialogue presents all persons in attendance with the opportunity to participate. However, one must revisit the observation of the unequal nature of the relationship that existed following the conflict as it influences the nature of the participation. The process must originate from a point wherein no party to the process has an advantaged or disadvantaged position. The arrival of the accused in pink, jail-issued attire, in the presence of an armed escort, to face the court, appears to violate this consideration of equality. It is interesting to note that the same happens in common law jurisdictions in which an accused is brought before the court because of the *prima facie* evidence of guilt. However, in a common law jurisdiction, the burden of proof remains the task of the prosecutor. In Gacaca, the burden is shared between the judges as well as the accused to find the truth. The right to remain silent appears irrelevant here.

It is hard to imagine how the accused can actually enter the process as an equal participant in the process. This position of original disadvantage may affect the defendant's participation from the outset to the point that he/she are more likely to agree with others in the process in light of his/her role as the accused. Despite this arguable concern, a survey completed by the National Unity and Reconciliation Commission (NURC) suggests that the vast majority of the Rwandan population at large, including the prisoners (both those who have confessed [over 90 percent] and those who have not [over 80 percent]) believe that the Inyangamugayo will be honest individuals who respect the truth and individual rights (Government of Rwanda 2003b: 49). This stated confidence in the judges provides evidence that the people believe that fairness will exist in the final decisions made by the judges.

Resulting from one of the Government of Rwanda's primary goals in achieving justice and putting an end to the culture of impunity, the Gacaca has a focus that directs its attention toward the determination of individualized guilt and responsibility of the offender. Accompanying this determination of guilt is the imposition of punishment upon the offender once guilt is established. The relationship between guilt and punishment, on the one hand, and attempting reconciliation through the reparation of the harm done, on the other hand, is problematic when one considers the relational aspects involved in the pursuit of justice. According to Llewellyn and Howse, a focus on both individualism and its resulting imposition of punishment on the offender, associated with the retributive justice approach, removes the relational aspect of the conflict from the equation of justice and, in doing so, reduces the likelihood of achieving justice (Llewellyn and Howse 1998: 23).

A restorative justice perspective, in comparison, seeks the active participation of all the stakeholders in an attempt to focus on repairing the harm done rather than a fixation on the guilt of an individual as a measure of success. Despite the observation that the Gacaca does operate within a framework that seeks individual guilt and imposes punishment on those determined to be guilty, the process by which this occurs involves dialogue and participation of all affected. Legislation provides some additional flexibility in the determination of an appropriate sentence. According to Llewellyn and Howse, this ability to choose what constitutes an appropriate punishment, or a 'set of practices,' challenges the arbitrariness of the system of punishing associated with the retributive approach (Llewellyn and Howse 1998).

The individualization of guilt and the punitive nature of the sentences are important for a number of reasons in the context of Rwanda. According to Daly, punitive measures are consistent with the wishes and expectations of the Rwandan people who perceive these measures as not only reasonable, but required for the crimes committed (Daly 2002). Additionally:

> Trials are also important, however, because they individualize responsibility. It is important for society to make individual determinations so as to minimize the tendency to demonize an entire group. Trials differentiate among members of a group so that it cannot be said that all Hutu are guilty of genocide. This in turn reduces the likelihood of mass, undifferentiated violence.
>
> (Daly 2002: 375)

Suspicion and rumour can deter the building of relationships in an environment in which the numbers of perpetrators are significantly high. The trials and individualization of guilt identifies the perpetrators while freeing others from the perception of guilt. This process allows for community building in an environment more conducive to dialogue. As stated by Kayitana:

> From the Gacaca process, that brings them together. They start to discuss. After they leave the Gacaca, they can continue to discuss informally. The Gacaca process begins the dialogue and forces them into dialogue which then they can take out informally and that will help bring them together.
>
> (Kayitana 2006)

An additional consideration in the active participation of the interested community lies in the use of the Inyangamugayo as lay judges. As chosen members of the community from all walks of life and, therefore, not professionals in the judicial field, the Gacaca judges represent the replacement of what Christie refers to as 'professional thieves' (Christie 1977: 3), by members of the community. Christie argues that within the familiar trial model, lawyers and other court personnel (and by extension the state) steal the conflicts from all those who are actually involved in the dispute. Resulting from the theft of their conflict by the system, the victims become double-losers (Christie 1977: 3). They are perceived as victimized by the offender in the first instance and by the court, in the second instance, through exclusion from the processes designed to resolve their conflicts. The offender and the community also lose in the process as everyone in society misses the potential benefits that Christie claims participation in resolving conflicts achieves: 'This loss is first and foremost a loss in opportunities for norm-clarification. It is a loss of pedagogical possibilities. It is a loss of opportunities for continuous discussion of what represents the law of the land' (Christie 1977: 6).

This process of engaging each other in discussion within the framework of the Gacaca, presents an opportunity for putting an end to the culture of impunity through a dialogue wherein all members of society search for what is considered acceptable within their community. There is considerable support of the Gacaca's ability to assist in eradicating the culture of impunity. The NURC survey reports that 84 percent of the population asserts a positive opinion on this issue (Government of Rwanda 2003b: 17). What this suggests is a strong communal sense that accountability for wrongdoing is crucial in moving the country towards reconciliation. Furthermore, it the collective search for justice 'creates a common experience in which everyone works toward a common goal. In a sense it aims to replace the divisive experience of the genocide with the cohesive experience of securing justice' (Daly 2002: 376).

Responsive regulation

Braithwaite discusses the concept of responsive regulation and its counterpart, regulatory formalism, as separate or distinct approaches to addressing crime (Braithwaite 2002: 29). However, both elements appear to be present to some degree in the Gacaca. The modernization of the traditional Gacaca has occurred within a legalistic framework in that the process is enshrined within law. In congruence with the concept of regulatory formalism, the law outlines pre-ordained categories of offences, as well as sentences that would apply to an individual convicted of a crime. It also articulates a confession and plea bargaining process that clearly states the sentence reductions in the event that the judges accept a confession as full and sincere. Furthermore, Thompson suggests that the Gacaca is a reflection of State power by imposing justice upon the Rwandese people (Thompson 2007: 2).

It appears that the Gacaca is formally regulated and, therefore, not consistent with the idea of responsive regulation. However, a number of factors suggest otherwise. The origin of the modern Gacaca (described previously) was the result of a process of dialogue and discussion, engaging a broad spectrum of society in its conceptualization. Despite these origins, the current model has become codified for consistency sake while the process remains inclusive and participatory. Another aspect that enforces the Gacaca's responsive adaptation to address the crimes, is the degree to which the government is reported to recognize and respect the importance of local ownership and adaptations to it: 'While gacaca is still a state process, it leaves as much power as possible to those outside the central state power structure' (Daly 2002: 377). The government's removal from undue influence over the process empowers citizens to address local concerns locally. Furthermore, Daly notes that the 'sheer number of tribunals operating simultaneously should protect the process as a whole from undue influence by the government' (Daly 2002: 377).

Despite the formalism observed in the codified categories and sentences, the process of information-gathering and subsequent categorization begin as dialogues. The gathering of the general assembly in the Gacaca offers an inclusive discussion for all people in attendance. Although the categories themselves are formally constructed, the process by which the courts categorize the accused is based on a dialogical approach consistent with the base of the regulatory pyramid.

The regulatory pyramid is dynamic in response to the character of the individuals and their responses to the intervention received. As an offender's thoughts and actions shift from incompetent/irrational to rational, and, finally, to virtuous, the intervention should be cognizant of this and adjust accordingly. The confession and plea bargaining procedures, although formalized, do represent a process of recognition for changes in the participants. A reduction in sentence and the opportunity to serve a large portion of the sentence in the community rather than jail is available to those who demonstrate remorse, accountability, and a desire for re-integration. The severity of the sentence and the type of sentence are representative of the type of offender that the system is facing. The system adjusts its penalties and the degree of State intervention in recognition of both the type of crime and the type of offender.

The different levels of sanction are based on the different degrees of severity of the crimes, and different levels of involvement clearly demonstrate the regulatory pyramid of intervention approach. For example, in the case of those accused of property crimes within category three offences, if the parties involved in the dispute can reach an agreement on their own concerning how to resolve the dispute, then they need only to submit this information to the Gacaca and the process ends there. The Gacaca is not involved in the case except to record it as completed. Thus, there are crimes for which government intervention, in the form of a more formal process, is not even required. A crime of greater severity necessitates a consideration for a greater level of intervention. The Gacaca, at this time, deals only with those third category offences that cannot be resolved by the individual parties themselves and the second category of accused that constitute a group with a lesser degree of complicity in the genocide. The Gacaca does not deal with the trials of the accused that are placed in the first category of listed offences. It appears that the overall plan for addressing the crimes of 1994 fit, to a limited degree, within Braithwaite's conceptualization of the pyramid of regulation (Braithwaite 2002).

Liberal-legalism in the Gacaca

One of the central factors that produced the decision to incorporate the Gacaca into the mix of judicial responses used in the Rwandan context was the high degree of complicity among the population in the commission of the crimes. Because of the staggering numbers of those accused of genocide crimes, the Rwandan national judiciary faced the difficult task of adjudicating the perpetrators. The creation of the Gacaca courts presents a somewhat middle-of-the-road, combinatory approach between the opposing poles of liberal-legalism and realism. On the one hand, the realist's approach exists within the Gacaca in the sense that Rwanda is seeking an expedient solution to a situation of system capacity overload and, in doing so, is, to some degree, abandoning due process. The courts, on the other hand, present a pseudo-legalistic model that incorporates the fully-insulated aspect of due process within the trials associated with the Western-style courtroom.

The flexible framework of the Gacaca is based on legislation that pre-determines the placement of individuals into specified categories, each with a prescribed range of sentences. This demonstrates the legalistic foundation upon which the process is oriented. However, the application of this foundation, moving from a strictly adversarial model focused on the strict application of due process, to one that is more dialogical in its methods, represents a departure from the legalistic model. The relaxed legalistic model presents the Gacaca with some advantages in attempting to achieve its stated goals, but also runs the risk of calling into question its ability to achieve others goals.

With its massive number of lay magistrates operating an equally sizeable number of courts, the Gacaca, even considering that they meet once per week as opposed to the daily functioning of the regular courts, does allow for the processing of many more accused in a compressed amount of time. It also permits the advantages and positive effects of a more restorative justice approach. Concerns have been noted, however, regarding the lack of due process protections for the offenders, especially given the gravity of the crimes of which they are accused, and the stiff penalties that they may be given if convicted.[31]

Rule of law

> A Management Systems International (MSI) team notes a general sense that there is a legitimate commitment to the rule of law on the part of most national leaders. Gacaca may present a sterling example of this commitment as well as some of the problems remaining in the justice sector.
>
> (Smith *et al* 2002: 46)

The MSI report states that the government's agency in continuing to adjust the law and the practice of the Gacaca, in response to issues arising from its operation, is an example of this commitment. That justice begets reconciliation, the cornerstone of the Rwandan government's mantra, suggests that, by extension, the potential significance of the Gacaca lies in its potential to reconcile, putting an end to the cyclical ethnic violence that has been a part of the Rwandan landscape for half a century. In an attempt to achieve this benefit, the population also shares the duties and obligations that accompany the process:

> Rwandans of all stations will literally be defining justice for the post-genocide society rather than it having it imposed on them. This may be valuable from a rule of law perspective, and it may also constitute an important mechanism for promoting democratic values.
>
> (Daly 2002: 376)

Within the Rwandan context, however, a country in which the majority of its citizens rely on subsistence farming, mandatory participation in the information-gathering phase in the Gacaca, once a week for a perceived extended period of time, places a huge burden upon the citizens.[32] This burden is especially onerous on the Gacaca judges as their commitment to the position is one that, albeit voluntary,[33] requires in some cases one full day of their time every week for an entire year, without financial compensation. It is difficult at this time to predict how successful the National Service of Gacaca Jurisdictions will be in recruiting a second, third, fourth, and possibly fifth, group of volunteer judges as the government estimates that the process will take between 3 to 5 years (Mukantaganzwa 2005). When asked why they would agree to accept such a demanding position, one judge responded, 'First of all, we are all touched and offended by what happened in the genocide. The only power we have is to build our country back again. There is a sense of responsibility' (Gacaca judge 2005).[34] The prospect of reconciliation, and the civic pride they express in participating in the rebuilding of their nations, appears to offset the shared burden of their participation.

It is interesting that Rwandans refer to their civic duty when discussing their obligation to take part in the Gacaca. This is a common experience for all Rwandans that is a part of their culture. From the forced labour in the pre-colonial and colonial times to the present day *umuganda* (a half day each month when everyone stops what they are doing to engage in labour for the good of the people), Rwandans are familiar with, and, for the most part, accept their civic responsibilities. Hatzfeld reports that many of the killers claimed that they were doing their civic duty when they engaged in the commission of their crimes (Hatzfeld 2005). Lambourne observed a similar phenomenon: 'Given the lack of remuneration and the huge responsibility of the task, I was impressed by the level of commitment displayed by all the judges I met and interviewed' (Lambourne 2005: 6).

One's citizenship in Rwanda demands active participation of all in the Gacaca process, leading to the development of a broad sense of community.

Regardless of ethnicity, wealth, or status within the community, all Rwandans equally carry the burden of participation in the Gacaca process. The participation of women, a previously disenfranchised group within Rwandan society, as judges in the Gacaca, has raised their social capital. Rossouw states that the majority of judges in the Gacaca are likely to be Hutu, resulting in an increased sense of inclusion for Hutus experiencing fear of exclusion with each shift in ethnic power (Rossouw 2002).

> This participatory process promotes national democratic and rule-of-law values as well, in that it shifts the power from the central government to the people. This is particularly important in a context where there is a significant rift between the people and the government.
>
> (Daly 2002: 376)

Active participation additionally ensures that justice is visible to Rwandans. All members of society are involved in the process, and, as such, they discuss issues pertaining to justice and are engaged in the rendering of judgements. This allows them to see that justice is being done, and, as a society, they are holding people accountable for their crimes.

The Tutsi victory in 1994, bringing the civil war to its conclusion, placed them, by default, in a position of elevated power within the country. In the search for justice, this unequal position and the politicization of the Gacaca has a deleterious effect in the framework under which the Gacaca operates. The law stipulates that the Gacaca have jurisdiction over 'the crime of genocide and crimes against humanity, committed between October 1, 1990 and December 31, 1994, or other crimes provided for in the penal code of Rwanda' (Government of Rwanda 2004d). However, there has been a noticeable absence of any former RPF accused of various crimes by the Gacaca courts.

Martin Ngoga, Deputy Prosecutor of Rwanda and former Rwandan envoy to the ICTR, explains the reasoning behind the politics of resistance by Rwandan authorities to investigate and bring to trial RPF soldiers at the ICTR, as well as in the Gacaca with reference to the notion of moral equivalence (Ngoga 2005). There had been a determination within the Government of National Unity that the acts committed by RPF soldiers are not considered morally equivalent to those committed by the genocidaires, and that individual acts by RPF members, therefore, should not be tried in the same venue as the master-minds of the genocide (Ngoga 2005). Although on some level of abstraction, this might present a reasonable view that, in accordance with the rule of law, a crime is a crime and all should be accountable as such.

Despite the specific reference to the non-inclusion of former-RPF at the ICTR, it is conceivable that the same underlying considerations may be present within the framework of the Gacaca proceedings. This politically-determined omission of a segment of the population undermines the essential conditions necessary to achieve justice. The concept of victor's justice appears within the

Gacaca courts, and, despite the other perceived advantages of the process, may be detrimental to attempts at securing justice. Engaging in a practice that involves the alienation of a select group of victims from the process of Gacaca can present an additional complication in the achievement of justice. It may undermine one of the goals of the Gacaca specifically outlined in the legislation – the eradication of the culture of impunity – by failing to adhere to the rule of law. This failure has ramifications beyond the social institution of the Gacaca since it calls into question both the judiciary as a whole and the government's stated commitment to the ideal of justice. Indeed, it undermines the establishment of substantive and procedural justice and the creation of a set of mutual expectations for all Rwandans.

Notes

1 In accordance with the latest figures that are available, 932,000 people were killed during the genocide in Rwanda. Recent projections from the National Jurisdiction of Gacaca estimate that the number of individuals who were involved in the commission of the various acts that are subsequently to be tried under the array of crimes specified within the three categories in the Gacaca law may be as many as 1,000,000.
2 See Amnesty International (2002: 6–8) for a commentary on the legality of arrests and the conditions of detention.
3 According to Karekezi, these meetings were 'a series of "meetings of reflection" to discuss the country's future' (Karekezi, Nshimiyimana, and Mutamba 2004: 71).
4 Philibert Kigabo is a Rwandan anthropologist who works for the Rwandan Commission for Human Rights and has been involved in certain aspects relating to the implementation of the Gacaca by the Rwandan government to deal with the genocide crimes.
5 Other research supports the claim that the Gacaca had not completely vanished from Rwandan society. Lambourne notes that '[w]hile its use diminished under colonization, the traditional form of Gacaca has survived and is still used today by people in rural areas' (Lambourne 2005: 2).
6 According to Amnesty International, 'Offenders voluntarily appeared before inyangamugayo. Their appearance before community elders demonstrated their desire to be re-integrated into the community' (Amnesty International 2002: 21).
7 Note that the process of institutionalizing the Gacaca had begun in previous decades. According to Amnesty International:

> During the colonial period, a western judicial system was introduced but Gacaca remained an integral part of customary practice. With independence, Gacaca became more institutionalized with local authorities sometimes assuming the role of Inyangamugayo and Gacaca sessions considering local administrative matters.
>
> (Amnesty International 2002: 21)

As is noted here, some degree of formalization had already begun in the post-colonial period.
8 According to Vandeginste, 'Conflicts amounting to criminal offences (generally of a minor kind, like theft) may also be settled, though they will not typically result in a typically criminal sanction (imprisonment) but in some sort of civil settlement' (Vandeginste 1999: 17).

9 See Amnesty International (2002) *Rwanda: Gacaca: a question of justice*, for a more detailed examination of the specific differences identified.

10 The Organic Law specifically addresses three UN Conventions: Convention on the Prevention and Punishment of the Crime of Genocide of 9 December 1948, the Geneva Convention relative to the Protection of Civilian Persons in Time of War of 12 August 1949 and its additional protocols, as well as the Convention on the Non-Applicability of Statutory Limitations to War Crimes and Crimes Against Humanity of 26 November 1968.

11 This initial process of categorization was changed in subsequent legislation combining elements of some of the categories resulting in a product that in the final version included only three categories of offence.

12 The research entailed a 1-year project in which 'they developed a questionnaire to see how Gacaca functioned in the past and one year later we presented our findings to the population and then the authorities' (Kigabo 2005).

13 Geographically speaking, Rwanda is separated into 12 provinces, each province is divided into 106 districts, then 119 sectors, and 9,100 cells. There is a great deal of difference in the population density across the country. For example, Umujyi Wa Kigali (Kigali City) is considered its own province and accounts for approximately 22 percent of the country's population; the provinces of Gitarama and Butare are on the other end of the population percentage at 7 percent and 6 percent respectively. With regard to the localization of governance, after the National Government, in each province there is a prefect, each district a bourgmestre, each sector the equivalent of a mayor, and then in the cells a responsible, an individual that is in charge of what is happening for a collection of approximately 10 households (Government of Rwanda 2005).

14 The general assembly refers to all Rwandans over the age of majority, 18, within a specified area. See Organic Law No 16/2004 of 19/6/2004 establishing the organization, competence, and functioning of the Gacaca courts (Government of Rwanda 2004d).

15 Double letters are being used to preserve the anonymity guaranteed to a number of individuals interviewed for this research (for example AA, BB, CC, and so on).

16 Observe that in the most recent Rwandan election, in 2008, that Rwanda became the first democracy in history to have more women elected to Parliament than men.

17 This is based on my observations of a number of Gacaca in which women were, albeit sometimes in the minority, well represented in each court visited.

18 According to Thompson, mandatory participation amounts to the government forcing justice on the people:

> the gacaca courts are an expression of the power of the post-genocide state. … The gacaca process resolves the case officially at the level of the individual while at the same time it re-enforces the image of the post-genocide state as one that tries to treat its citizens fairly in the pursuit of national unity and reconciliation.
>
> (Thompson 2007: 2)

19 The categories, presented in the 2007 Organic Law, are based on the results of the categorization observed in the pilot-project of Gacaca. Under this law, the second and third categories, present in the first law, are collapsed into a single category (Government of Rwanda 2007a).

20 In a recent development, the Rwandan government is giving consideration to having the Category 1 offences remain within the jurisdiction of the Gacaca courts (Mutangana 2005).

21 For more detail, see Section II of Organic Law No 16/2004 of 19/6/2004 establishing the organization, competence, and functioning of Gacaca courts (Government of Rwanda 2004d).

22 For a more in-depth discussion of the criticisms arising from these processes, see PRI Document Penal Reform International 'PRI research on Gacaca report: Report IV: "The guilty plea procedure, the cornerstone of the Rwandan justice system"' (Penal Reform International 2003).

23 See Section III Organic Law No 16/2004 of 19/6/2004 (Government of Rwanda 2004d) for specific details.

24 This was prior to 2008 when the death penalty was removed from Rwandan penal law.

25 Note that at the time of the legislation, the death penalty was still in force in Rwandan law. However, as reported by Amnesty International, the law banning the death penalty has passed. Furthermore, Amnesty International reports that 'it is the first country in Africa's Great Lakes region to call a halt to executions and the 100th country worldwide to abolish the death penalty in law' (Amnesty International 2007).

26 These sentences apply to those placed in the two most severe sub-categories of the second category (see Article 51, 2nd Category 1° and 2° Organic Law, Government of Rwanda 2004d: 15).

27 In the move toward decolonization, the Catholic Church has been said to support the Hutu rule from the pulpit, supporting the notion of the right of majority rule (see Mamdani 2001).

28 The observation that the Church was involved in the prelude to the genocide is corroborated by Caplan in a speech presented October 2005: 'Genocide Generation: Remembrance and Reconciliation or Repetition'.

29 However, there has been a concern that, given the Rwandan historical context wherein the Hutu population was forced into indentured service of the Belgians, and, by extension, the Tutsi population, who have been observed to have benefited from the position granted to them by the Belgian colonialists, the community service may be perceived to be a return to the past; locating the Hutu population in an inferior social position and status within the country undermines the whole notion of social equality. However, the fact that it is only those Hutu who have been convicted of a crime, and not the general Hutu population, these concerns may be overstated.

30 This observation is based on the author's attendance at Gacaca proceedings on a number of occasions.

31 See Amnesty International (2002) for a more detailed discussion of these concerns.

32 In accordance with Section IV of Organic Law No 16/2004 0f 19/6/2004 establishing the organization, competence, and functioning of Gacaca courts (Government of Rwanda 2004d). Refusing to testify can result in prison terms ranging from 3 to 6 months for a first offence and up to 1 year for a second.

33 An individual could turn down the assignment if, by accepting it, they, and their family, would experience a great hardship.

34 They refer to their civic duty when discussing their obligation to take part in the Gacaca. This is a common experience for all Rwandans as part of their culture. From the forced labour in pre-colonial and colonial times, to the present-day umuganda (a half-day each month when everyone stops what they are doing to engage in labour for the good of the people), with which Rwandans are familiar, and, for the most part, accept their civic responsibilities. Hatzfeld reports that some of the killers claimed that they were forced into doing their civic duty when they engaged in the commission of their crimes (Hatzfeld 2005 [2003]: 71–6).

4 The Rwandan national judiciary

> In Rwanda we are trying our best. We are really trying our best as far as the judiciary is concerned ... in post-genocide traumatized society ... you will not expect us to be on international standards like that in the U.S. or Canada, but you will expect us to be on international standards on the continent of Africa.[1]
>
> (Mutangana 2005)

The history of the Rwandan national judiciary with regard to adjudicating those accused of genocide crimes occurred in three distinct periods: (1) the pre-genocide judiciary; (2) the judiciary in the immediate aftermath of the genocide; and (3) the current state of the national judicial system. The historical progression of the courts has involved attempts to address three major issues with regard to the judiciary's role in the adjudication of the perpetrators of the genocide. The first deals with the lack of legitimacy stemming from the previous history of the courts, including the lack of properly-trained personnel, as well as accusations of corruption and unfair practices. The second issue requires the total reconstruction of the judiciary in the immediate aftermath of the genocide. Despite the efforts to deal with the first two issues, the third issue is the need to accommodate an enormous caseload of genocide crimes resulting from the policy of maximal accountability and the categorization process in the Gacaca courts, whilst still adjudicating ongoing criminal activity in the country.

Historical issues impacting the current judiciary

The history the Rwandan judiciary tells a story that is antithetical to the promotion of the rule of law and justice. Schabas states that, 'in fact, the Rwandan legal system had never been more than a corrupt caricature of justice' (Schabas 1996: 531). Accusations of corruption and political tampering within the courts were rampant: 'The pre-genocide Rwandese judicial system was weak, possessing limited resources, insufficiently trained personnel and a lack of judicial independence' (Amnesty International 2002: 12). The concepts of fair treatment, impartiality, and independence on the part of the justice professionals were non-existent. According to Ngoga, 'Rwanda hardly had a legal system worth the name. Its judiciary was basically dominated by the executive power, and it was neither independent nor impartial but tools of a dictatorial regime' (Ngoga 2005). In addition to this concern was the lack of any form of legitimate legal training on the part of most of the professionals working in the system. Samuel Rugege, the current Vice-president of Rwanda's Supreme Court stated that, 'in fact, about eighty percent of judges did not have legal qualifications' (Rugege 2005). For those who did possess the requisite legal training, the interference by political authorities rendered them virtually ineffective. Schabas states that 'even well-meaning lawyers and judges within the system were powerless to prosecute numerous atrocities during the years that foreshadowed the genocide' (Schabas 1996: 531). The systemic issues that plagued the Rwandan judicial system prior to the genocide were exacerbated following the events that transpired in the fateful months of 1994. Immediately following the genocide, the newly-established government faced the dual issues of the need for justice and the need to construct a legitimate, as well as an effectively-functioning, justice system. According to Schabas, '[T]he term rebuilding is often used to describe the challenge facing Rwandan justice, but it is not well chosen' (Schabas 1996: 531). The previous justice system did not provide a foundation upon which the government could rebuild the desperately needed social institution. The Rwandan judiciary would have to be constructed from scratch in an environment that presented extraordinary conditions.

Another significant historical hurdle for the government and, specifically, the judiciary to overcome is the judiciary's *complicity* in creating the culture of impunity. The amnesty laws, discussed in Chapter 2, represent the judicial non-response to the wave of massacres that occurred in the decades prior to the 1994 genocide. These laws created an environment in which the concept of individual accountability did not exist. Hatzfeld, in his study of Bugersera genocidaires, eloquently relays the impressions of judicial immunity shared by many accused: 'Since I was killing so often, I began to feel it did not mean anything to me. It gave me no pleasure, I knew I would not be punished, I was killing without consequences' (Hatzfeld 2005 [2003]: 51). That ethnically-based killing did not receive judicial condemnation created a culture conducive to such events taking place. If crimes of this magnitude can proceed without attracting any form of judicial intervention, the entire system is called into question. The need to re-establish a functioning judiciary worthy of its name is critical to eradicating the culture of impunity and establishing the rule of law.

Problems facing the judiciary in the immediate aftermath of the genocide

The immediate concerns following the defeat of the genocidal regime were the establishment of order and the prevention of continued violence. Only under these conditions would it be possible for the government to even begin to attempt to engage in the business of creating a justice system that could address the need for justice. The pressing need for an end to the violence did not present the government with the luxury of time, a crucial factor required in any attempt to reconstruct social institutions of any kind, let alone a justice system that required highly-trained and specialized personnel.

Massive arrests and burgeoning prison population

To address the primary and immediate concern of establishing security and creating some semblance of order, the government employed its military to expediently round up suspected genocidaires *en masse*. 'In order to stop widespread revenge, and in response to the public demand for accountability for genocide, the R.P.A. arrested and detained genocide suspects on testimony by their communities' (Government of Rwanda 2000: 5). In describing the Rwandan government at this time, Amnesty International states that 'massive arrests combined with a non-functioning judicial system characterized the first two years of the Government of National Unity' (Amnesty International 2002: 5). The circumstances surrounding the arrests and detentions of these accused were focal points of concern for international human rights organizations.

On 16 April 1975, Rwanda officially ratified the International Covenant on Civil and Political Rights, as well as the Convention on the Prevention and Punishment of the Crime of Genocide (United Nations 2007). The International Covenant on Civil and Political Rights outlines a number of standards regarding acceptable practice in the arena of justice. Rwanda, as a signatory to the Covenant, presented itself as accepting of these international standards for fair trials that they were being accused of violating. According to Vandeginste, '[G]iven the massive number of criminal offences that had been committed in combination with the nearly complete breakdown of the law enforcement and justice system after the genocide, a massive number of people had been arrested illegally' (Vandeginste 1999: 10). Other issues raised by Amnesty International (2002) with regard to this process include: (1) the lack of legal dossiers that would be considered sufficient under the International Covenant to allow for the detention of an accused; (2) the time that an individual could be held before appearing before a magistrate; (3) the separation of minors and adults; and (4) the legalization of unlawful arrests and detentions (Amnesty International 2002: 6–8). Amnesty International (2002) states that despite the ruling of the Constitutional Court in 1995, the Transitional Government of National Unity voted for alterations to the Constitution, enacting Articles 4, 38, and 41 that suspended provisions in the CCP (the Code of Criminal Procedure) in September 1996.[2] These measures effectively legitimized the practices that were being undertaken that violated individual's rights with regard to arbitrary arrests and detentions. In response to these allegations, the Rwandan Government responded that:

[They] could not respond to the crisis by ordering the release of all the genocide suspects in detention. We were, and still are, of the view that the failure to respect procedural requirements for the arrest and detention of the suspects was the result of a very grave and unprecedented national crisis which could not, and had not, been foreseen. We took the view that the legislation should be passed to extend the period within which prosecutors could complete formalities legalizing the detention of these suspects.[3]

(Government of Rwanda 2000: 6)

By 1996, the Rwandan prison population had swollen to an alarming size; the majority of its inmate population were accused of crimes committed in the 1994 genocide. Despite government efforts in the recruitment and training of judicial personnel, the state of the judiciary was still far from what was required to address the estimated 120,000 inmates accused of genocide crimes.[4] The concern for expediting such an immense number of trials was additionally exacerbated by the overcrowded and unsanitary conditions observed in the detention facilities. According to an Amnesty International report:

[p]rior to 1994, the capacity of Rwandese prisons was 18,000. Between mid-1994 and mid-1996, the population in Rwandese detention facilities quintupled to slightly more than 90,000. By mid-1997 new prisons and extensions to the existing prisons had raised the capacity to 49,400. Nonetheless, the number of detainees continued to outstrip prison capacity. New facilities were overfilled as soon as they were constructed. The prison population levelled out at around 124,000 during 1997 and 1998. Their have been annual, albeit slight, declines in the prison population since then. Rwanda today has a prison population of around 112,000.

(Amnesty International 2002: 8)

The International Covenant on Civil and Political Rights, Part III, Article 7 dictates that no human being should be subjected to cruel and unusual treatment or punishment. The conditions that were observed to exist within these severely overcrowded detention facilities were argued to be in violation of that Article. Amnesty International reports that:

[p]reventable diseases, malnutrition, and the debilitating effects of overcrowding have resulted in a reported 11,000 deaths between 1994 and the end of 2001. There have also been reports of deaths in custody resulting from the physical abuse of detainees by prison officials.

(Amnesty International 2002: 8)

Despite the unsavoury conditions observed in the prisons, the tens of thousands of prisoners being held in the local detention centres (or *cachots*) were subjected to even worse conditions than in the prisons.

The concerns of outside groups regarding the situation in Rwanda did not go unnoticed. The government recognized the severe shortfalls in judicial personnel, but also stated that despite the challenges they were facing, they:

> concede that the trial of persons suspected of having participated in committing genocide crimes is slow indeed. However the report fails to take into account the fact the system has to cope with a caseload of unprecedented proportions. It overlooks the fact that the system of administration of justice in Rwanda had to be rebuilt from scratch.
>
> (Government of Rwanda 2000)

A consequence of genocide: a depleted judiciary

The Rwandan judiciary, like all government institutions, was not immune to the devastating impact of the genocide. An assessment of the judiciary painted a gloomy picture with regard to their capacity to address the genocide crimes. The genocide had left the numbers of judicial personnel severely depleted; the material resources and the avenues required for training were also virtually non-existent. The physical structures and facilities necessary for holding trials were all but destroyed. Table 4.1, presented by Ngoga, depicts the state of judicial personnel in Rwanda following the genocide.[5] Before the genocide, 1459 personnel were involved in judicial operations as judges, prosecutors, or support personnel, the majority of whom were Tutsi. In the months following the genocide, that number was 393, a nearly 75 percent reduction in personnel capacity.

Domestic Rwandan law did not include genocide crimes

Another factor that was involved in the lengthy process of proceeding to trials was the fact that, despite their signatory status in 1976 to the Convention on the Prevention and Punishment of the Crime of Genocide, the government of

Table 4.1 Judicial personnel in Rwanda

Reference time	Judges	Prosecutors	Other support staff
Before 1994	758	70	631
November 1994 (available information, shortly after the genocide)	244	12	137
After training sessions carried out at different times (before the judicial reform of 2004)	841	210	910
After judicial reform	235	237	230

Source: Mukantaganzwa (2004)

Rwanda had not established the requisite legislation regarding crimes of gen-ocide or crimes against humanity.[6] A criticism that haunted the Nuremburg trials, and would undoubtedly want to be avoided in Rwanda given the simi-lar scope of international interest, was that it proceeded with the trials despite the concern for the international legal principle that established the doctrine of *nullum crimen sine lege* (no crime without law).[7] As stated in the previous chapter, the law that provided the foundation for all prosecutions of genocide crimes was enacted in August 1996 (Government of Rwanda 1996).

The specialized chambers for genocide trials

For the purpose of dealing with the genocide crimes, the Organic Law, in accordance with Chapter V, Section 1, Articles 19–21, established specialized chambers within both the tribunals of first instance and the military courts. In an attempt to address the ever-worsening conditions in the prisons as more and more individuals were being incarcerated, as well as to begin a process of rebuilding or creating the judiciary, the government embarked on a 2-year recruitment and training programme. Ngoga states that 'in response to both domestic and international concerns, Rwanda chose to begin the trials using lay magistrates, rather than wait until new judicial personnel had received years of training' (Ngoga 2004). Utilizing the lay magistrates, the trials of the accused genocidaires began in 1996.

It was the task of these designated chambers to undertake the massive numbers of genocide cases. The use of lay magistrates is outlined in Article 20 of the Organic Law, specifically:

> [e]ach Specialized Chamber shall be comprised of such numbers of career or auxiliary magistrates as are deemed necessary and they shall be placed under the directions of a Vice-President of the Tribunal of First Instance or the military courts. ... Career magistrates and Presidents of the Spe-cialized Chambers of the Tribunals of First Instance shall be named by order of the President of the Supreme Court, following a decision of the College of the President and the Vice-President of the Supreme Court.
>
> (Government of Rwanda 1996)

That the President of the Supreme Court is appointed by Presidential Order and, therefore, potentially subject to political bias, has brought forth further concerns with regard to the appointments of the magistrates to the specialized chambers. The conceptualization of political interference within the structure and functioning of the courts has been criticized repeatedly. According to the *Country Assessment for Rwanda* performed by the Netherlands Organization for International Development Cooperation (NOIDC):

> [t]he distinction between the courts on the one hand and the RPF-led government and army on the other hand is not clear cut. According to

documents obtained from the UN, more than 60 judicial officials have been detained, beaten, or suspended, most of them Hutus. Often it appears that they have been deemed too sympathetic to genocide suspects. Some have refused to make arrests without proper evidence. Others had freed suspects. ... Such officials have been charged with mismanagement, corruption, and genocide.

(NOIDC 1997: 15)

This concern, and allegations of political interference by the government within the realm of what should ideally be an independent judiciary, calls into question the legitimacy of any decisions that arise from the trials. 'Government employment practices in the re-establishment of the judiciary, however, exacerbated a problem that it claims it wants to resolve and undermines public confidence in the new judiciary' (Amnesty International 2002: 13).

Giving consideration to the gravity of both the offences with which the accused were charged as well as the fact that those convicted of the most serious crimes faced the death penalty, the use of lay magistrates was highly criticized by the international community:

The most serious problem with the genocide trials now underway in Rwanda is the lack of defence attorneys. Judges have been unwilling to grant postponements for suspects to find counsel, and in any case, few of Rwanda's 33 private attorneys want to defend genocide suspects.

(NOIDC 1997: 13)

An additional observation of the 1996 Organic Law is that while it does indeed recognize the right for all accused to have an attorney, in accordance with Article 36, this guaranteed right is not provided at the expense of the State.[8]

The lack of available resources and competent legal professionals, although improving, continues to present an inadequate solution to the overcrowded prison population and cries of human rights and due process violations. Drumbl asserts, 'Any legal system which, in almost five years, has only determined the guilt or innocence of 1 percent of all detainees cannot be said to be dispensing "justice"' (Drumbl 2000: 291). The notion of dispensing justice is further complicated by the criticism that even those trials that have been completed are questionable with regard to appropriate legal representation for the defendants and the impartiality of the judges in delivering a fair sentence. It has been reported that 'conviction sometimes rests more on public acclaim than on the incontrovertible evidence of guilt' (Amnesty International 2002: 16). The highly-volatile and contentious socio-political environment existing in Rwanda has entered into the courtroom and influenced its proceedings, which further questions the possibility of a defendant receiving an objective and fair trial. These concerns become exacerbated with the recognition that many of these trials are capital cases. Recent projections suggest that approximately 76,000 individuals (and possibly as many as

100,000) will face trial for genocide crimes in the criminal jurisdiction (Mukantaganzwa 2005).[9]

Amnesty International additionally cites concerns with the operations of the specialized chambers that relate to the use of lay magistrates and their inexperience and ability to manage a court:

> Court proceedings continue to reflect the hostile socio-political environment outside of the courtroom. The climate of fear affects judicial personnel, defendants, and witnesses. Defence counsel and witnesses are intimidated causing the former to withdraw from trials and the latter to refuse to testify.
>
> (Amnesty International 2002: 15)

While attempting to fulfill the judicial mandate of maximal accountability for the crimes of genocide, the operation of the domestic trials has been a slow-moving process fraught with allegations of: (1) corruption (Amnesty International 2002: 24); (2) due process violations (Drumbl 2005: 601); (3) lack of competent legal professionals (Mukantaganzwa 2004); (4) detention of numerous suspects without any kind of judicial review, arrested by individuals without the requisite authority (Vandeginste 1999: 10); and (5) perceptions of the court as an example of victor's justice (Sarkin 2000: 5). In summary, the court environment was an unhealthy and seemingly unprofessional one.

In attempting to balance the need for justice and security with ongoing international pressure regarding the issues surrounding the lack of perceived fairness noted above, the specialized chambers proceeded, beginning in December of 1996, with the trials of those accused of genocide crimes. Additionally, the attempt by the Rwandan government to repatriate those individuals residing in the refugee camps outside the borders of Rwanda (having fled Rwanda as a result of the campaign of fear of reprisal instilled by the former regime) was of great significance in moving forward with the trials. 'It [was] a political imperative to convince the returnees that the RPF's version of justice is not to let inmates rot in prison' (NOIDC 1997: 16).

With an understanding of the scope of the challenges facing the Rwandan judiciary, the trials of the accused were a significant and progressive step forward to balance the need for justice while engaging in the re-building process. From December 1996, to the next phase in the Rwandan judicial development in 2001 of judicial reforms, a large number of cases were heard before the specialized chambers. One additional challenge that remains to the present day is the process of creating and maintaining the judicial archives and court statistics. As such, precise data with regard to the numbers of trials and the range of dispositions that were handed down is difficult to attain.[10] Nevertheless, according to Ngoga:

> figures show that by the end of 2001 only, approximately 41220 persons had been judged on genocide-related charges. During the first nine months of 2001, approximately 1005 had been judged in local courts on

genocide related charges, 88 receiving death sentences, 288 were sentenced to life imprisonment, 459 received sentences for less than life, 205 were acquitted, while 25 were fined for property crime.

(Ngoga 2004)

The figures stated by Ngoga indicate that, in those early years of the adjudication process, an average of 7,000 individuals were tried each year. The trials themselves, conducted by lay magistrates, employed a strategy of mass trials to deal with the enormous caseload of accused persons.[11] The use of mass trials continued during the following few years as well. The figures obtained from the Supreme Court for the period of 2000–3 demonstrate that 5490 accused individuals came in front of the courts during 595 trials, representing an average of approximately nine persons on trial in each case.[12] The court statistics also suggest a number of trends with regard to the severity of the sentences that have been handed out over time. In the first year that the specialized chambers for the genocide crimes were in operation, the sentences delivered to those convicted tended towards the most severe sanctions. According to a statistics sheet received from RCN Justice and Democratie, in 1997, the percentage of accused who received the death penalty was approximately 36 percent, life sentences 34 percent, all prison terms less than life accounted for approximately 25 percent, and those acquitted 5.6 percent.

Table 4.2 suggests that there has been a significant and steady reduction of the use of the death penalty and life imprisonment, as well as a significant increase in the percentage of those acquitted of their charges. It is difficult, given the limited amount of data available, to create and support hypotheses as to whether: (1) these trends are the result of a change in the overall environment of the social context in Rwanda; and/or (2) they reflect a significant acceptance and increased use of plea bargaining as a result of the government's attempts to *educate* the prisoners on the plea bargaining process. Nevertheless, it remains a significant trend in the adjudication process of the accused.[13]

Table 4.2 Genocide trials in the specialized chambers 2000–2003

| | Accused | | Acquitted | | Imprisonment | | | | | | Death penalty | |
| | | | | | Under 15 years | | 15–20 years | | Life sentence | | | |
Year	(N)	(%)	(N)	(%)	(N)	(%)	(N)	(%)	(N)	(%)	(N)	(%)
2003	1162	–	318	27.4	445	38.3	179	15.4	122	10.5	39	3.4
2002	1173	–	302	25.7	255	21.7	179	15.3	190	16.2	43	3.7
2001	1429	–	292	20.4	284	19.9	222	15.5	324	22.7	112	7.8
2000	1726	–	226	13.1	147	8.5	341	19.8	251	14.5	146	8.5
Total	5490	–	1138	20.7	1131	20.6	921	16.8	887	16.1	340	6.2

Note: percentages have been rounded.
Source: Government of Rwanda (2005)

The sheer volume of cases that have come before the courts is additionally significant given the number of judicial personnel. The fact is that each genocide case that came before the specialized chambers required three magistrates to sit on the bench (Government of Rwanda 1996). In addition, the regular operations of the justice system on new cases arising as a result of ongoing criminal activity were simply added to what might be argued as an already overworked judiciary groaning with the high backlog of the old genocide cases. Between the start of 2000 and end of 2003, the adjudication of genocide cases amounted to approximately 14 percent of the total number of trials that were adjudicated in Rwanda during that time period. According to Mutangana, the specialized chambers were eventually closed as a result of two main factors: (1) the rise of the Gacaca courts, which replaced the specialized chambers; and (2) the process of judicial reform and renewal that was undertaken by the government in 2004 (Mutangana 2005).

A system in transition: judicial reform

The initial enterprise of constructing a judicial system from a virtually non-existent foundation, while at the same time addressing the high priority objective of the adjudication of those responsible for the commission of genocide crimes, was well underway by the end of 2001. In addition, a greater sense of stability and security throughout the country presented the government with one of the vital aspects that was not available in the initial period immediately following the genocide: time. With time as an ally rather than a constraint, the Rwandan government embarked on a period of judicial reform. The creation of a number of commissions whose task it was to evaluate and provide direction to the future of the judicial and other closely related social institutions was the starting point. The awareness of the Rwandan judicial personnel that their approach to addressing the genocide crimes is subject to great interest and scrutiny worldwide cannot be understated in their pursuit of reforms and justice. 'The eyes of the world are all focused on Rwanda; to see how justice is developing and to see how the personnel working in justice are really developing' (Mutangana 2005).

Constitutional reform

One of the prerequisites for the government to achieve judicial reform was the re-drafting of the Rwandan Constitution. In preparing for this task, the government held public meetings designed to both educate the public with regard to the constitution and to receive their input. One of the results of this effort was the publishing of an informational book for public consumption.[14] According to the Legal and Constitutional Commission:

> The Legal and Constitutional Commission set up in accordance with the Arusha Peace Agreement and the law n° 23/99 dated 24/12/1999 provides for the following in Article 2:

The Commission for preparing the Constitution and revising other laws' has the mission to: (1) Prepare the draft-bill of the Constitution, (2) Search for, receive, and collect thoughts given by the population and to make use of examples from other countries, (3) Explain to the population what the Constitution is and the main ideas which it is comprised of, (4) Prepare the draft-bills of laws that govern the last transition period, and (5) Put together all the laws which must be notified in order to adapt them to the Constitution.

(Legal and Constitutional Commission 2002: 3)

The culmination of this process of public consultation, sensitization, and education was a newly-written Rwandan constitution that came into force on 2 June 2003.[15] The importance of the memory of the genocide and its devastating effects, along with the stated national goal that the conditions that led to its occurrence are never again to be allowed to permeate Rwandan society, is clearly outlined within Part 2° of the Preamble of the new constitution which states, 'Resolved to fight the ideology of genocide and all its manifestations and to eradicate ethnic, regional, and any other form of division' (Government of Rwanda 2003c).

The newly-constructed constitution demonstrates the protection from discrimination for all Rwandan citizens, Under Title II, Article 11:

All Rwandans are born and remain free and equal in rights and duties,

Discrimination of whatever kind based on, inter alia, ethnic origin, tribe, clan, colour, sex, region, social origin, religion or faith, opinion, economic status, culture, language, social status, physical or mental disability or any other form of discrimination is prohibited and protected by law.

(Government of Rwanda 2003c)

The constitution also presents a declaration of the desired objective of national unity and a single national identity, and, therefore, the eradication of the ethnic divide that existed in Rwanda prior to the genocide is found in the statement of the National Motto found in Article 6: 'UNITY, WORK, PATRIOTISM' (Government of Rwanda 2003c), as well as in the declaration of the Fundamental Principles of the Constitution in Article 9, which includes 'equitable sharing of power; building a state governed by the rule of law, a pluralistic democratic government; ... the constant quest for solutions through dialogue and negotiation' (Government of Rwanda 2003c).

In addition to constitutional guarantees, the deeply-seated concern to address the discriminatory and divisionist historical conditions believed to have been a key factor in the genocide are further observed in two additional changes. The first was the removal of the *ethnic* classification from both the data collected in the Rwandan Census as well as from the identity cards carried by Rwandan citizens.[16] The second was the creation of Organic Law N° 47/2001 of 18/12/2001, instituting punishment for offences of discrimination and sectarianism[17] prior to the coming into force of the constitution in February 2002.

Guarantees specifically relevant to the trials of those accused of genocide and the provision of legal rights are presented in Articles 15 to 21 of the constitution. These include: (1) the principle of the rule of law; (2) guarantees regarding personal liberties and freedom from arbitrary detention; (3) the right to be informed of the charges laid; (4) the presumption of innocence; (5) the right to appear before a competent judge in a fair and public hearing; and (6) guarantees for the providing of a defence (Government of Rwanda 2003c).

The Constitutional and Legal Commission also gave consideration to the work being performed by other commissions by making a number of changes within the structure and functioning of the judiciary. These changes are reflected in the constitution itself, specifically Organic Law N° 03/2004 of 20/03/2004 determining the organization powers, and function of the prosecution service, and Organic Law N° 13/2004 of 17/05/2004 relating to the code of criminal procedure. A number of changes have also been in the structure of judiciary as part of the process of judicial reform.

Judicial restructuring

One concern that is being addressed by the current regime deals with the structure and functioning of judicial institutions. Noted by Human Rights Watch, '*Gacaca* looked to the past, supposedly joining elements of customary institutions with some concepts and practices of formal punitive justice. The new conventional courts looked to the future, fusing elements from Anglo-American law with the existing Belgian-created judicial system' (Human Rights Watch 2008: 23). Based originally on the French and Belgian systems, the judicial system in Rwanda did not previously incorporate a system of judicial precedents as employed in English common law systems. The Supreme Court was, according to Rugege:

> a review court that would hear cases based on procedure and declared that the case had been properly adjudicated or if it was not properly adjudicated and that would send it back to the lower court – to the court of appeals.
>
> (Rugege 2005)

Under the newly-created judicial structure,[18] the Supreme Court would become the highest court of the land. Judicial restructuring continued well into 2006, and, according to Human Rights Watch, the judiciary was streamlined in an effort to increase judicial efficiency:

> The March 2006 law reduced the number of courts established under the 2004 law, providing for 60 lower instance courts with jurisdiction over less serious criminal and civil cases, and 12 higher instance courts dealing

with criminal and civil cases involving heavier penalties or higher monetary value, as well as category one genocide crimes.

(Human Rights Watch 2008: 24–5)

A High Court sits atop the aforementioned review courts and the Supreme Court over the High Court. 'The Supreme Court, including 14 judges, heads the system with appellate jurisdiction over the High Court and the Military High Court' (Human Rights Watch 2008). The Supreme Court has been established as the highest court of the land. The one distinct *missing link* in the judicial chain is the Gacaca, in which no appeal to the highest court of the land is possible.

In accordance with Article 144 of the Constitution, 'decisions are binding on all parties concerned whether such are organs of the State, public officials, civilians, military, judicial officers or private individuals' (Government of Rwanda 2003c). This judicial structure establishes the Supreme Court as the court of final authority and begins the process of setting precedents, which, according to Rugege:

> there wasn't before. There are now plans to do it. We have set up a committee to compile important decisions of the High Courts and the Supreme Court and probably by the end of July [2005], we might have the first compilation of cases.
>
> (Rugege 2005)

Another facet of the process of constitutional and judicial reform concerns the existence of the specialized chambers and specialized courts. The specialized chambers for the genocide trials have been closed and replaced by the Gacaca courts which, now, serve as the specialized courts with the responsibility for adjudication of the majority of the genocide crimes. According to prosecutor Mutangana:

> The reason why these chambers were closed, you know, these chambers were directly administrated by the Prosecutor General for genocide cases, were instituted within the 1996 Organic Law to try genocide cases as opposed to ordinary crimes. And there were specific prosecutors to try genocide cases so this was a disadvantage, not all prosecutors are competent to try genocide cases. ... We wanted all prosecutors to have the same competence for all cases; that is point one. Secondly, the inception of Gacaca law, because the Gacaca law came in 2000 and we didn't see the logic of having specialized chambers in the Gacaca cell and district and we did see the significance of that because we wanted the Gacaca to be global in one way, as far as the trials are concerned. So first of all some prosecutors are not competent to try genocide cases and some judges are not competent, in the specialized chamber there was a specialized chamber judge, and it was usually the vice-president of the Provincial

Court ... We wanted to bring the whole thing together, secondly there was Gacaca, so the logic of specialized chambers was no longer necessary.

(Mutangana 2005)

The creation of the Gacaca and their administration by community members may have resulted in confusion between the operation of the Gacaca and the previous specialized genocide chambers once the latter were permanently closed.

Competency of judicial personnel

The concern of competency among the judiciary is recognized as a government priority and the government has begun a lengthy process to address this concern. The process of reviewing the competency of those who were employed by the judiciary, as well as the recruitment of properly-trained personnel, was in and of itself a major undertaking; the process actually involved the complete shut down of all the courts for an extended period of time. According to Rugege:

The courts resumed in October [2004] because the old courts were discontinued around May of 2004 and then we started the recruitment process of new judges, new court clerks, and then we took them for training on the new laws and they finally resumed October 2004.

(Rugege 2005)

The process required that the judicial personnel essentially re-apply for their previously-held positions. They would re-apply, be interviewed for the position, and then it was determined by the judicial commission as to whether or not they would be approved for future employment. 'So they went through that process. The law automatically terminated their employment. They reapplied for their jobs. Some were retained, others were not retained' (Rugege 2005).

In addition to this process, according to Rugege, the government and the judiciary have been involved in other ways to address this concern (Rugege 2005). They have created a training school for judges where recent graduates of the law school will be given training with regard to the practices of the court. For those who were retained as a result of the re-application process, the government has engaged in a programme by which the individuals may be financially compensated for the cost of their tuition when acquiring the necessary educational certification:

For those people we have donor support to put them through school and eventually they will come back to the system. So they will have the experience [gathered in their previous work in the courts] and now they will have the credentials.

(Rugege 2005)

Ngoga further detailed another plan by which the government was sponsoring a number of students for their law school education in exchange for an agreed upon time of employment within the Parquet General upon their graduation (Ngoga 2005).

In total, the current judicial system has approximately 330 trained lawyers and judges with another 90 having been recently recruited. The present judiciary has qualified personnel at the national and district levels. Furthermore, they have developed a 3-year plan whereby this level of competence will be extended to all levels of the judiciary:

> The judiciary in Rwanda, as far as human growth and resource development is concerned, in three years time we will be 100 percent in all sectors of justice … which will be okay, because in some countries in East Africa they don't have 100 percent. They just have lay magistrates.
>
> (Mutangana 2005)

From the perspective of those working within the judicial system, the advances made in the training of judicial personnel to an unprecedented standard represents a significant achievement.

Relationship to the Gacaca

Despite the independence of the Gacaca from the national judiciary, which was noted in the previous chapter, there remains an interesting connection between the Gacaca court and the ordinary court. That connection is the transfer of cases from the Gacaca court to the national judiciary of all persons suspected of Category 1 genocide crimes as defined in the Gacaca Organic Law. Other than the transfer of these cases, there is no institutional link between the Gacaca and the ordinary courts that leaves conspicuously absent an avenue for appeal to the highest court of the land, the Supreme Court. Within the specific guidelines of Gacaca Law, there is only one avenue for appeal, the Gacaca appellate court at the sector level. The decision of the sector appeal court of the Gacaca is final. This demonstrates the separation of the two avenues for adjudicating those accused of genocide crimes since there is no method of appeal from the Gacaca to the national judiciary. Given the judicial reform process, this brings into question the notion of creating a system of precedents. The development of case precedents within the Gacaca is non-existent as the committee compiling the cases for precedence are focused on decisions rendered by the High and Supreme Courts. It also raises concerns with regard to the guarantees of due process outlined in the constitution.

Three final concerns regarding the relationship of the Gacaca to the ordinary courts and Rwandan law are issues regarding the constitutionality of the Gacaca Organic Law, specifically the concepts of competency and a fair hearing, double jeopardy, and the placing of the burden of proof. The first issue that presents itself is that of the constitutional guarantee to a fair trial with a competent judge. The use of lay magistrates within the Gacaca framework, despite the training that they receive through Avocats Sans Frontières, is questionable when considering the gravity of both the charges and the sentence that may result upon conviction. Additionally, the absence of legal representation in the process may undermine the guarantee for a fair trial in that the accused is not presented with legal advice in preparation for their defence or during the process. Second, the observation has been made that those who were previously not convicted within the ordinary courts may nevertheless be subjected to trial within the Gacaca process which is a violation of the principle of double-jeopardy.[19] Finally, the Gacaca may present a reversal of the burden of proof established for the ordinary courts in the Rwandan Penal Code. In the ordinary judicial process, the burden of proof lies with the prosecutor while in the Gacaca, based on my observations of the Gacaca proceedings,[20] it is apparent that the accused were forced to defend the veracity of their confessions rather than the judges being forced to demonstrate the validity of the accusations.[21] These concerns need to be remedied in a coherent manner if there is to be clarity and consistency in the application of the judicial reforms.

Despite developments in the legal framework of the constitution, other relevant laws, and the significant training of personnel within the judiciary, the judicial system still faces the task of an unprecedented number of cases. The National Jurisdiction of the Gacaca estimated that they expect some 760,000 new cases of which 10 percent (76,000) may be forwarded for prosecution by the ordinary courts.[22] The current state of the judicial system will very likely be overwhelmed with these cases while still attempting to deal with both the backlog of cases of those already incarcerated for the crimes of genocide and for ongoing criminal matters that arise in the normal course of events. The limitations observed in terms of both human resources and the financial predicament[23] that Rwanda continues to face will remain a source of ongoing concern in the courts' attempt to address these cases. Finding a way to address the prospect of system capacity overload remains an issue to be addressed.

Relationship to the ICTR

The *relationship* between the Rwandan judiciary and the ICTR in adjudicating those accused of genocide is both interesting and complex. The ICTR Statute (in Article 8) states that the ICTR and Rwanda have concurrent jurisdiction over the genocide crimes. The same section of the statute, however, states that the ICTR will have primacy over national courts of all states. Despite the suggestion of concurrent jurisdiction, the relationship that exists in practice has been one where the ICTR has asserted primacy.

In what might be considered recognition of the concept of Westphalian sovereignty, the ICTR does not get involved in cases heard before any Rwandan courts (including Gacaca, judicial, or military courts). Non-involvement, however, does not suggest that they are unaware of, or do not pay attention to, the cases heard in Rwanda. According to Obote-Odora (2005), when statements are made, or decisions rendered, that relate to a case within which the ICTR is involved, they will use that information in the prosecution of accused at the ICTR. The ICTR makes a request of the Rwandan government for transcripts of the trials, as well as access to the witnesses involved in specific cases.

The constitutional guarantee protecting an accused acquitted of a crime against double-jeopardy is another prickly factor in the relationship between Rwandan courts and the ICTR. The primacy of the ICTR for the prosecution of accused genocidaires, as well as concerns about the competency of the Rwandan courts, are both considered with respect to double-jeopardy and ICTR involvement in Rwandan court cases. Obote-Odora (2005) states that because the tribunal takes precedence over criminal trials, even if the latter take place in Rwanda, once the prosecutor takes the opinion that the trial was not properly conducted he or she could take over the case. Additionally, an individual acquitted at the ICTR cannot be tried in Rwanda or any other national jurisdiction because of the primacy of the ICTR over national courts.

Another issue has arisen out of the ICTR completion strategy and served as an impetus for the Rwandan government to address concerns regarding the competency and functioning of the judiciary. The ICTR is assessing the potential of the Rwandan courts to effectively adjudicate as many as 25 cases for trial that are currently under ICTR jurisdiction (Obote-Odora 2005). Under Rule 11*bis* of the ICTR Statute, the prosecutor has discretion to transfer selected cases to national jurisdictions. A recent decision in Trial Chamber III at the ICTR states the factors given consideration in the transfer of a case to Rwandan courts:

(i)   The case is appropriate for transfer to the authorities of another State;
(ii) Rwanda has jurisdiction; and
(iii) Rwanda is an appropriate referral State in that (a) the death penalty will not be imposed and the Accused will receive an appropriate punishment if convicted of the crime with which he is charged; and (b) the Accused will receive a fair trial.

(Prosecutor v Munyakazi 2008: 3)

The decision rendered in this case denied the transfer of the accused to Rwandan jurisdiction. The court recognized that the case was appropriate for selection for transfer stating, 'The Chamber is satisfied that the level of responsibility of the Accused makes his an appropriate case for referral to authorities of a State' (*Prosecutor v Munyakazi* 2008: 6).[24] The decision additionally recognized Rwanda to have jurisdiction over the case since it met the criteria outlined in Rule 11*bis* (A)[25] and the non-imposition of the death penalty under Article 3 of Organic Law No 31/2007 of 25/07/2007 Relating to the Abolition of the Death Penalty Law, was consistent with the ICTR penalty structure. The ICTR trial chamber did take issue, however, with the *special provisions* outlined in the law that implements solitary confinement for those convicted of genocide, crimes against humanity, murder, and torture. According to the decision, the sentence of life imprisonment in isolation is considered an inadequate penalty structure 'as required by the jurisprudence of the ICTY and the Tribunal, thus precluding referral to Rwanda' (*Prosecutor v Munyakazi* 2008: 12).

The second issue debated in Trial Chamber III was the determination of the ICTR Statute's guarantee to a fair trial. Munyakazi's defence counsel argued against the transfer to Rwanda on the basis that the single judge configuration of Rwandan courts did not meet the international requirement that 'persons accused of serious crimes under international humanitarian law appear before a panel of three judges in the first instance and before five judges at the appellate level' (*Prosecutor v Munyakazi* 2008: 12). It is argued that a panel of judges alleviates any political interference in the judiciary. The Trial Chamber thus focused its discussion to questions surrounding the independence of the judiciary in Rwanda. It examined the Rwandan government's past exploits, including:

> the interrupted cooperation with the Tribunal following a dismissal of an indictment and release of an appellant, as well as its negative reaction to foreign judges for indicting former members of the Rwandan Patriotic Front ('RPF'). The Chamber is concerned that these actions by the Rwandan Government ... show a tendency to pressure the judiciary, a pressure which a judge sitting alone would be particularly susceptible.
>
> (*Prosecutor v Munyakazi* 2008: 14)

The availability and safety of potential defence witnesses was another issue raised with respect to the accused receiving a fair trial if transferred to Rwanda. Citing a number of sources that questioned the safety of witnesses, as well as raising their own concerns about the ineffectiveness of the witness protection programme and the ability of the courts to produce the witnesses requested by the defence, the Trial Chamber concluded that these factors would impede the accused receiving a fair trial if transferred to Rwanda. In their concluding statements, nevertheless, the judges did take note of Rwanda's progress in addressing many judicial concerns:

> The Chamber would like to emphasise that it has taken notice of the positive steps taken by Rwanda to facilitate referral. The Chamber is of the view that if Rwanda continues along this path, the Tribunal will hopefully be able to refer future cases to Rwandan courts.
>
> (*Prosecutor v Munyakazi* 2008: 26)

In response to this decision and another case involving the possible transfer of Gaspard Kanyyarukiga to Rwanda, Chief Prosecutor Hassan Bubacar Jallow

(ICTR) cooperated with Martin Ngoga (Prosecutor General in Rwanda) to appeal the Tribunal's decision (Kimenyi 2008a). Additionally, Aloys Mutabingwa (Rwanda's Special Representative to the ICTR) also stated in a news report that the Government of Rwanda would be discussing these concerns in Parliament: 'These discussions will include examining how solitary confinement can be avoided when handling the cases that have been shifted from the ICTR or cases from other States that don't allow the solitary confinement punishment' (Muramira 2008).

The concern regarding the politicization of the judiciary in Rwanda has drawn additional attention from Human Rights Watch. The accusation of political interference and resulting lack of judicial independence is evident in their critique of the judicial reforms in Rwanda:

> Judicial authorities operate in a political context where the executive continues to dominate the judiciary and where there is official antipathy to views diverging from those of the government and the dominant party, the Rwandan Patriotic front (RPF). A campaign against 'divisionism' and 'genocidal ideology' imposes the risk of serious consequences on persons who question official interpretations of the past and who would prefer other than the official vision for the future.
>
> (Human Rights Watch 2008: 2)

Restorative and/or retributive justice

The newly-revised and restructured conventional courts in Rwanda are premised on a foundation that draws from both the civil and common law systems. They are designed to mete out punishment in response to establishing an offender's guilt. The main theme of the government in addressing crimes that occurred during the genocide has been that no reconciliation can occur without justice, more specifically, punishment. Based on their structure they function in a manner very similar to that found in Western conventional courts. That is, they are retributive in nature. They do not seek active participation of the various stakeholders that are affected by the crimes they adjudicate. They do not engage in dialogical processes in an attempt to come to a consensus with respect to the harm caused by crime. Rather, they engage in an adversarial process that removes the stakeholders from the process, for the most part, placing the process in the hands of professionals which, as Christie (1977) would argue, steals the conflict from those who should own it. The State acts on behalf of the victims and the community and the defendants are represented by counsel.

Responsive regulation

The Rwandan conventional courts represent Braithwaite's (2002) notion of regulatory formalism and, as such, do not respond, in and of themselves, in a manner that reflects responsive regulation. The process of referring those placed in Category 1 in the Gacaca reflects a more responsive system than the operation of conventional courts alone, albeit it in a limited sense. Because the initial processes of information-gathering and categorization in the Gacaca are dialogically-based, the actual starting point for addressing these genocide crimes is not the standard means typically incorporated into regular courts. However, it is at this juncture in the process that the responsive aspect ends. Once transferred to the conventional courts, the procedures for actually dealing with the crime operate within a framework that reflects regulatory formalism.

However, looking beyond the adjudication of genocide crimes, the suggestion posited by members of the Rwandan judiciary that the Gacaca courts may continue to operate after the completion of the genocide trials may imply that the conventional courts have a role to play in helping the overall judicial system to become a more *responsive* system. For this to occur there would need to be additional structural changes made to the entire judicial system.

To reflect a system incorporating responsive regulation, the starting point for addressing crime would become the responsibility of the Gacaca courts operating is a less formalized manner, a system more reflective of the traditional Gacaca. This would be a system without formalized categorization of crimes and pre-ordained punishments. There would be a focus on dialogue, involving those impacted by crime, seeking consensus among themselves in reaching a means to address the harm caused by the crime. If an agreement could not be reached, or if the offender did not alter his/her behaviour as a result of this quasi-judicial intervention, then the case could be referred up the regulatory pyramid to the conventional courts.

Liberal-legalism

The main theme present within post-dictatorial rule in Rwanda is that of a shift towards a liberal-legalistic model for the conventional courts. In the post-genocide era, there is an abundance of challenges that must be overcome in order for justice to flourish and a sound judiciary to emerge. Despite these roadblocks, there remains evidence that the Rwandan government is seeking to create an environment conducive to the realization of a justice system worthy of its name. The re-conceptualization of the key ideas upon which the constitution was founded implicitly makes a case for creating conditions that are conducive to the principles of justice. Recent evidence suggests that the domestic judiciary has taken serious strides aimed at achieving significant improvement in several areas including, but not limited to, the acquisition of qualified and impartial staff resulting in an increase in the annual number of cases adjudicated, the elimination of the death penalty, and increased acquittals in genocide cases. The elimination of *ethnicity* from the State identity cards and the participation rates of women elected to Parliament, serving in government (at rates above the international average) and in the Gacaca, both present important concrete steps towards engaging in practices that support the ideals of justice. However, these conditions are not likely to appear suddenly and require time to take root and blossom throughout Rwandan society. The significance of the progress that these steps have made is of little value if there remains a distrustful and negative perception of the overall judicial process (Vandeginste 1999; Drumbl 2000).

Rule of law

The advance of the *rule of law* accompanies the establishment of the liberal-legalistic approach with its protections of *due process* and respect for *individual rights*. There remain questions, however, that have yet to be resolved with regard to the accountability of RPF soldiers who committed reprisal killings and crimes against Hutus in the wake of the genocide. For there to be a realization of justice, there must be accountability on the part of all who were involved in the violation of law regardless of their position, ethnicity, or other factors. As noted previously, there are additional concerns with the current configuration of the justice system that need to be addressed if there is to be a true realization of the *rule of law*. It must be recognized, however, that the Rwandan justice system remains in a state of transition that is nowhere near completion. With the constitution as a foundational guide for future developments, there exists the potential for positive outcomes in the future.

Unfortunately, the spectre of victor's justice remains as a dark cloud hanging over the trials in both the national courts as well the Gacaca. This perception is based on a number of factors, including the failure to prosecute the war crimes of the Rwandan Patriotic Front, the exclusion of former Hutu judges and prosecutors from the judiciary, and the perceived unfair treatment of Hutu defendants. These factors support the view that victor's justice continues to be ever present, thereby continuing to severely undermine the government's efforts in operating fair trials. The perceived and real operation of fair trials is crucial in progressing towards national reconciliation.

Notes

1 John Bosco Mutangana is a Rwandan Prosecutor of National Competence. The quotation was provided in an interview in Kigali, Rwanda, 7 June 2005.
2 These specific violations are in contradiction to the International Covenant on Civil and Political Rights, Part III Article 9 (ICTR 2007).
3 In 1994, the Government of Rwanda had invoked Article 4 of the International Covenant on Civil and Political Rights, wherein:

> 1. In time of public emergency which threatens the life of the nation and the existence of which is officially proclaimed, the States Parties to the present Covenant may take measures derogating from their obligations under the present Covenant to the extent strictly required by the exigencies of the situation, provided that such measures are not inconsistent with their other obligations

under international law and do not involve discrimination solely on the ground of race, colour, sex, language, religion or social origin.

2. No derogation from Articles 6, 7, 8 (paragraphs 1 and 2), 11, 15, 16 and 18 may be made under this provision.

3. Any State Party to the present Covenant availing itself of the right of derogation shall immediately inform the other States Parties to the present Covenant, through the intermediary of the Secretary-General of the United Nations, of the provisions from which it has derogated and of the reasons by which it was actuated. A further communication shall be made, through the same intermediary, on the date on which it terminates such derogation.

(ICTR 2007)

However, according to outside observers, while accepting this initial invocation of this Article, by the end of 1995, it was argued that the need for its continuance was no longer necessary and the Rwandan Government continued to use this article as a defence for its illegal and inhuman actions. As noted by Vandeginste, despite the reasonable argument put forth by the Rwandan Government with regard to the invocation of this article in the Covenant, 'the adopted derogations were excessive ... some suspects will have spent over 5 years without a judicial review of their pre-trial detention by a judge' (Vandeginste 1999: 10).

4 This estimate is provided by the Rwandan government (2000) in their response to Amnesty International's publication.

5 This table was recreated from a copy of the speech presented by Martin Ngoga (2004) obtained personally in Rwanda. In the original, the table was credited to Domitilla Mutanganzwa, Executive Secretary Gacaca Jurisdiction *Organization, Genesis, Functioning Achievements and Future Prospects* paper presented at Kivu sun workshop, October 2004.

6 Convention on the Prevention and Punishment of the Crime of Genocide: Approved and proposed for signature and ratification or accession by General Assembly resolution 260 A (III) of 9 December 1948, *entry into force* 12 January 1951, in accordance with article XIII: *Article 5*: The Contracting Parties undertake to enact, in accordance with their respective Constitutions, the necessary legislation to give effect to the provisions of the present Convention, and, in particular, to provide effective penalties for persons guilty of genocide or any of the other acts enumerated in Article III (United Nations 1948).

7 The 1948 Convention claimed that genocide had always been a crime in customary law (United Nations 1948).

8 According to Article 36 of the No 8 of 30 August 1996: Organic Law on the organization of prosecutions for offences constituting genocide and crimes against humanity committed since 1 October 1990, persons prosecuted under the provisions of this organic law enjoy the same rights of defence given to other persons subject to criminal prosecution, including the right to the defence counsel of their choice, but not at government expense (Government of Rwanda 1996).

9 Domitilla Mutanganzwa is the current Executive Secretary of the National Service of Gacaca Jurisdictions in Rwanda.

10 As a result of this issues concerning the collection and organization of the court data, there is a range of numbers that have been presented by various organization. Within the data that I was able to collect for the years 2000–3, there remains a large number of missing cases that affect the overall integrity of the reported findings.

11 It is interesting to note that the trial of multiple accused within one trial is reminiscent of the Nuremberg trials and is also the same prosecutorial strategy initially developed and incorporated at the ICTR.

12 This estimate based on statistics received from the Supreme Court may be a relatively low estimate. Another set of figures received from RCN Justice and Democratie

actually suggests that the number of accused per trial may actually be upwards of 19 accused (Government of Rwanda 2005).

13 Within the Organic Law the guilty plea procedure has additionally been argued to serve an additional purpose for the Government beyond speeding up the trial process. According to Vandeginste, 'this procedure was seen as an instrument to overcome the main obstacle for the prosecution of genocide suspects: the lack of evidence' (Vandeginste 1999: 9).

14 Members of the Legal and Constitutional Commission traversed the whole country from January up to June gathering ideas on the Constitution from Rwandans of all categories. This book follows the one the Commission published in January 2002, which contained fundamental ideas on the Constitution which were conducted countrywide.

15 Although officially adopted on 2 June 2003, the final steps in the process of arriving at the new Constitution was that is was publicly adopted first, through a referendum process on 26 May 2003.

16 The last Rwandan Census to collect data with regard to the ethnic origin of the citizenry was collected in 1991. In the process of obtaining a copy of this document, a discussion regarding the accuracy of the census figures regarding ethnicity revealed that in the past efforts to collect the census information there were different rules regarding the ability of the census-takers to check the identity cards of those they were interviewing to verify the data that they were being presented (Mugabo 2005). This may potentially call into question the veracity of the data as over the multi-year history of the census taking it was at different times reportedly more advantageous to report that one was either a Hutu or Tutsi. It was stated that a large number of individuals may have presented false information with regard to their ethnic origin based on the relevant time in history that they were asked for the information. The results of the 1991 Census, as reported and it must be noted that there is considerable possible error, calls into question the accuracy of the number of Tutsis who were killed in the 1994 genocide. The 1991 Census data does not report the presence of a high enough number of Tutsis living in Rwanda that would reflect the estimates of those killed. This observation does not in any way attempt to discredit the occurrence of the genocide but does possibly question the numbers of Tutsi killed and possibly, therefore, demonstrate that the numbers of Hutus killed in 1994 may have been much higher than reported.

17 In Chapter One: Article 1 of this law it states the definitions of the terms discrimination and sectarianism. According to this law:

> 1° Discrimination is any speech, writing, or actions based on ethnicity, region or country of origin, the colour of the skin, physical features, sex, language, religion or ideas aimed at depriving a person or group of persons of their rights as provided by Rwandan law and by International Conventions to which Rwanda is party;
> 2° Sectarianism means the use of speech, written statement or action that divides people, that is likely to spark conflicts among people, or that causes an uprising which might denigrate into strife among people based on discrimination mentioned earlier in article one 1°;
> 3° Deprivation of a person of his/her rights is the denial of rights provided by Rwanda Law and by International conventions to which Rwanda is party.
>
> (Government of Rwanda 2004d)

18 Chapter V: Section 2: Article 143 of the Constitution establishes the judicial structure in Rwanda: 'Ordinary Courts are the Supreme Court, the High Court of the Republic, the Provincial Courts and the court of the city of Kigali, the District

Courts, and the Municipality and town courts. Specialized courts are the Gacaca courts and Military courts' (Government of Rwanda 2003c).

19 In an interview with a member of the judiciary, it was expressed that this concern has come to the awareness and that it is something that will be dealt with in the near future.

20 It must be noted, however, that the cases that were personally observed, at the trial phase of the Gacaca courts that were part of the pilot-project, did involve individuals who had pled guilty through the plea bargaining process established by the Organic Law. Therefore, it is reasonable that there was in fact a presumption of guilt that followed from their confession and guilty plea. Nevertheless, in the process of the Inyangamugayo determining the veracity of the confession it was certainly evident that the accused was forced to *prove their innocence* with each attack made on their confession rather than the judges proving that their confession was not complete or true.

21 Additionally, the use of hearsay evidence was frequently not only used but encouraged. The judges would ask those in attendance if they had heard from others regarding the events in question and would also further question the defendant with regard to additional events that were not involved in the immediate case that was being heard.

22 Strauss questions the estimates of the number of perpetrators that have been produced by both the Rwandan Government, as well as other observers. The significance of attempting to find a reliable estimate lies in the implications that it has for the Rwandan people with regard to the idea of collective blame: 'The high-end estimate effectively criminalizes the entire adult Hutu population at the time of the genocide. The low-end estimate is equivalent to a small fraction of the adult male Hutu population' (Strauss 2004: 85). Strauss estimates that the number of perpetrators (using his own definition of "perpetrator" that does differ from that used by the Rwandan Government in the legislation) is approximately 200,000; a number significantly less than that of the Government. If his estimate is more empirically reliable then there will be significant consequences for the judicial processes that are occurring in Rwanda.

23 According to Samuel Rugege, the entire judicial budget for 2005 was approximately 2.5 billion Rwandan francs, or about US$5 million (Rugege 2005).

24 In the decision of this case the ICTR presents the level of responsibility of the accused as a relevant factor for considering transfer. The primacy of the ICTR over national jurisdictions is reflected in the cases for which it retains jurisdiction and those considered for transfer. According to this discussion surrounding this issue, in this particular case, the Chambers note, 'the Tribunal is mandated under Security Council Resolution 1503 and 1534 to transfer *intermediate* and *low-rank* accused to competent national jurisdictions' (*Prosecutor v Munyakazi* 2000: 4).

25 Rule 11*bis* (A) governing the transfer of cases states:

> If an indictment has been confirmed, whether or not an accused is in the custody of the Tribunal, the President may designate a Trial Chamber which shall determine whether the case should be referred to the authorities of a State:
> (i) in whose territory the crime was committed; or
> (ii) in which the accused was arrested; or
> (iii) having the jurisdiction and being willing and adequately prepared to accept such a case,

so that the authorities should forthwith refer the case to the appropriate court for trial within that State.

(*Prosecutor v Munyakazi* 2000)

5 The International Criminal Tribunal for Rwanda

> One of the reasons that people swear a blood oath to stand by their colleagues is not just because they respect them professionally, but there's a belief that the overall process has some real value to it. ... For me, in the larger picture, what I see this process here as doing is taking some baby steps that I'm hoping the ICC will eventually turn into some toddler steps and be able to start moving more quickly.
>
> (White 2005)

With the adoption of UN Resolution 955 on 8 November, 1994 by the UN Security Council, the 'International Criminal Tribunal for the Prosecution of Persons Responsible for the Genocide and Other Serious Violations of International Humanitarian Law Committed in the Territory of Rwanda and Rwandan Citizens Responsible for Genocide and Other Such Violations Committed in the Territory of Neighbouring States between 1 January and 31 December 1994' (ICTR) was created under Chapter VII of the United Nations Charter. The creation of an *ad hoc* tribunal as a response to violations of international humanitarian law is but one response among the many available to the United Nations. According to Yacoubian, the international community has historically responded to the various instances that have encompassed a number of violations of international humanitarian law (Yacoubian 2003). Included in the list of methods for dealing with such violations are '1) doing nothing; 2) granting amnesty; 3) creating a truth and reconciliation commission; 4) domestic prosecutions; and 5) creating ad hoc international criminal tribunals' (Yacoubian 2003: 135). Indirectly, the ICTR seeks to provide response mechanisms, on the part of the international community, that include both the creation of the *ad hoc* tribunal as well as support for domestic prosecutions. According to the ICTR Statute, the stated purpose and mandate of the tribunal are:

> To contribute to the process of national reconciliation and to the restoration and maintenance of peace ... contribute to ensuring that such violations are halted and effectively redressed ... strengthen the courts

and judicial system of Rwanda, having regard in particular to the necessity for those courts to deal with large numbers of suspects.

(ICTR 2007: 6)

Factors contributing to the creation of the ICTR

Discussions among United Nations officials and other international participants regarding the creation of an international criminal tribunal in the aftermath of the events that transpired in Rwanda had their beginnings shortly after the massacres had begun. According to Des Forges and Longman, those persons engaged in these discussions, were 'fed by their sense of guilt; the fact that the International Criminal Tribunal for the former Yugoslavia (ICTY) was already in existence made the creation of a tribunal an obvious route to administer justice for the Rwandan genocide' (Des Forges and Longman 2004: 51). Des Forges and Longman also made reference to an additional aspect that the UN wished to avoid, allegations of racism: 'Further, since the crimes in Rwanda were so much more blatant and grievous and large[r] in scale than those committed in the former Yugoslavia, failure to create a mechanism comparable to the ICTY would almost certainly have led to accusations of racism' (Des Forges and Longman 2004: 52). Regardless of the veracity of the notions of guilt and the avoidance of racist allegations,[1] such discussions, and the UN Security Council resolution that eventually created the tribunal, were based on a number of different factors of which the existence of the ICTY was most certainly one. Two other factors within the ICTR Statute were given great consideration in the decision to create the tribunal: the findings of the special rapporteur for the United Nations and the request by the Rwandan government for an international tribunal.

Prior to the creation of the ICTR, and long before the end of the hostilities in Rwanda, the first group of investigators of the Rwandan genocide included a number of human rights organizations including Human Rights Watch, Amnesty International, African Rights, and the soldiers of the UN peacekeeping force UNAMIR, including Major General Romeo Dallaire (Obote-Odora 2005). These sources brought into the public realm a great deal of evidence of the mass slaughters of innocent people that occurred during the fighting of the civil war. Based on these initial and incredibly disturbing reports, the United Nations engaged in a special mission to Rwanda to assess the situation first-hand. The results of this mission presented the United Nations with undeniable evidence of mass slaughter. A UN report discovered that:

> [t]he number of Rwandan children, women, and men who were murdered in the frenzy of the massacres over the past seven weeks will likely never be determined accurately. As time passes evidence erodes and witnesses vanish. The estimate is that between 250,000 and 500,000 were killed – a substantial portion of Rwanda's population of 7 million.
>
> (United Nations 1994g: 2)

This report laid the foundation for Security Council Resolution 935 that:

> [r]equests the Secretary-General to establish, as a matter of urgency, an impartial Commission of Experts to examine and analyze information submitted pursuant to the present resolution, together with such further information as the Commission of Experts may obtain through its own investigations or the efforts of other persons or bodies, including the information made available by the Special Rapporteur for Rwanda, with a view to providing the Secretary-General with its conclusions on the evidence of grave violations of international humanitarian law committed in the territory of Rwanda, including possible acts of genocide.
>
> (United Nations 1994e: 2)

The conceptualization of possible acts of genocide was substantiated on the basis of the reports filed by the Special Rapporteur, Rene Degni-Ségui. He states in one report, dated 25 May 1994, 'The massacres do seem to have been planned. There are various pieces of evidence pointing to this conclusion' (Degni-Ségui 1994: np) Furthermore, in a summation of these reports to the UN General Assembly on 14 November 1994, just 6 days following the creation of the tribunal, the alleged acts of genocide were presented as confirmed.[2] The investigation and subsequent reports, which include information presented to the special rapporteur by the other sources mentioned by Obote-Odora, laid the foundational basis for the investigations that were to proceed at the ICTR.

The final significant consideration in the creation of the tribunal, one that has since been a matter of much discussion, differs greatly from that of the ICTY. As stated in UN Resolution 955, the UN '*[d]ecides* hereby, having received the request of the Government of Rwanda (S/1994/1115), to establish an international tribunal ... and to this end to adopt the Statue of the International Criminal tribunal for Rwanda' (United Nations 1994f). Akhavan states that '[i]n contrast to the origin of the ICTY, the initial proposal for the establishment of the ICTR came from the Rwandese Government and not the international community' (Akhavan 2001: 23). However, as noted by Uvin and Mironko, the situation had changed in the meantime: the ICTR 'is the product of the international community; it is fully managed and funded by it and exists to no small extent over the objections of the government of Rwanda' (Uvin and Mironko 2003: 219). Despite the eventuality whereby Rwanda voted against the creation of the ICTR after the discovery of a number of concerns with regard to the organization and the operation of the ICTR,[3] Akhavan additionally discusses the primary reasons behind their initial request and support for the tribunal: 'The government supported such an institution, inter alia, because of its desire to avoid "any suspicion of its wanting to organize speedy, vengeful justice"' (Akhavan 2001: 23).

There is a strong connection between the ICTR and the ICTY. According to Chief Prosecutor of the ICTR Hassan Bubacar Jallow, in a speech made at the Prosecutor's Colloquium in Arusha in 2004, '[B]oth the ICTR and ICTY were created as organs of the United Nations, which had hitherto not undertaken administration of international criminal justice' (Jallow 2004). With the exception of the Nuremburg and Tokyo trials, no modern-day model was present for consideration in the creation of the tribunals, and the circumstances surrounding each of them were significantly different from those observed at the conclusion of the Second World War. As discussed by Dicker and Keppler, some of the differences are such that the Nuremburg and Tokyo courts did not provide an adequate model for the current tribunals (Dicker and Keppler 2004). For example, they state that as a result of those trials being completely operated by the victorious countries of the Second World War, 'while not absent, fair trials safeguards in these prosecutions would probably not pass muster under today's standards. Most strikingly, there was no right to appeal' (Dicker and Keppler 2004).

Despite the technicality that the two tribunals were created under their own individual security council resolutions and are specifically responsible for responding to very different conflicts both in terms of geography and circumstance, the two have commonalities. The ICTY and the ICTR are often referred to as 'sister tribunals.' However, it might be fairly argued that the ICTY represents the 'big' sister in that it was created and began its operations at an earlier time, and, therefore, potentially provided the ICTR with some framework upon which it could be constructed.[4] The intertwined nature of the two tribunals is evident in a number of ways. Dieng, Registrar of the ICTR states that 'it is also important to keep in mind that the structure of the Registry of Special Court Sierra Leone (SCSL)[5] was largely designed according to the ICTR model while the latter was simply copied from the ICTY Statute and Rules' (Dieng 2004).[6]

In the initial conceptualization of the ICTR, the chief of prosecution was the same for both tribunals. With regard to this initial situation, Obote-Odora states that 'in the minds of many of these individuals the answer would seem more as subsidiary ... they don't actually see them as completely separate' (Obote-Odora 2005).[7] The ICTR, from its inception in 1994, had three chief prosecutors, Richard Goldstone, Louise Arbour, and Carla Del Ponte, in common with the ICTY. It was not until the passing of Security Council Resolution 1503 (United Nations 2003c: 3) and the assigning Hassan Bubacar Jallow as prosecutor for the ICTR, that there was an independent prosecutor for each of the tribunals.[8]

A final aspect of the relationship between the ICTY and the ICTR is the continued sharing of the appeal chamber of the courts. According to Stewart, the ICTR Appeal Council, the appeal chamber for both the ICTR and the ICTY is composed of a rotating panel of five judges who will hear appeals for both courts (Stewart 2005). The judges travel between the courts, often in conjunction with various plenary sessions, and hear the appeals in the location of the original trial. Despite the observed separation of the prosecutor's office between the two tribunals, Stewart additionally stated that he does not anticipate this occurring with the appeal chamber: 'I think it would be very difficult at this stage to constitute a new appeals court, or appeals chamber, additionally, I think there would be a disadvantage, well a potential disadvantage, and that is a potential divergence in jurisprudence' (Stewart 2005).[9] In order to maintain consistency of jurisprudence and in an attempt to formulate concrete international case law for these crimes, Boed observes that 'the ICTR Appeals Chamber's approach in *Musema* mirrors the approach now entrenched in the ICTY Appeals Chamber jurisprudence' (Boed 2003: 174).

Despite the observation of a familial relationship between the ICTY and the ICTR, the circumstances surrounding the different conflicts have resulted in a significant difference in the cases being presented in each jurisdiction:

> You are dealing with very different conflicts, although the bottom line, I suppose is human cruelty, and there is a certain universality there. I think the scale of what happened in Rwanda is enormous, it far surpasses what the ICTY is dealing with, but the ICTY has a very complex conflict to deal with because it is not a single conflict it is a number of conflicts that sort of came up and down over the years and that creates a great deal of complexity.
>
> (Stewart 2005)

As a result of the nature of the different conflicts, the prosecution's focus at the two tribunals can be observed to lean more heavily in one of two legal directions, and the international statutes that specifically refer to those conflicts: the ICTY on war crimes, and the ICTR on genocide. According to Stewart:

> The law of armed conflict and the violations of armed conflict figure very largely in the ICTY cases in some ways they kind of have a military side to them that may be not as obvious here in the Rwanda conflict. ... Also a strong emphasis on crimes against humanity in the context of the former Yugoslavia but genocide is much rarer, now it has been proven. ... Here, at the ICTR the 'big' crime is genocide, but there are crimes against humanity and war crimes.
>
> (Stewart 2005)

These observed differences had an effect on the entire process of managing the cases from the investigation through to the prosecution. For example, there is a difference in the definition and determination of responsibility. According to Obote-Odora, there will be a differential examination of the concept of 'superior responsibility' as opposed to 'command responsibility' as outlined in the various conventions, depending on the context of the case (Obote-Odora 2005). He further noted, 'When you are investigating war crimes you focus more on command responsibility and yet for genocide talk about mass participation and superior responsibility' (Obote-Odora 2005).[10]

One final difference, arising from each tribunal having its own chief prose-cutor, is a difference in trial strategy that is forming one aspect of the com-pletion strategies for each tribunal. At the ICTY, there has been a move toward group trials of many accused at once, while at the ICTR, the opposite has occurred. Based on some of the struggles that the ICTR has noted with regard to the management and progress of group trials, they are now moving to a completion strategy that will focus on single-accused trials as opposed to the previous method of group trials (Obote-Odora 2005). In the overall scheme of the ICTY and the ICTR, despite the variances noted above, they do continue to work towards a common goal: 'Although each of these insti-tutions formally independent from the others, James Crawford ... demon-strates how they draw strength from each other and weave together to form the tapestry of international criminal law' (Drumbl 2005: 1302).

The ICTR: organizational structure

Article 10 of the Statute of the ICTR provides the framework for the orga-nizational structure of the tribunal:

The International tribunal for Rwanda shall consist of the following organs:
(a) The Chambers, comprising three Trial Chambers and an Appeal Chamber
(b) The Prosecutor
(c) A Registry.

(ICTR 2007)

Although working under the same statute and towards the successful com-pletion of the ICTR mandate, each organ of the tribunal is granted some degree of autonomy. The structure is organized along these lines of indepen-dence in order to avoid any perception of impropriety among the various branches of the tribunal when a case appears before the court.

The chambers

Employing a civil law judicial structure rather than the structure familiar in common law countries, the ICTR chambers consist of two branches: the three trial chambers and the appeals chamber. Within the ICTR Statute, Articles 11–14 outline the composition, qualifications, and election of officers of the chambers, as well as the determination of and the status of *ad litem* judges (ICTR 2007). Note that the judges were the first individuals hired at the ICTR.[11] The statute specifically states that '[t]he Chambers shall be composed of sixteen permanent independent judges, no two of whom may be nationals of the same State' (ICTR 2007: 50). Although this criterion of not having two individuals from the same nation-state is stated specifically with regard to the appointment of judges, there is an apparent desire, throughout the ICTR, to represent as many UN member-states as possible across the various posts that need to be filled. In the chambers specifically, this broad approach to hiring has yielded a grouping of people with an incredibly diverse range of legal traditions and backgrounds that have to be continually reconciled during the process of operating a trial. According to Des Forges and Longman, '[I]n the course of trials, judges often interpret the Rules of Evidence and Procedure in different ways according to their background, resulting in debates that consume a great deal of time and slow proceedings' (Des Forges and Longman 2004: 52). Former Prosecutor Drew White stated that:

> ... some of the major reasons behind the slowness of the daily proceedings relates to the procedural tension between the civil and common law backgrounds of the judges, and that while there are standard Rules of procedure, the Rules do not have the benefit of having been litigated and settled in their practical usage, with the result that the daily application of even simple Rules is frequently in dispute and unevenly administered. Those challenges are magnified by the high degree of variability in courtroom experience amongst the judges, some of whom have never been judges before, or have never controlled their own courtrooms or have no criminal trial experience as judges.
>
> (White 2005)

Concerns have also been raised about the quality of the judges resulting from their appointment to the bench. 'The quality of the judges has also created problems. ... Elected by the UN General Assembly, the judges appear to often pay more attention to political concerns than to experience or competence in judicial matters' (Des Forges and Longman 2004: 53). The possible politicization of the trials within the chambers may also have a detrimental impact on the pace of the trials as well as on the perception of the overall quality of the justice dispensed by the tribunal.

The slow pace of the trial proceedings has an effect on the overall length of the trials themselves, which, within the forum of an international court, has additional effects regarding a potential for changes in the personnel involved in the various trials. The chamber has not been immune to this systemic concern. At the outset of the trials, according to one prosecutor, the judges in his specific case:

> took a very low-key approach to controlling the courtroom. They wanted to let things work their way out, sort of an academic sit-back. It was not what you would normally see in a Canadian courtroom where a judge takes control and says 'you'll do this and this and this.' A submission by the defence would go on and on and on with no testimony from the witness for hours and hours. ... And one of the things that happened is, I think, that the defence strategy to operate at that pace took a toll on at least one of the judges. One of the things that happened was that by the

next year, one of the judges wasn't re-elected, one of the judges had to retire, and one of the judges just got worn down. ... By the spring of 2003, we had lost all three judges.

(AA 2005)

Personnel turnover amongst those directly involved in the actual court proceedings has a serious effect not only on the pace of the trials, but also on the whole continuity of the case.

Over the course of time, the chambers have significantly expanded their operational capacity. When the trials first began, there was only a single courtroom from which they were to operate. This was due to the incredible expense associated with the construction of the courts associated with the unique requirements including: (1) the various security measures that had to be taken in light of the gravity of the offences for which the defendants were accused, and the protection of witness anonymity when on the stand; (2) the simultaneous translation of the three official languages of the tribunal (Kinyarwanda, English, and French); (3) the audio and video requirements; and (4) the need to accommodate upwards of 50 individuals in the courtroom at any given time given the nature of the multi-accused trials. 'It's a very expensive courtroom; I've been told that on average they cost about a million dollars to create these courtrooms' (White 2005). Since then, there have been three additional courtrooms added in 1998/1999, 2001, and 2005, respectively. This has, and will continue to, expand the amount of time and the number of cases that the chambers can simultaneously address. In addition, at least one chamber hears two cases each day, one scheduled for the morning session and a different one for the afternoon session. There is an attempt to make sure that the courtroom space is maximally utilized.

An additional observation made by a number of individuals who were interviewed at the ICTR was that, when compared to trials operating in national jurisdictions and what has transpired at the ICTY, there was a noticeable lack of plea discussions and informal case resolutions at the ICTR.[12] The use of plea bargaining is a method often utilized in order to increase the efficiency of the courts by expediting trial processes (Brannigan 1984: 136). It further may allow for the potential to develop insider witnesses or informants whose testimony facilitates prosecutions against other defendants (Fyfe and Sheptycki 2006: 320). This strategy has not appeared to find favour amongst the members of the bench in the Trial Chamber at the ICTR. Even more significantly, as a direct result of the events that transpired in the *Kambanda* case, it has not been utilized in many cases since. Judge Erik Møse, President of the ICTR, stated in an address to the UN Security Council that, 'as you know, the number of guilty pleas at the ICTR is low compared to the ICTY; It will be interesting to see whether the number will increase further' (Møse 2005).

Furthermore, despite the early precedent set in the Kambanda trial, there has been a recent development in the use of a guilty plea:

Francois Roux, a French lawyer who achieved the first acquittal here of bourgmestre Bagilishema, managed to persuade his client that he believed the lessons had been learnt by the judges and the [Office of the Prosecutor] O.T.P., the prosecutor, and negotiated a plea bargain by which his client ended up getting, I think, six years.

(BB 2005)

These may be signs that there is a re-evaluation being undertaken of the plea bargaining issue at the ICTR and, if so, it may significantly impact the expediency with which the ICTR can address the caseload that they are facing. This is especially significant in light of the completion strategy outlined by the Security Council. As well, there may further be an increase in the potential for convictions of some of the key accused at the tribunal for which the use of an insider witness may be a key aspect of the prosecution.[13]

The Office of the Prosecutor (OTP)

In accordance with Article 15 of the ICTR Statute:

The Prosecutor shall be responsible for the investigation and prosecution ... The Prosecutor shall act independently as a separate organ of the International Tribunal for Rwanda. He or she shall not seek or receive instructions from any government or from any other source.

(ICTR 2007: 27)

The original formulation of the OTP, as stated above, involved a sharing of the chief of prosecutions between the ICTR and the ICTY. In addition to the concerns raised previously, the major concerns with regard to the sharing of the chief prosecutor centre on the logistical and operational shortcomings that result from the challenges of running essentially two offices simultaneously. One significant challenge that has impacted the work of the OTP throughout the operation of the tribunal is the initial lack of a definitive prosecution strategy from the outset. The first chief of prosecution for the ICTR was Richard Goldstone who used, according to Obote-Odora, what 'was referred to as the *global approach*' (Obote-Odora 2005), which essentially attempted to look at the entirety of the genocide and look at all of those thought to be guilty in the commission of the crimes within the government and the military.[14] Following Goldstone was Louise Arbour, 'who was greatly influenced by the Nuremburg Trial. ... The first indictment, the *Bagasora* indictment, was comprised of twenty-nine accused persons. But the logistics, they could not even fit into one courtroom physically, not based on the legal part of it. Logistically, it was not even possible' (Obote-Odora 2005).

The initial indictment of 29 people went through a process involving a series of severances into some of the key cases operating today referred to, for example, as 'Government I' and 'Government II', 'Military I' and 'Military

II', and the 'Butare Case'. The process of severance was not fully systematic because of the considerations involved in the process included the state of the evidence against each accused at the time of the decision to sever the indictment (Obote-Odora 2005). The final result was the operation of multi-accused trials which, it has been argued have had a significant negative impact on the progress of the trials.[15] This contrasts with the previously noted move at the ICTR towards single-accused trials. Many advantages of the single-accused trials were espoused during the interviews conducted with one recurring theme being the avoidance of delays on the part of any attorney for a defendant in a multi-accused trial. If one attorney became ill, and there was not a second trial attorney on that defence team, the entire trial would be delayed until that attorney was well enough to attend court.

The geographical arrangement of the ICTR, with its investigations based in Kigali, Rwanda and the prosecutors in Arusha, Tanzania has presented the OTP with a wide variety of challenges. In the early days of the tribunal, the lack of contact with the prosecutors in Arusha, the investigators were often left to create their own strategies for gathering relevant information. According to one investigator, 'Before 2004, all our missions were convicted on the initiative of us. I will read the file, read the indictment and see where the gaps are to be filled in the file' (CC 2005). Since the OTP has moved into the trial support stage of the case, the situation has changed and they are given more direction by the senior trial attorney as to what evidence each case will require.

The process of investigation in the early days of the tribunal was also severely hampered by the prosecution beginning the thrust of their investigations on the basis of a list of accused and, then, seeking the evidence to convict them.[16] According to one senior investigator, this was a procedural error (LL 2005). In performing an investigation, 'you start with the witnesses, not with the suspects, it's the witnesses that bring you the suspects and bring to you the evidence against the [suspects]. You know, we never start [from] the top to the bottom, we start [from] the bottom to the top' (LL 2005). In addition to the procedural issue regarding the investigations, other concerns that had a negative impact on the progress and quality of the investigations manifested themselves during the course of the investigations.

The hiring of qualified staff by the registry to outfit the investigation teams affected the work of the ICTR. So, too, did the ICTR methods for the evaluation and possible advancement of staff also affect the work of the OTP:

> They don't hire on the system of merit; theoretically, you know there are too many other criteria, one of which is the idea that you have to have certain percentages of representation from as many nations as possible. I can understand this kind of 'affirmative action' on a philosophical level, ... but what you need in a system of justice is people who know what that is, know how it works, and can get in and produce the end result. The end result here, of course, is the courtroom.
>
> (AA 2005)

When asked about his background qualifications, and how he came to work for the ICTR, one of the investigators was quite taken aback. He stated that he had been there almost 5 years and that, until that moment, no one had ever asked that of him, including the people who hired him (CC 2005). In another interview, examples of suspected patronage appointments were made for which the individual did not have the requisite qualifications as an investigator:

> That's the problem they have here. They have a friend of a friend. Then they have somebody come here. We had a girl we thought was a lawyer and it took almost a year and a half and we find out she was not a lawyer at all and she stayed here about another two years.
>
> (DD 2005)

Another senior investigator claimed that fully one-half of those hired to work as investigators lacked the requisite qualifications (LL 2005).

Within discussions of recruitment and personnel, other issues, such as salaries and the annual evaluations of ICTR employees, arose that have deeply impacted the work of the OTP. From a western viewpoint, the salaries for those working in the ICTR are comparable with those found in North America for similar positions. However, when one gives consideration to what a western salary would mean to an individual from a developing nation the impact of salary becomes an issue. 'If you [were to do] a survey you will realize that some people here are [earning] between 30 to 68 times their [normal annual] salary' (DD 2005). Additionally, other factors, such as free or greatly subsidized education of the children of UN employees, the provision of a pension after 5 years of continuous service with the United Nations and so forth, create an environment that may in fact reduce efficiency as individuals are more prone to maximize their benefits without achieving their professional objectives.[17]

The process of annual evaluations is the final aspect with regard to personnel issues that will be addressed here. The 'ePAS',[18] as it is called, is an annual evaluation process for employees of the ICTR. It is the measure of their production within their given position over the previous year. At issue with this procedure are the measures used to make the assessment. It has been observed that the measurement tool is inherently quantitative in nature, which has impacted the quality of the work that has been accomplished (AA 2005). This has had a very real impact on the evidence that has been produced on the part of the OTP. Since the measure for evaluating an investigator was based primarily in quantitative terms, quantity was what they strove to achieve in a number of instances: 'I will bet you $100 that of all the statements taken before 1999, that 80% of those statements have no value. At that time it was quantity, not quality. The criteria for promotion were based on the number of statements you did not the quality of the statements produced' (DD 2005). This process of evaluating the investigators, coupled with the lack of an overall investigative framework, had an impact of the direction that the investigations took:

> Many of these witnesses are witnesses who are relevant for many trials so they get contacted by a collection of different teams; and very often those teams do not review what else the witness has said. There is one famous witness who has produced over thirty statements. Now, when you take that witness into court, you have to do a disclosure, and you are facing potential cross-examination on prior inconsistent statements, you know what that's going to mean.
>
> (AA 2005)

The last challenge presented within the context of the OTP, and which very likely impacts every part of the ICTR and its ability to efficiently operate, is the issue of language and culture. Jallow asserts, 'Most witnesses speak only Kinyarwanda, as are most of the documentary exhibits retrieved from Rwanda. This slows down the investigation process as interpreters are used during the interviews so that statements can be recorded in either French or English' (Jallow 2004: 3). The concern for the accuracy of the translations is a point that was also raised by a number of the defence attorneys who were interviewed in Arusha: 'Astonishingly, in my view, it is still the case now, after 13 years of investigations, that when a statement is taken from a witness who speaks only Kinyarwanda there is no record made of what the witness actually says in that language' (BB 2005).

In addition to this added chore of translation is the influence of cultural effects during the process. One noted example of a cultural effect in the process involved witnesses responding to investigator's queries about 'colours and distances' in a way that was not comprehensible to the investigators requiring significant work to gain an understanding (EE 2005). This recognition of cultural factors having an impact is additionally noted in the *Akayesu* trial by Ruzindana. Among the cultural effects, based on the Rwandan oral tradition and the indirect method of questioning, is the tendency to share second-hand information as if it is first-hand (*Prosecutor v Akayesu* 1998). 'They say word for word, tell you, and then you take it down. But that's not always the case, and some of these translators have been doing it for so long, they know what to ask' (EE 2005).

The Registry

Article 16 of the ICTR Statute outlines the responsibilities of the registrar: 'The Registry shall be responsible for the administration and servicing of the International Criminal Tribunal for Rwanda' (ICTR 2007). According to Dieng, 'It is widely accepted that the Registry, as an organ of a court, is in all latitudes vested with the mission to provide the court and litigants with the administrative services necessary for fair and prompt resolution of cases'

(Dieng 2004: 1). The registry is designed to provide all of the logistical support for the ICTR that would normally be achieved by the administration of the State within national jurisdictions. These include such matters as hiring personnel, providing all necessary office space and equipment, managing the finances of the tribunal, making travel arrangements, managing the victims and witnesses, and managing both internal and external communications, including security.[19]

Over the course of the ICTR's history, especially in its early years, the registry has come under much criticism, from the other organs of the tribunal, the defence teams, and also from the UN Security Council. In fact, in 1996, as a result of the accumulation of concerns about the entire tribunal addressed to the Secretary-General of the United Nations, an audit was ordered on the overall functioning of the ICTR (United Nations 1996a). This report, later referred to as the Paschke Report, highlighted some of the major concerns with regard to the tribunal in general.[20] In the overall findings of the report, 'the evidence did not confirm allegations of corrupt practice or misuse of funds. The review however, has disclosed mismanagement in almost all areas of the Tribunal and frequent violations of United Nations rules and regulations' (United Nations 1996a).

With specific reference to the issues surrounding the registry, the report states:

> In the Tribunal's Registry not a single administrative area functioned effectively: Finance had no accounting system and could not produce allotment reports, so that neither the Registry nor the United Nations Headquarters had budget expenditure information; lines of authority were not clearly defined; internal controls were weak in all sections; personnel in key positions did not have the required qualifications; there were no property management systems; procurement actions largely deviated from United Nations procedures; United Nations rules and regulations were widely disregarded; the Kigali office did not get the administrative support they needed, and construction work for the second courtroom had not even started.
>
> (United Nations 1996a)

The findings of this report, although specifically related to the situation in 1996, appear to, still exist, albeit to a slightly lesser degree, despite the provisions taken to correct the noted concerns. One of the concerns that relates to the overall functioning of the registry as a support organ of the ICTR is that a tremendous portion of the ICTR's operating budget is focused on the work performed by the registry itself rather than the trials and trial support. Des Forges reports:

> By 1998, the tribunal was receiving regular funding on a yearly budget, which facilitated its operation. Although the sum available for 1998 was

substantial, some U.S. $50 million, considerable more than half of this amount was allocated to the registrar's office, about U.S. $34 million, while the office of the prosecutor, responsible for investigating and preparing the cases, was allocated only U.S. $14 million.

(Des Forges 1999: np)

Speaking with regard to the work that the ICTR has done and can possibly do, one defence counsel stated that when describing the functioning of the registry:

It is hampered by inefficiency, incompetence, a certain amount of corruption, and that it is perceived by most of its employees as a milk cow. ... It seems to me to be an enormous administrative tail wagging a tiny little dog.

(BB 2005)

Others interviewed stated that the ICTR represented an extension of the United Nations's typical paramilitary structure that is applied seemingly to all configurations of UN missions, and to a very specific circumstance for which it is not adequately suited.

When concerns with respect to the functioning of the registry are discussed, the somewhat harsh and frank criticisms relating to issues of trial support tend to take centre stage. However, there are many additional activities in which the registry is involved that are not linked directly to the overall judicial functioning of the ICTR. According to Moghalu, the first priority of the newly appointed registrar, Agwu Ukiwe Okali in 1997, resulted in the ICTR 'embark[ing] on institutional administrative and quasi-judicial reforms, which combined with the parallel reforms by the judges in the tribunal's judicial rules, put the institution on a much firmer and more effective footing to render justice for Rwanda' (Moghalu 2005: 65). The registry engaged in extra-legal programmes in addition to their administrative and trial support functions. According to Moghalu, Okali was responding to pleas for assistance, a stated perception of discrepancy in the treatment of the witnesses compared to the accused, the feelings of witnesses being *used* by the tribunal for its purposes and possible backlash from the witnesses (Moghalu 2005: 69). Mandiaye Niang, Special Assistant to the Registrar, outlined a number of these programmes: (1) involvement in teaching at the National University in Butare; (2) training members of the Parquet General in Rwanda; (3) providing internships for the training of individuals interested in furthering their understanding of international law; and (4) setting up an information centre in Kigali designed to provide information to the citizens of Rwanda of the activities of the ICTR (Niang 2005). Given the sensitive political nature of the programmes 'Okali was careful to stress that the tribunal's restitutive justice program was neither a generalized economic and social assistance for the people of Rwanda nor a compensation programme for the genocide (Moghalu 2005: 69).

Elsie Effange-Mbella, the gender advisor to the ICTR in 2005, provided information with regard to the services provided to the confirmed witnesses that testify at the ICTR. These included everything from medical support – especially given the high rate of AIDS transmission that took place as a result of the massive number of rapes that occurred during the genocide – to psychological counselling, and the protection and security of witnesses. In accordance with the programme mandate, many of these programmes, although funded by the ICTR would be operated by NGOs already providing many of these services in Rwanda. Another role that they perform is the support for victims and witnesses while transporting them from Rwanda to Arusha as well as with the navigating trial procedures themselves:

> They are well briefed before they come about what to expect, but even when they are, they are accompanied by witness support assistance in their travels and when they get here … they are accompanied everywhere … and in some really traumatic cases, the psychologist comes with them as well and even may be allowed to be in the witness box.
>
> (Effange-Mbella 2005)

As a neutral branch of the ICTR, the registry provides these services to all confirmed witnesses brought to the tribunal regardless of whether they are called by the prosecutor or the defence. For those called as defence witnesses the major concern, according to Effange-Mbella, is their safety and fear of reprisals as they may be denounced upon their return to Rwanda as genocide deniers or conspirators (Effange-Mbella 2005). The imminent closure of the tribunal raises concerns with respect to these individual's anonymity/confidentiality. Although the United Nations continues to bear the cost of the various programmes after the close of the tribunal, all logistics and operations will be transferred to the Rwandan government and this process remains to be addressed (Effange-Mbella 2005).

It is often noted that for justice to be done, it must be *seen* to be done. 'Without the benefit of a significant number of Rwandans to attend and witness the trials, a sense of the court's presence in the lives of the average Rwandan citizen was doubtless impaired' (Peskin 2005: 951). This was certainly a stumbling block for the ICTR in its rendering of justice for the people of Rwanda. According to Moghalu, Okali's 'second priority was to correct the obvious disconnect between the tribunal and Rwandan society, with its judicial procedures distant and seemingly irrelevant to ordinary Rwandans' (Moghalu 2005: 65). One measure taken to address this concern was the ICTR's outreach programme designed, in essence, to take the tribunal to Rwanda by attempting to overcome the geographical barrier created by its location. In addition to the geographic barrier faced by the ICTR, Peskin also recognizes the political context of the relations between the Rwandan government and the ICTR as an additional roadblock:

> From the start, some officials at the Tribunal envisioned an outreach programme not only to keep Rwandan citizens abreast of the court's

goals and accomplishments, but as a strategy to repair the institution's deteriorating image. An effective outreach programme might also mitigate the government's distrust.

(Peskin 2005: 961).

The time and effort put into the outreach programme by the ICTR appears to have achieved limited success. 'A 2002 survey of 2,091 Rwandans found that 87 per cent either were "not well informed" or "not informed at all" about the Tribunal' (Stover and Weinstein 2004: 334 as cited in Peskin 2005: 955). That some Rwandans have been able to familiarize themselves with the events transpiring at the ICTR suggests that some progress has been made. There appears much work to be done, however, if the ICTR is to achieve its stated goals.

The ICTR Statute and the concept of jurisdiction

The initial concept of universality of jurisdiction over the crimes being explored in the Rwandan context is historically located in the Nuremburg trials and the paradigm that it created for the future of international criminal law. Drumbl claims, 'This paradigm, which has gained currency since the Nuremburg trials, casts mass violence as something blatantly transgressive of universal norms' (Drumbl 2005: 1297). In accordance with this paradigm, extreme violations of these universal norms 'necessitates thorough investigation, effective prosecution, and retributive punishment' (Drumbl 2005: 1297). Article 1 of the ICTR Statute states:

> The International Criminal Tribunal for Rwanda shall have the power to prosecute persons responsible for serious violations of international humanitarian law committed in the territory of Rwanda and Rwandan citizens responsible for such violations committed in the territory of neighbouring States between 1 January 1994 and 31 December 1994, in accordance with the provisions of the present Statute.

(ICTR 2007)

According to Sriram, '[W]hile the principle of universal jurisdiction is well established in customary internal law, its application is developing in a piecemeal fashion, with many judges unsure of the scope and power of the principle' (Sriram 2002: 49). The means by which the ICTR appears to claim jurisdiction over these crimes was originally established in the UN Security Council Resolution 955, which states:

> *Determining* that this situation continues to constitute a threat to international peace and security ... *Believing* that the establishment of an international criminal tribunal for the prosecution of persons responsible for genocide and the other above-mentioned violations of international

humanitarian law will contribute to ensuring that such violations are halted and effectively redressed ... [the U.N, enacts this resolution].

(United Nations 1994f: 1)

The notion of violation of international humanitarian law and the effects that these violations may have on the international community – both in terms of continued violations that result in the further undermining of such laws as well as the more immediate aspect of concerns relating to international stability and peace – are reflected in this concept of universal jurisdiction. According to Sriram, '[I]t is claimed that such jurisdiction signals that certain crimes are so heinous that that they both threaten the international community and are forcefully condemned by it; it is in the interest of justice everywhere that the perpetrators are brought to justice' (Sriram 2002: 50).

Within the specific context of Rwanda, the concept of jurisdiction requires further delineation with regard to balancing the efforts of the Rwandan national judicial system operating at the same time as the ICTR. The use of both domestic and international courts remains an option for the international community as measures through which these crimes can be redressed. As evident in this situation, both methods are being incorporated into an overall strategy to redress the crimes committed in Rwanda. The Statute of the ICTR clearly identifies the concept of jurisdiction as it relates to the 'dual' approach observed in Rwanda. Article 8 of the ICTR Statute states:

1. The International Tribunal for Rwanda and national courts shall have concurrent jurisdiction to prosecute persons for serious violations of international humanitarian law committed in the territory of Rwanda ...
2. The International Tribunal for Rwanda shall have primacy over the national courts of all States. At any stage of the procedure, the International Tribunal for Rwanda may formally request national courts to defer to its competence in accordance with the present Statute and the Rules of Procedure and Evidence of the International Tribunal for Rwanda.

(ICTR 2007: 47)

The issue of jurisdiction has, at times, been a source of conflict between the ICTR and Rwanda as the two partners in this endeavour have argued about jurisdictional primacy in specific cases (Renaud 2005). Given the statements made in Article 8, there appears to be a discrepancy between concurrent jurisdiction and the idea of primary jurisdiction that is at the root of the issue. When asked who may have the ultimate jurisdiction, Renaud responded, 'It's really easy. The ICTR has the [ultimate] jurisdiction on any targets involved in the genocide' (Renaud 2005).

A mediating factor in the overall question of jurisdiction is related to the concept of targets put forth by Renaud. The targets of the ICTR represent a model of 'selective prosecution'. The influence of the Nuremburg trials is readily apparent in the adoption of this model of prosecution in those trials. According to Akhavan, '[T]he ICTR is not intended to substitute for the Rwandese judicial system, but to serve as a jurisdiction with limited resources focusing on the arrest and prosecution of the most senior accused' (Akhavan 2001: 26). The selective nature of the prosecutions occurring at the ICTR is certainly evident when one looks at the list of those whom the ICTR has placed within its list of targets. The senior members of the former political and military regime are prominent figures in the ICTR's attempt at what Akhavan notes above as the ICTR's role in the overall judicial process.

Jurisdictional mandate of the ICTR and the suspected crimes of the RPF

Within the scope of the jurisdictional disagreements between the ICTR and the Government of Rwanda, the most controversial issue that has arisen is that of the crimes that were committed by forces of the RPF during the liberation of Kigali in July 1994. The nature and severity of the conflict between the two parties reached its climax during the tenure of Carla del Ponte as the chief prosecutor for the ICTR[21] According to a report printed by the International Crisis Group:

> The Rwandan government provoked a serious crisis in its difficult relationship with the court when it prevented the travel of witnesses whose presence was required for cases to proceed because it objected to the prosecutor's inquiries into war crimes presumed to have been committed by the RP[F] in 1994.
>
> (International Crisis Group 2003: 1)

The result of this specific confrontation was two-fold. First, there was the near shutdown of the ICTR, which seriously jeopardized the tribunal's ability to continue its prosecution of ongoing cases. Second, the establishment of separate prosecutors for the ICTY and the ICTR resulted in Carla del Ponte no longer operating within the ICTR. 'The formal suspension of Carla del Ponte's investigations in September and the establishment of a U.S.-sponsored deal between the prosecutor's office and the Rwandan government seemed to improve the situation' (International Crisis Group 2003).

In addition to being a source of tension between two partners in the judicial response to the crimes committed in 1994, the void in prosecutions created by the absence of any RPF individuals accused of crimes has also been the source of much criticism regarding the achievement of justice on the part of the ICTR. According to Renaud:

> If you take a look [at the] different sides you will see that people [don't necessarily] agree [as to] what is going on [at the] ICTR because all the accused persons are only Hutus. ... When we conduct an investigation we learn [about] both sides [of the conflict]. The prosecutor has information

[about RPF alleged crimes]. He has said to the UN Security Council and to the Rwandan government, 'We have information. We have files. We are working to analyze the files and we will see after we finalize our investigations what we can do.' It's still pending, but for the citizens, they do not know [this information]. The world doesn't know [this information], and the Rwandans who left the country [of Hutu origin]. They cannot understand what is going wrong because they [say] the world will fight, but none of them were prosecuted by the ICTR, none of them [RPF war criminals] were convicted.

(Renaud 2005)

Furthermore, one defence attorney noted that within his role of a defence attorney he calls into question the entire notion of justice on which the ICTR is premised:

You can't have prosecution on one side in a war like that because then you're exonerating, you're testifying the crimes of the other and it's not a step forward for me. ... That's not justice. That's revenge. Then you're deciding to charge one side for political reasons not for criminal justice, juridical reasons.

(HH 2005)

The crimes that were alleged to have been committed by the RPF during the course of their victory, in fact, do fall under the mandate of the ICTR and yet, up until the time of this writing, there has not been a single indictment carried out toward any RPF individual accused of allegedly participating in the reprisal killings or other noted acts that fall under the ICTR's mandate. Despite the ongoing debate, one defence attorney stated, 'I give you a pound-to-a-penny that there never will be any indictments against anybody from the RPF' (BB 2005).

The objections noted in the previous chapter on the part of officials within the Rwandan government are that the crimes committed by select few RPF soldiers were not of the same moral equivalence and, as such, do not belong in the same tribunal as those who orchestrated, facilitated, and carried out the genocide is widely debated amongst individuals working at the ICTR According to one attorney:

From my part, moral equivalence isn't really, isn't an issue. Nobody's saying that somebody that plans and organizes the killing of 10,000 people is morally equivalent to the commander of some unruly troops who allows them to burn down a village and in the process of which 75 people lose their lives. One is much worse than the other is. But to suggest that as a result of one being worse than the other, the less bad should not be punished, or that the authority that is charged with punishing the people shouldn't, is in my view nonsense, and the kind of thing that guilty people say, or people covering up for guilty people say, trying to get them off the hook.

(BB 2005)

From another perspective, Obote-Odora, Special Advisor to ICTR Prosecutor, did recognize that the issue of moral equivalence can produce difficulties that may result from mixing war crimes and genocide crimes in the same tribunal. He disagreed that issue alone should prevent the ICTR from fulfilling its mandate:

I think that the mandate of the tribunal cannot be disputed in the fact that it can try both the RPF and the others in the same court; and no one can argue that trying them together is about moral equivalence. What I do say is that, when there is an impression that the RPF are also being prosecuted for genocide, it is [important] to make it clear that the RPF in the investigations that are being conducted it is in relation to war crimes and crimes against humanity, [and not genocide].

(Obote-Odora 2005)

As an aspect of the stated complementary relationship that is said to exist between the domestic trials and the ICTR within the framework of concurrent jurisdiction, there remains a potential explanation for the continued non-indictment of accused RPF by the ICTR. Repeated statements by the Rwandan Government that it has indeed tried these perpetrators within its own military judicial system make charges at the ICTR redundant. Despite the observation that the ICTR Statute does provide itself with primacy over all states, it does not require the ICTR to supersede the efforts of domestic prosecutions with regard to this matter.[22] Within this framework, if indeed the Rwandan Government has undertaken the trials of the accused RPF individuals, then essentially there would be no necessity on the part of the ICTR to engage in a repetitive process. However, the long-standing, strained relationship between the ICTR and the Rwandan Government over this matter may be viewed as possibly calling into question whether the Rwandan Government actually undertook such trials and punished offenders appropriately.

Regardless of how this jurisdictional matter may affect the current positive working relationship between the Government of Rwanda and the ICTR, there remains the fact that these alleged crimes remain within the prosecutorial purview of the ICTR. According to Obote-Odora, there may be future prosecutions for the alleged crimes of the alleged RPF members:

Ordinarily [the prosecution of both the genocide crimes and those committed by the RPF] should have continued contemporaneously. The only thing is that at the early stages this investigation, for whatever reasons, [was] focused on genocide and they did not focus on these other areas. When the investigations on these war crimes committed by the RPF were intensified then we also get this issue of completion strategy. So now it appears that we are rushing because of the completion strategy, but when the decision for the completion strategy came, these investigations were almost completed.

(Obote-Odora 2005)

Whether the completion strategy put forward by the Security Council or the logistics of the relationship between the Rwandan Government and the ICTR play a role in the eventual decision as to whether or not those RPF members accused of war crimes will face international justice remains to be seen. However, the intention of the ICTR to fulfill the entire scope of their mandate appears to be without question.

ICTR cases and budget

The initial estimate from the office of the prosecutor regarding the number of targets that the ICTR was investigating for the purpose of adjudicating was approximately 200 (AA 2005). However, this figure has been drastically reduced with regard to the number of individuals who will be brought to court at the ICTR. Obote-Odora states that it would be 'not more than 80. If you are going to consider individuals that we are going to transfer to national jurisdictions, for example those which are indicted here but transferred under [Rule] 11 bis., [there will likely be another 25 cases]' (Obote-Odora 2005). Even given the provision of transferring cases, the ICTR has fallen short of its initial estimated number of trials by nearly 43 percent. To date, the ICTR has completed 34 cases resulting in 29 convictions and five acquittals. There are currently 29 cases in progress (one of which is on appeal), nine accused remain in detention awaiting trial, 13 accused remain at large, and two cases have been transferred for trial from the ICTR to France. If one assumes – and given the struggles the ICTR has had in apprehending a number of those at large it remains just an assumption – the resultant number of cases that the ICTR will have had a hand in adjudicating is 87 (ICTR 2008).

The production of the ICTR, in terms of sheer numbers at least, appears to be miniscule. This is even more remarkable when one considers the vastly different financial resources given the relative difference between the ICTR and the trials held in Rwanda. According to the United Nations General Assembly budget report:

The resources for the biennium 2004–5, before recosting, amount to [U.S.] $208,768,800 gross ... including growth of [U.S.] $4,806,200 gross ... or 2.4 per cent, compared with the revised appropriation for 2002–3 ... In nominal terms, the estimate for the biennium 2004–5 amounts to [U.S.] $235,177,100.

(United Nations 2003a)

The annual cost for the operation of the ICTR over the 4-year period is approximately US$116,368,000. According to Rugege, Vice-president of the

Supreme Court in Rwanda, '[O]ur budget for all the courts [including the Gacaca is] this year [2005] about 2.5 billion Francs [Rwandan] not dollars, so that is about five million dollars and that sounds disastrous' (Rugege 2005). There is no doubt that some of the provisions required for the ICTR to function, such as the use of international personnel (and their commensurate salaries), the security measures, the cost of building the courtrooms ($1,000,000 each), and the transportation expenses due to their location in Arusha, do indeed amount to significant expenses. Nevertheless, there appears to be a substantially disproportionate expenditure by the ICTR given the caseload that they are expected to address compared with the caseload of the Rwandan courts.

Furthermore, given the mandate of the ICTR under UN Resolution 955,[23] which states, 'Stressing also the need for international cooperation to strengthen the Courts and Judicial System of Rwanda, having regard in particular to the necessity for those Courts to deal with large numbers of suspects' (United Nations 1994f: 2), the budget and the spending of the ICTR seems at odds with the mandate under which it is to operate.

One defence attorney mentioned a comment made by a former colleague at the ICTR regarding the vast sums of money spent at the tribunal:

> There was a lawyer who was here for a while ... [XX] was interviewed by the BBC a couple of years ago and they asked him about spending all this money on the tribunal: is it a good investment? [XX] said actually it would be better to spend the billion dollars plus you are spending on the tribunal, and use it to provide clean drinking water.
>
> (FF 2005)[24]

Given its substantially disproportionate financial resources, the ability of the ICTR to adjudicate genocide crimes becomes an important consideration. The foundation upon which the ICTR presents its major contributions is liberal legalism.

Restorative and retributive justice at the ICTR

The ICTR mandate includes both retributive and restorative justice elements in the achievement of two of its stated goals of eradicating the culture of impunity and facilitating reconciliation in Rwanda. The retributive element is found within the actual trials. The trials are premised on the notion of establishing individualized guilt and applying the requisite punishment upon conviction. There is no dialogical participation on the part of the offender, victim, or community. In applying this retributive philosophy, the goal of eradicating the culture of impunity through punitive sanctions for the convicted is pursued.

The restorative element has been suggested to exist within the extra-legal programmes argued to make the ICTR a more victim-oriented court. It has been suggested that these programmes, responding to the needs of victims, will assist in the process of reconciliation by *restoring* the victims to their previous state prior to the genocide through processes that are restitutive in nature. The issue that requires clarification is that restitutive justice is not the equivalent of restorative justice:

> Restitution as a common law concept denotes the idea that a gain or benefit wrongly taken or enjoyed should be returned. ... Restitution then interprets our moral intuition that 'something must be done' as demanding that things be returned to the way they were before the wrong occurred.
>
> (Llewellyn and Howse 1998: 16)

That the ICTR seeks to right the wrongs to the victims of the genocide is certainly laudable and undoubtedly a worthwhile endeavour. However, it does not mean that the ICTR is engaged in restorative justice as suggested by Okali (Moghalu 2005: 68). Restitution can be part of a restorative justice approach to addressing crime, especially given its focus on the victim, but it is not restorative justice in and of itself. Restorative justice looks at the harm done by the crime in a much broader context, including a consideration of the harm to both the community and the perpetrator resulting from the act. Furthermore, restorative justice, unlike restitutive justice, is forward-looking and 'does not take restoration of the *status quo ante* as its goal' (Llewellyn and Howse 1998: 17). Restorative justice does not seek to simply return things to the way they were before as the way things were before were conducive to the act being committed. It seeks restoration beyond that which existed before; it seeks to create a new order that promotes a greater ideal. 'It stands juxtaposed to the to the backward focus of restitution as it attempts to address a wrong by transforming relationships between those involved such that the same situation could not rise again' (Llewellyn and Howse 1998: 18).

Furthermore, restitution requires the quantification of losses and 'because restitution requires quantification and valuation of that which must be transferred between perpetrator and victim it cannot account for the non-material harms a victim can and often does suffer' (Llewellyn and Howse 1998: 16). The perpetrators being tried at the ICTR transfer nothing to the victims. It is the ICTR taking this action, essentially providing restitution on behalf of the perpetrators based on the moral need that something must be done. The convicted themselves assume accountability for their actions via one single means, serving their sentence, the result of retributive justice. That the ICTR has incorporated the programmes seeking to address many of the issues and concerns of the victims and the wider Rwandan population is a positive step. However, it does not address the relational aspect of the harms caused by the genocide. In failing to do so, restitution at the ICTR is seen as a worthy addition to its retributive function. However, the limited success that it might achieve with respect to its first goal of assisting with the eradication of impunity in Rwanda through accountability through retribution is at odds with its success in achieving its second goal of reconciliation.

The ICTR and responsive regulation

Although not technically *associated* with the Rwandan judicial system, it is plausible that the ICTR as an international court engaged in adjudicating those accused of crimes in Rwanda can be considered an extension of the overall effort to address the genocide (notwithstanding the relationship problems between the Rwandan Government and the ICTR). If conceived in this way, one can consider the place of the ICTR within the regulatory pyramid. The selective prosecutions taking place at the ICTR focus on individuals that have been accused of the highest level of complicity in the genocide. Furthermore, they are no longer within the grasp of the Rwandan courts, barring the cooperation of other States in executing Rwandan warrants and returning them for trial in Rwanda.

According to one defence attorney at the ICTR, among the defence tactics at the trials held at the ICTR is the argument that the alleged genocide in Rwanda never happened (GG 2005). He argues that although there may have been massacres, there was not an orchestrated genocide. Another defence attorney argues that, 'the RPF was used as a proxy force by the British and Americans to invade Rwanda and then to be used later to invade the Congo. ... The other aspect is this; it's really a war between France and the US for control of central Africa' (HH 2005). In conjunction with the regulatory pyramid, the accused at the ICTR (assuming that these defence strategies are their positions and not merely a strategy for acquittal) would fall into the category of the incompetent/irrational actor. The accused in this category are not demonstrating any degree of culpability or remorse and certainly are not about to make amends for their wrongdoing. As such, the regulatory pyramid would suggest that, if the other methods have failed (or are destined to fail), then a trial and incapacitation of the offender is a justifiable response. Drumbl notes that 'After all, some perpetrators may are simply beyond being shamed and consequently may be immune from the effects of restorative justice initiatives' (Drumbl 2000: 1278).

Liberal-legalism

Giving recognition to the international community's previous judicial efforts at addressing mass atrocities, the ICTR has incorporated the liberal-legalistic model and its incumbent trial method into its *modus operandi* in adjudicating genocidaires. According to Drumbl:

> This deontological approach, which is *au courant* among international lawyers, posits that trials of selected individuals (preferably undertaken at the international level) constitute the favored and often exclusive remedy to respond to all situations of genocide and crimes against humanity.
>
> (Drumbl 2000: 1228)[25]

The adoption of the liberal legalistic framework provides the ICTR with a model to engage in a process of seeking justice for the victims of the genocide. Furthermore, it attempts to accomplish this goal within a process that provides fair trials, avoiding the criticisms and arguments levied against the expedient method of totalitarian show trials that would, in and of themselves, undermine the achievement of a just outcome.

Indeed, if the process of addressing the atrocities committed in 1994 is deemed a fair and just process, then the decisions emanating from the trials will provide not only justice in the immediate context and a degree of redress for the victims affected by the perpetrators, but also a clear statement to the international community of what is and is not considered acceptable conduct, and what consequences can be expected if these guidelines for conduct are violated. The liberal-legalistic approach to justice presents an opportunity for norm clarification through the setting of legal precedent.

The ICTR and the rule of law in Rwanda and internationally

The ICTR's trials have thus far produced 34 verdicts during its tenure. It is also predicted to render another 43 verdicts before the completion of its mandate. These verdicts contribute to the development of the rule of law both in Rwanda as well as in the international realm of justice. With respect to those who favour trials as the quintessential model for dealing with crimes of this nature, Drumbl notes that 'these individuals underscore the fact that, in the wake of mass atrocities, trials may have a significant declaratory value' (Drumbl 2000: 1277). The world will respond to genocide, if not in the first instance to prevent its occurrence, then, by holding those complicit in its commission individually accountable and rendering severe punishments as a step towards establishing the rule of law in the international arena. A non-response may have contributed to exacerbating the culture of impunity, not only within Rwanda, but also around the world.

Regarding its impact on Rwanda, the ICTR has undoubtedly contributed to the overall search for justice. As a result of the trials, the ICTR has denounced the genocide. It has *put on record* the events that transpired in 1994 and clearly stated that they were unacceptable. Further, it has contributed to maintaining peace by managing to secure the arrest, conviction, and detention of a number of individuals complicit in the genocide. These individuals are no longer in a position to further their cause; they have been rendered ineffective in the continuation their fateful mission. Indeed, those who remain at large, but for whom warrants have been issued, while avoiding prosecution for the time being are also no longer free to engage in the same activities they might otherwise were it not for the outstanding warrant.

However, as Peskin states, '[T]he Tribunal's failure to make its courtroom accomplishments more known to the domestic legal system is a lost opportunity for international law to have a direct and lasting impact on the rule of law in Rwanda' (Peskin 2005: 957). For the rule of law to take root in a society there must be conscious awareness of the law in action. The limited segment of the Rwandan population that knows about the proceedings and findings of the ICTR is likely not sufficient for the ICTR to have a significant impact within Rwanda in this regard.

On a more global level, the impact of the ICTR in raising the bar of accountability is associated with the precedents and achievements that it has made in international law. When asked what the success of the ICTR will be when it is all over, one attorney responded:

> I think the successes of the tribunal is that it exist[ed] at all ... and that if it does result in people who were active in or complicit in mass murders being tried in proper courts, having a proper defence, had a fair trial hearing, and being punished in appropriately humane, but severe way, that will be an achievement.
>
> (BB 2005)

Furthermore, in conjunction with the work of the ICTY in The Hague, the model that has been used in these two courts is likely to contribute to the work at the International Criminal Court (ICC) as well as other attempts at international justice. A trial attorney at the appeal level at the ICTR stated that the ICTR and ICTY have 'created an established body of law from which they can now draw, and although the precedents set may not be technically binding on the ICC, they will not be able to dismiss them' (JJ 2005). With consideration of the work of the ICTR in this regard, the following chapter examines the key precedents established during its operations.

Notes

1 These possible reasons, as discussed by Des Forges and Longman (2004), while possibly containing a degree of merit given the obvious lack of international involvement in the prevention of and ending of the Rwandan genocide, are nevertheless not given any credence within the context of the Statute of the ICTR nor in the resolutions leading up to it.

2 UN Doc A/49/508/Add.1,S/1994/1157/Add.1, 14 November 1994 clearly states that:

> [a]lthough the existence of the genocide has been confirmed, there is considerable delay in conducting the investigation. The various elements constituting genocide appear to be increasingly confirmed by on-the-spot investigation that has been carried out. Such elements include the discovery of mass graves, the existence of evidence and proof indicating that the massacre of the Tutsi was planned and the identification of those primarily responsible.
>
> (United Nations 1994c)

3 According to Yacoubian, there were four reasons why the government of Rwanda voted against the UN Resolution 955 to create the tribunal:

> First, the Rwandan government believed that the temporal jurisdiction of the tribunal was too restrictive; ... Second, ... the 'composition and structure' of the tribunal was 'inappropriate and ineffective'; ... Third, the Rwandan

government could not accept the fact that individuals convicted by the tribunal would be imprisoned outside of Rwanda, and that issues of confinement would be determined by host states; ... Fourth, the strongest punishment available at the tribunal was life imprisonment, whereas Rwanda permits capital punishment.

(Yacoubian 1999: 188)

4 The ICTY was created in 1992 upon the adoption of United Nations Security Council Resolution 808, 48th session, 3217 meeting, UN Document S/RES/808 (1992). Although adopted in 1992, the tribunal did not get underway until 1993.
5 SCSL refers to the Special Court for Sierra Leone. Dicker and Keppler write, 'In 2002, taking a different "hybrid" approach, the United Nations signed an agreement with government of Sierra Leone to create the Special Court for Sierra Leone' (Dicker and Keppler 2004: 4). See Dicker and Keppler (2004) for a more detailed comparison of the SCSL and ICTR/ICTY.
6 This statement is clearly spelled out in the ICTR Statute: Article 14: Rules of Procedure and Evidence, which states:

The Judges of the International Tribunal for Rwanda shall adopt, for the purpose of proceedings before the International Tribunal for Rwanda, the Rules of Procedure and Evidence ... of the International Tribunal for the former Yugoslavia with such changes as they deem necessary.

(ICTR 2008)

7 The interview took place 22 June 2005, Arusha, Tanzania, at the International Criminal Tribunal for Rwanda.
8 The move to having separate chief prosecutors for each of the tribunals came partly as a result of the desire on the part of the UN Security Council to see the completion strategies for both tribunals become effectively carried out. Logistically, therefore, it became apparent that the best means for achieving the strategies was to have two separate prosecutors with a sole focus on each tribunal.
9 The interview took place 23 June 2005 in Arusha, Tanzania, at the International Criminal Tribunal for Rwanda.
10 In defining the difference between the two, Obote-Odora stated:

In Rwanda, for me, I read our Article 6–3 I try to distinguish superior responsibility from command responsibility, because command responsibility you need a structure and a clear unequivocal order. In superior responsibility you don't need that structure and some orders can come through nuances, not a direct order, and because in many of the crimes, in the Rwandan situation, there was an overlap between the work of the military and the civilians. And there were very many retired senior military officers who became senior administrators, so they combined both the military and civilian authority.

(Obote-Odora 2005)

11 On two separate occasions during my interviews (Renaud 2005 and Obote-Odora 2005), it was discussed how the hiring process could be considered 'backwards' with regard to the process by which typically a case is likely to be dealt with, in that the last people hired were the investigators (who should have been the first) and the judges were the first to be hired, then the registry, followed by the prosecutors. This process of hiring was also a key consideration in the observed 'slow start' of the ICTR in prosecuting the accused.
12 The topic of plea bargaining as it relates to the processes all three levels of the judicial response discussed in this work will be more fully examined in Chapter 7.

At this time, just a brief overview of plea bargaining as it has affected the work of the ICTR is presented.

13 According to Renaud, the use of 'insider witnesses' has been an ongoing aspect of the work of the investigators and has the potential to play a key role in the conviction of other key individuals who participated at the highest levels of the organizers and planners of the genocide (Renaud 2005).

14 Under the tenure of Goldstone, very little was accomplished at the ICTR. The main reason for this, according to Obote-Odora, was the way in which the Security Council undertook the challenge of staffing the tribunal. The ICTR was established in 1994, but the judges were not in place until 1995. Furthermore, this process resulted in hampering the investigations and as a result Goldstone focused his attention to the work being carried out at the ICTY (Obote-Odora 2005).

15 In many of the interviews conducted at the ICTR, it was commonly stated that the logistics and time required to process these multi-accused trials were significantly less efficient than operating a single-accused trial. As a result of this observation, there has been a change in the prosecution strategy with regard to the completion of the trials at the ICTR. While focusing on the completion of the multi-accused trials already in progress, it has been stated that future trials are much more likely to take the form of single-accused trials in an effort to increase efficiency in dealing with the cases.

16 Obote-Odora stated that perception of the prosecution strategy was only partially true (2005). There had already been some evidence collected by various human rights organizations, as well as the Special Rapporteur for the United Nations. However, with reference to the state of the investigation, it appears that this previous evidence was very general in nature in that it was a record of what happened and when, but not necessarily tied to any specific individual.

17 This allegation was alluded to, but without substantiation, by two of the individuals interviewed. Due to the potential ramifications of such an allegation will remain nameless.

18 This stands for 'electronic performance appraisal system'.

19 See Dieng (2004) for a more detailed understanding of these various functions.

20 With regard to the chambers, there were no findings of any significance that they were not operating in a substandard way. The OTP was deemed to be hampered by reasons expressed in the previous section of this writing, namely that of a lack of leadership and operational problems.

21 At the time that Carla Del Ponte was the active Chief of Prosecution for the ICTR, there was only one Chief Prosecutor for both the ICTY and ICTR.

22 In the previous chapter, it was stated that there has been a sense of awareness on the part of the Rwandan Government that it is likely time that they make public the records of the cases whereby accused RPF were tried and convicted within their military courts. However, until such a time as that it has taken place, this notion of injustice on the part of the entire judicial effort will remain an ongoing source of discontent and accusations of partiality.

23 UN Resolution 955 and many others are contained within the ICTR Statute.

24 XX inserted to protect the name of the individual to whom the interviewee referred to in the quotation.

25 See Drumbl (2000) for an in-depth discussion of the deontological approach and its limitations for policy application when considering the social context of the occurrence of these crimes.

6 International jurisprudence: definitions of the crimes and the key precedents

These tribunals have really broken ground. In a sense that you have these conventions and treaties and things like that sitting up there on the shelves gathering dust and we took them off, dusted them off, put them into the Statutes that create the two tribunals; and the judges have now applied them in real fact situations, so you have a development that is extraordinarily important and I don't think that the International Criminal Court will ignore it. I think they may differ in the future on interpretations, but they've got a hugely valuable body of law to apply.

(Stewart 2005)

During the past 12 years, the ICTR has come under a great deal of criticism, concerning the process of delivering judgments against some of the key figures alleged to be responsible for the events that took place in Rwanda in 1994. The uphill battle engaged in at the outset of the tribunal's efforts to get underway was further exacerbated by inefficiency and poor management that threatened the tribunal's operations (BB 2005). A key criticism facing the ICTR has been its lack of progress, especially given the budget under which that they have been operating. Despite these criticisms, the ICTR has made some significant advances both in terms of achieving its declared mandate as well as laying a foundation of international jurisprudence that is believed will have a direct impact on any future cases that may present themselves before the International Criminal Court.[1] This chapter specifically addresses the nature of the crimes that the ICTR is mandated to prosecute, some of the key elements of those crimes as well as some of the key precedents developed within the context of specific cases.

The ICTR Statute and the crimes it is charged with prosecuting

In constructing its explicit provisions regarding the crimes that fall within its mandate and determining said crimes, the statute of the ICTR drew upon a number of international humanitarian laws and treaties. The statute specifically incorporates the definition of certain acts as criminal from: (1) the London Charter of the International Military Tribunal; (2) the Convention on the Prevention and Punishment of the Crime of Genocide; (3) the Geneva Convention Relative to the Treatment of Prisoners of War; and (4) the Protocol Additional to the Geneva Conventions of 12 August 1949 and Relating to the Protections of Victims of Non-International Armed Conflicts (Protocol II).[2] Each grouping of crimes involved certain logistic and legal qualifications in the process of successfully finding defendants guilty of the specific crime for which they are indicted.

Genocide

In the context of the ICTR, it has already been noted that genocide is the central crime of the majority of the prosecution's cases. According to Akhavan, the 'ICTR Chambers have felt compelled to justify the inclusion of genocide in the Statute by reference to its universal criminality' (Akhavan 2005: 990). In the early days, the tribunal's efforts to secure convictions of this crime were difficult because there was no case law or precedent from which to prove that the genocide occurred or to assign individual responsibility. According to Stewart:

> In the early days of prosecuting the crime of genocide ... of course one of the fears that we had is that we wouldn't prove the genocide, that everybody in the world would know that there was genocide in Rwanda in 1994, except the Trial Chamber.
>
> (Stewart 2005)

Article 2 of the ICTR Statute outlines the various elements of the crime of genocide that are considered central in the attempts by the prosecution to convict alleged perpetrators within the Rwandan context.[3] 'The definition of genocide, as stated in Article 2 of the Tribunal's Statute, is taken verbatim from Articles 2 and 3 of the Convention on the Prevention and Punishment of the Crime of Genocide' (*Prosecutor v Akayesu* 1998: para 494). Article 2(2) outlines the mental element of the crime, or *mens rea*, while Article 2(3) describes the *actus reus*, or the specific acts for which the accused may be charged. The demonstration of the *mens rea* required to secure a conviction of an alleged offender of genocide is what separates the crime of genocide from the other crimes in the Statute. According to Akhavan, 'ICTR jurisprudence correctly recognizes the mental element of genocide in the *chapeau* of Article 2(2) and its distinguishing feature, namely the requirement of a specific intent (*dolus specialis*)' (Akhavan 2005: 989). As stated in the judgement of the Trial Chamber in *Prosecutor v Akayesu*:

> Genocide is distinct from other crimes inasmuch as it embodies a special intent or *dolus specialis*. Special intent of a crime is the specific intention, required as a constitutive element of the crime, which demands that the perpetrator clearly seeks to produce the act charged. Thus, the special

intent in the crime of genocide lies in 'the intent to destroy, in whole or in part, a national, ethnical, racial, or religious group, as such.'

(*Prosecutor v Akayesu* 1998: para 498)

The special intent of the perpetrator, in the case of genocide, places it in a category in and of itself. According to Akhavan:

> It is this specific intent which distinguishes the crime of genocide from the ordinary crime of murder. Thus, in addition to defining genocide, the requisite mental element also delineates the normative sphere of international criminal law from that of domestic law.
>
> (Akhavan 2005: 992)

In an effort to prove that the *dolus specialis* was indeed present, the prosecutor must place the actions and intentions of the accused within the wider context of the entire event:

> We tried to put in evidence, we focused very much on the individual accused, as is the focus of any trial, but we did try to put in evidence of the context and in the end, you know we were very successful. But when you're dealing with someone who is a bourgmestre in Gitarama, you know he's not in Kigali, he's not connected to the top level of power structure; all you can do is say 'look, at a particular moment in time, he switches the way in which he is operating and now he's gone from resisting the penetration of the Interahamwe, ... to actively promoting the destruction of Tutsi in his commune'.
>
> (Stewart 2005)

Furthermore, even having established within the context of each trial[4] that genocide did occur in Rwanda in 1994, there remains the necessary provision of proof on the part of the prosecutor that the accused are found individually responsible for the acts with which they are charged. When looking at the actions of individuals in order to achieve the *dolus specialis* within a specific time period or geographical area, it is necessary to contextualize the actions within the broader scope of the events across the whole country. In the cases that are presented later in this chapter, additional specifics surrounding the crime of genocide and the application of the law will be examined in detail.

Crimes against humanity

The next cluster of offences that is found within the context of the indictments written at the ICTR involves those in which civilians have become the target of a multitude of acts of violence (ie crimes against humanity). The historical antecedent of these crimes in international law can be traced back to the Hague Conventions of 1899 and 1907.[5] The Hague Conventions 'acknowledged the existence of certain basic principles of humanity, which have to be respected under all circumstances, even if they are not put into treaty form' (Schiessl 2002: 203).

Following the Second World War, the Charter of the International Military Tribunal in London stipulated, for the first time, the notions of war crimes and crimes against humanity. Indeed, the concept of crimes against humanity is clearly outlined in the London Charter in Article 6(c), which states:

> CRIMES AGAINST HUMANITY: namely murder, extermination, enslavement, deportation, and other inhumane acts against any civilian population, before or during war, or persecution on political, racial, or religious grounds in execution of or in connection with any crime within the jurisdiction of the Tribunal, whether or not in violation of any domestic law where perpetrated.
>
> (London Charter of the International Military Tribunal 1945)

Finally, the creation of the Geneva Conventions and the subsequent Protocols demonstrated the need for the protection of civilians based initially on the events that transpired in the Second World War. According to Schiessl, 'besides the acts of opposing armies, [the Geneva Convention] included the protection against persecution by their own government or regimes' (Schiessl 2002: 205). Given the circumstances in Rwanda, it is not difficult to see the relevant nature of these progressive steps in defining certain behaviours as crimes against humanity and hence their inclusion in the ICTR Statute. These crimes are outlined in Articles 3 and 4 of the ICTR Statute:

Article 3: Crimes against Humanity

The International Criminal Tribunal for Rwanda shall have the power to prosecute persons responsible for the following crimes when committed as part of a widespread or systematic attack against any civilian population on national, political, ethnic, racial or religious grounds. (a) Murder; (b) Extermination; (c) Enslavement; (d) Deportation; (e) Imprisonment; (f) Torture; (g) Rape; (h) Persecution on political, racial, and religious grounds; (i) Other inhumane acts.

Article 4: Violations of Article 3 Common to the Geneva Conventions and of Additional Protocol II

The International Criminal Tribunal for Rwanda shall have the power to prosecute persons committing or ordering to be committed serious violations of Article 3 common to the Geneva Conventions of 12 August 1949 for the Prosecution of War Victims and of Additional Protocol II thereto of 8 June 1977. These violations shall include, but shall not be limited to: (a) Violence to life, health and physical or mental well-being of persons, in particular murder as well as cruel treatment such as torture, mutilation or any form of corporal punishment; (b) Collective punishments; (c) Taking of hostages; (d) Acts of terrorism; (e) Outrages upon human dignity, in particular humiliating and degrading treatment, rape, enforced prostitution and any form of indecent assault; (f) Pillage; (g) The passing of sentences and the carrying out of executions without previous judgement pronounced by a regular constituted court, affording all the judicial guarantees which are recognized by civilised peoples; (h) Threats to commit any of the foregoing acts.

(ICTR 2007)

As a measure of contrast with the crime of genocide, crimes against humanity do not require the same mental element:

> The term *dolus specialis* refers to the *degree* rather than the *scope* of intent. By way of comparison, *dolus generalis* requires that the perpetrator 'means to cause' a certain consequence 'or is aware that it will occur in the normal course of events.'
>
> (Akhavan 2005: 992)

Observed within the definitions regarding the *intent* of the accused when comparing genocide and crimes against humanity, the key difference remains that genocide requires the intent to *destroy in whole or in part a definable group of people* whereas for crimes against humanity it is the intent *to cause a certain consequence or awareness that a consequence will occur* (ie murder, extermination, etc).

Crimes against humanity, like genocide require an additional qualifier beyond the intent necessary for each of the individual crimes noted in the above lists. In order to secure a conviction, the proven act must be *part of a widespread or systematic attack against any civilian population*. As a reflection of this requirement, an incident that is observed to have occurred in isolation would not qualify as such a crime. As with genocide, crimes against humanity must have a connection between the specific crimes indicated in the indictment and the larger picture of the transpiring events. Given the close ties between the ICTY and the ICTR, the prosecution strategy for finding individuals guilty of crimes against humanity in the ICTY, for example, demonstrate that requirement.[6] In the Foca rape trials which began in 2000, 'Hildegard and Tej did not want to prosecute single individuals for isolated rapes but rather to build a case that reflected the organized way in which rape was a part of the ethnic cleansing that occurred in Foca' (Hagan 2003: 178). This case demonstrated, within the context of an armed conflict, that violence against the civilian population (in this specific case, rape) is construed as a part of a greater evil; when viewed in concert with each other as part of a larger plan, these individual acts deserve the designation as a *crime against humanity*.

Hierarchy of crimes?

The result of the designation of crime against humanity appears to speak to the circumstances under which the crimes took place, assuming a graver nature than one might observe in an isolated incident within a domestic context. The notion that a crime has occurred which offends and affects all of humanity, or at a minimum the entirety of the group of which the specific victim is a member, is suggested by this declaration. Nevertheless, it is doubtful when presenting a possible hierarchy of crimes, that there is any intention to downplay the impact of the crime on a single victim. For example, according to Karekezi there were different ways that rape has been used as a means of genocide in Rwanda and the former Yugoslavia:

> In Yugoslavia, for example, it was used as – sexual violence was used as ethnic cleansing too. The Serbian was trying to have children from Muslim women. Here it wasn't like that. Pregnancy was a consequence, but not aimed to have children through them. But the goal of the men ... was to weaken, to destroy, in this case the Tutsi, in Rwanda.
>
> (cited in Sharlach 2000: 100)

This concept of a hierarchy of crimes was further elucidated in the chamber's decision[7] in the case of the former Prime Minister Jean Kambanda. The chamber discussed the three categories and concluded that crimes that fall under the ICTR Statute derived from the Geneva Conventions and Additional Protocol II are 'considered lesser crimes than genocide and crimes against humanity' (*Prosecutor v Kambanda* 1998: para 14). The difficulty that the chamber had in *ranking* crimes of genocide and crimes against humanity is further discussed in the chamber's decision. With regard to genocide and crimes against humanity, but specifically applied in the process of sentencing, 'the Chamber is of the opinion that genocide constitutes the crime of crimes' (*Prosecutor v Kambanda* 1998: para 16). This sentiment appears to persist within the framework of the *ad hoc* tribunals as noted by Stewart:

> Well, I don't know that there is a strict hierarchy of crimes. I think generally speaking that war crimes are seen as somewhat lesser, although very serious, than genocide or certain crimes against humanity, but I think that the sentencing policy at the ICTR has generally been tougher than that of the ICTY, and I don't know why that is.
>
> (Stewart 2005)

The key precedent-setting cases of indictments handed down by the ICTR are discussed in the following section.

Precedent-setting cases at the ICTR

'In a real sense, the Arusha tribunal is attempting to evolve a system of international criminal justice out of nothing, and it is simply unfair not to appreciate the magnitude of their task and the absence of simple solutions' (Caplan *et al* 2000: 179). The prosecutors are delegated the responsibility with investigating and prosecuting crimes of a scale that are themselves unprecedented in recent history. Furthermore, with the exception of the Nuremburg trials and the handful of cases that were completed in the ICTY at the time that the ICTR was beginning its trials, there was no body of law from which to draw. This was especially significant since genocide was not recognized in law at the Nuremburg trials neither had anyone been tried for genocide in the ICTY. The early cases at the ICTR have additionally proved to be a source of reference for those cases that followed and demonstrated their usefulness in creating international jurisprudence.

Prosecutor v Akayesu (Jean-Paul) *(Case No ICTR-96-4-T)*

On 2 September 1998, the ICTR Trial Chamber 1, composed of Judges Laïty Kama (Presiding), Lennart Aspergren, and Navanethem Pillay, handed down a monumental decision when they unanimously pronounced Jean-Paul Akayesu guilty of nine of the 15 counts laid out in the indictment.[8] Akayesu served as a bourgmestre in the commune of Taba, located in the Prefect of Gitarama, during the period of the genocide in 1994. On 2 October 1998, he was sentenced to life imprisonment for the crimes of which he was convicted:[9]

> The verdict is the first handed down by the Rwandan Tribunal; the first conviction for genocide by an international court; the first time an international court has punished sexual violence in a civil war; and the first time that rape was found to be an act of genocide to destroy a group.
> (Human Rights Watch 1998: 1)

The elements of that case present some of the details surrounding the precedents that have been set as a result of this conviction. These include the finding of genocide and its requisite elements, the allocation of individual responsibility for the crimes of which he was convicted, and the finding that rape, for the first time, was considered a constituent element of genocide.

Genocide

With regard to the alleged crime of genocide, the first task for the Chamber in the Akayesu trial was to establish the *actus reus* of the crime, despite the obvious occurrence of mass murder in Rwanda in 1994. Nevertheless, the question remained as to whether or not these murders actually constituted the crime of genocide. Referring to Article 2 of the ICTR Statute, in addition to proving the mental element (*dolus specialis*), the factual elements of the acts of the crime – namely that the actions of killing or causing serious bodily harm were actually perpetrated – must be proven to confirm the crime of genocide. After giving consideration to the testimony of many witnesses, particularly a number of experts including Dr Zachariah,[10] Major General Romeo Dallaire,[11] and Dr Alison Des Forges,[12] and the photographic evidence provided by a British cameraman Simon Cox,[13] the chamber made the following pronouncement:

> Consequently, in view of these widespread killings the victims of which were mainly Tutsi, the Chamber is of the opinion that the first requirement for there to be genocide has been met, the killing and causing serious bodily harm to members of a group.
>
> <div align="right">(<i>Prosecutor v Akayesu</i> 1998: para 116)</div>

The second aspect of the act requires that the crimes were taken against either individuals or groups, solely on the basis of their membership within a specified group and not for any other reasons. After reviewing the relevant testimony and evidence[14] presented during the trial, the chamber stated with regard to identifying the Tutsi as a protected group and thereby falling under the requirement of the statute's guidelines, that:

> In the opinion of the Chamber, there is no doubt that considering their undeniable scale, their systematic nature and their atrociousness, the massacres were aimed at exterminating the group that was targeted. Many facts show that the intention of the perpetrators of these killings was to cause the complete disappearance of the Tutsi.
>
> <div align="right">(<i>Prosecutor v Akayesu</i> 1998: para 118)</div>

After the judgement, they further stated:

> In the opinion of the Chamber, all of this proves that it was indeed a particular group, the Tutsi ethnic group, which was targeted. Clearly the victims were not chosen as individuals but, indeed, because they belonged to the said group; and hence the victims were members of this selected group as such.
>
> <div align="right">(<i>Prosecutor v Akayesu</i> 1998: para 124)</div>

The finding of Trial Chamber 1 had declared in this judgment that the events which transpired in Rwanda in 1994 were of such a character that they met the requirement of the statute and, as such, constituted genocide. This is an especially significant finding since the context in which the genocide had taken place – an armed conflict between two opposing forces of a civil war – was argued to provide an alleged motive for the killings and thus the actions would not fall within the definition of genocide, but should be considered war crimes. When considering the differential sentences imposed for genocide and war crimes, this observation could be of significant probative value. The chamber dismissed this challenge stating, instead, that:

> The Chamber replies in the negative, since it holds that the genocide took place alongside the conflict. The execution of the genocide was probably

facilitated by the conflict, in the sense that the fighting against the RPF was used as a pretext for the propaganda inciting the genocide against the Tutsi, by branding RPF fighters and Tutsi civilians together, Inkotanyi.[15] Very clearly, once the genocide got underway, the crime became one of the stakes in the conflict between the RPF and RAF. ... In conclusion, it should be stressed that although the genocide against the Tutsi occurred concomitantly with the above-mentioned conflict, it was, evidently, fundamentally different from the conflict.

(*Prosecutor v Akayesu* 1998: paras 127–8)

As was previously mentioned, having established the *fact* that the *actus reus* (the genocide) had indeed occurred in Rwanda, the prosecutor nevertheless still had the responsibility for proving, beyond a reasonable doubt, the individual responsibility and intent of Akayesu in the commission of these crimes.

Individual responsibility

Akayesu's indictment recorded the grounds upon which the prosecutor established Akayesu's personal responsibility for the atrocities that took place in the Taba commune. Paragraph 12 of the indictment read:

As bourgmestre, **Jean Paul Akayesu** was responsible for maintaining law and public order in his commune. At least 2000 Tutsis were killed in Taba between April 7 and the end of June, 1994, while he was still in power. The killings in Taba were openly committed and so widespread that, as bourgmestre, **Jean Paul Akayesu** must have known about them. Although he had the authority and the responsibility to do so, **Jean Paul Akayesu** never attempted to prevent the killing of Tutsi in his commune in any way or called for assistance from regional or national authorities to quell the violence.

(*Prosecutor v Akayesu* 1998: bold in original)

Based on a number of witnesses who testified during the trial, the chamber found that the role of a bourgmestre was one that held a great deal of respect and authority within a commune. The bourgmestre is given the task of maintaining order within the commune. As part of his defence, Akayesu stated that despite his position within the community, once the events began to transpire they essentially took on a life of their own and he was powerless to stop them.[16]

The issue, according to the chamber, was 'whether he ever attempted to do so' (*Prosecutor v Akayesu* 1998: para 182). It was discovered, in fact, that there was a turning point in the manner in which Akayesu acted during the time in question: 'There is a substantial amount of evidence establishing that before 18 April 1994 the Accused did attempt to prevent violence from taking place in the commune of Taba' (*Prosecutor v Akayesu* 1998: para 184). After a meeting in Gitarama, involving the Prime Minister, the Prefects, and the bourgmestres, there was a significant change in Akayesu's behaviour: 'Many witnesses, including witnesses E, W, PP, V, and G, testified to the collaboration of the Accused with the Interahamwe in Taba after that date' (*Prosecutor v Akayesu* 1998: para 187). Akayesu was charged under section 6(1) and 6(3) of the ICTR Statute.

Article 6: Individual Criminal Responsibility

1. A person who planned, instigated, ordered, committed or otherwise aided and abetted in the planning, preparation or execution of a crime referred to in Articles 2 to 4 of the present Statute, shall be held individually responsible for the crime.
2. The official position of any accused person, whether as Head of state or government or as a responsible government official, shall not relieve such person of criminal responsibility nor mitigate punishment.
3. The fact that any of the acts referred to in Articles 2 to 4 of the present Statute was committed by a subordinate does not relieve his or her superior of criminal responsibility if he or she knew or had reason to know that the subordinate was about to commit such acts or had done so and the superior had failed to take the necessary and reasonable measures to prevent such acts or punish the perpetrators thereof.
4. The fact that an accused person acted pursuant to an order of a government or of a superior shall not relieve him or her of criminal responsibility, but may be considered in mitigation of punishment in the International Tribunal for Rwanda determines that justice so requires.

(ICTR 2007)

In their written judgment, the judges examined the nature of Akayesu's position as bourgmestre and the differences between the *de jure* and *de facto* powers associated with this position in the context of Rwandan society. Resulting from a historical investigation into bourgmestre positions as well as the statements of a number of witnesses, the chamber concluded that:

'The bourgmestre had exclusive control over the communal police, ... [and authority over] any gendarmes put at the disposal of the commune.' The Chamber does find it proved that '[the bourgmestre] was responsible for the execution of laws and regulations and the administration of justice, also subject only to the prefect's authority.' The Chamber does find it proved that, 'In Rwanda, the bourgmestre is the most powerful figure in the commune. His *de facto* authority in the area is significantly greater than that which is conferred upon him *de jure*.'

(*Prosecutor v Akayesu* 1998: para 187)

Intent: dolus specialis

Having provided the requisite evidence for the accused to be held criminally responsible for murder, the final requirement for a genocide conviction of remains the establishment of *dolus specialis*. After referring to the Tadic case at the ICTY and examining the elements of the *dolus specialis*, the chamber recognized the difficulty of establishing the intent of an accused in the absence of a confession. Therefore, they argued that:

> In the absence of a confession from the accused, his intent can be inferred from a certain number of presumptions of fact. The Chamber considers that it is possible to deduce genocidal intent inherent in a particular act charged from the general context of the perpetration of other culpable acts systematically directed against that same group, whether these acts were committed by the same offender or by others.
>
> (*Prosecutor v Akayesu* 1998: para 523)

The previous establishment of the existence of genocide in Rwanda, coupled with the specifics of the crimes within the Taba commune for which Akayesu was determined to be responsible under Article 6(1) of the ICTR Statute, provided the necessary context from which the chamber could infer the intent of Akayesu. For the first time in history, the prosecution substantially fulfilled all of the requisite elements and succeeded in obtaining a conviction for the crime of genocide.

Rape as a crime of genocide

Beyond the significance of the first conviction for the crime of genocide, the Akayesu case also provided ground-breaking international jurisprudence in the arena of crimes of sexual violence, namely, the classification of rape as a crime of genocide. It could be argued that this substantive finding that occurred by happenstance.

The original indictment of Akayesu did not include any charges pertaining to sexual violence within the commune of Taba. It was not until these crimes became apparent over the course of the trial that the indictment was changed to include them: 'In introducing this amendment, the Prosecution stated that the testimony of Witness H motivated them to renew their investigation of sexual violence in connection with events that took place in Taba at the bureau communal' (*Prosecutor v Akayesu* 1998: para 417).

Despite this statement by the prosecutor, there was some debate as to the legitimacy of this claim, instead suggesting that the addition to the indictment was the result of pressure from a number of human rights groups. Indeed, this was the position put forward by the defence: 'The Chamber notes that the Defence in its closing statement questioned whether the Indictment was amended in response to public pressure concerning the prosecution of sexual violence' (*Prosecutor v Akayesu* 1998: para 417). Others have argued that the absence of the crimes of sexual violence in the original indictment was due to 'a lack of political will among some high-ranking officials' (Human Rights Watch 1998). Taking these various arguments into account, the chamber stated that 'the Chamber understands that the amendment of the Indictment resulted from the spontaneous testimony of sexual violence by Witness J and Witness H during the course of this trial and the subsequent investigation of the Prosecution, rather than from public pressure' (*Prosecutor v Akayesu* 1998: para 417).

The importance of this decision in the Akayesu trial cannot be overstated given the widespread use of rape as a tactic of destruction within the context of armed conflict.[17] Additionally, this clarification by the Trial Chamber is of great interest given that the ICTR Statute, as written, did not include rape as one of the crimes of genocide under Article 2 and, therefore, the decision represented an *interpretation* of the statute rather than a strict application of the law. Within the ICTR Statute the crime of rape is explicitly only indictable as a crime against humanity in conjunction with Article 3 and, in the case of the indictment of Akayesu, the charges of sexual violence originated from this interpretation.[18] The specifics of the case made against Akayesu for sexual violence are found in charges 12A and 12B.[19]

In conferring the judgment, the chamber made clear (paras 731–4) its conclusion that rape does constitute an act of genocide.[20] The crime of rape, in the Rwandan context, constituted an attempt to destroy, in whole or in part, the Tutsi ethnic group. It further met the conditions as laid out in Article 2(b) and 2(c): the 'causing of serious bodily harm to members of the group' and 'inflicting on the group conditions of life calculated to bring about its physical destruction in whole or in part', respectively (ICTR Statute). The chamber noted that rape may be considered among the worst harms that can be inflicted upon an individual, and, as reported by a number of witnesses, this harm may lead to the desire for the end of their lives.

The incorporation of the crime of rape into the realm of a crime of genocide represents a significant advance in international jurisprudence. It also may provide an impetus for the international community to take note of what Hagan referred to as the 'gendered nature of the reality of war' (Hagan 2003: 176). Discussing the Srebrenica and Foca rape trials at the ICTY, Hagan stated that '[w]hereas men tend to get killed, women and children more often are forcibly detained and deported, and young women in particular are at risk of sexual assault and rape' (Hagan 2003: 176). Although Hagan was referring to the circumstances that may arise during a war, the genocide in Rwanda appeared to have involved a similar pattern of killings.[21] Finally, as a result of this precedent-setting case, there may need to be an explicit inclusion of rape to as a revision to the Convention on the Prevention and Punishment of the Crime of Genocide that would reflect the significance of this finding. According to Sharlach, this suggestion is long overdue and is in great need of being addressed as it is observed that 'all of the definitions of genocide presented here are gender-neutral. None treat crimes against men or crimes against women separately' (Sharlach 2000: 92).

Prosecutor v Kambanda (Jean) *(Case No ICTR-97-23-A)*

A mere 2 days following the landmark conviction of Akayesu, on 4 September 1998, former Rwandan Prime Minister Jean Kambanda pleaded guilty to all counts of the indictment in which he was charged.[22] The conviction of Kambanda, a head of state, for crimes committed during his tenure as leader of the country, albeit brief, was another first for international criminal justice. Furthermore, Kambanda's case represented the first time that anyone had pled guilty to the crime of genocide and bolstered the ICTR's attempts to prove that the genocide as a matter of legal fact, did occur. In addition to the conviction of a head of state, the Kambanda plea presented ICTR prosecutors with the opportunity to attack the main line of defence used by a number of other accused, namely that there was no planned and orchestrated genocide:

> Given that denial remains a favourite tool of Hutu Power advocates even to this day, Kambanda's confession is of vital significance. Not only did he fully concede the existence of a deliberate genocide against the Tutsi population of Rwanda, he equally acknowledged that it was planned in advance.
>
> (Caplan *et al* 2000: 180)

Kambanda's guilty plea on all counts of the indictment and subsequent allocution to the events that transpired in Rwanda were given great consideration during the process of sentencing: 'Kambanda's lawyer argued that he should be sentenced to only two years since he had been such a cooperative defendant and had pleaded guilty. The prosecutor joined in asking the judges to take his cooperation into consideration' (Caplan *et al* 2000). In rendering their decision, Judges Kama, Aspergren, and Pillay addressed the various factors to be considered in sentencing an individual within the context of the crimes for which the accused was charged and to which he pled guilty. Their discussion of the relevant factors to be considered in arriving at a sentence and the imposition of a sentence of life imprisonment is a key decision that has affected all subsequent sentences of the ICTR.

Factors relevant in sentencing at the ICTR

The first element that was given consideration by the chamber in rendering their decision was that Article 23 of the ICTR Statute provides consideration to the relevant sentencing practices of the country wherein the alleged crimes took place:

Article 23: Penalties
1. The penalty imposed by the Trial Chamber shall be limited to imprisonment. In determining the terms of imprisonment, the Trial

Chambers shall have recourse to the general practice regarding prison sentences in the courts of Rwanda.

2. In imposing the sentences, the Trial Chambers should take into account such factors as the gravity of the offence and the individual circumstances of the convicted person.

(ICTR 2007)

The chamber stated in their judgment that the decisions at the ICTR should observe the sentences determined by Rwandan courts as a reference for their consideration, but that they should not be a strict guideline *per se* (*Prosecutor v Kambanda* 1998). The maximum penalty that an accused can be sentenced to at the ICTR is life imprisonment and was a source of tension between the Rwandan government and the ICTR as the death penalty could formerly be imposed under Rwandan law and had been imposed by Rwandan courts upon many of the individuals convicted of this most heinous crime. This lack of concordance in the sentencing practices of the ICTR and the Rwandan courts remains a contentious issue within Rwanda as citizens do not understand how the selective prosecutions of the most prominent figures in the genocide may result in sentences of life imprisonment at the ICTR while those who carried out their orders are liable to receive the death penalty from Rwandan courts. While equivalent sentencing may not exist, the chamber did note that 'Rwanda, like all the States which have incorporated crimes against humanity or genocide in their domestic legislation, has envisaged the most severe penalties in the criminal legislation for these crimes' (*Prosecutor v Kambanda* 1998: para 18).

In addition to observing Rwandan sentencing practices, Article 23 of the ICTR Statute addresses additional factors that are to be considered when imposing a sentence on those convicted under its authority. Rule 101 of the Rules of Procedure and Evidence is also applied when undertaking sentencing considerations.

The judges in Trial Chamber 1 gave consideration to the applications made by both the prosecutor and the defence while also considering Rwandan sentencing practices and the ICTR Statute requirements for sentencing. The gravity of the crimes is relatively self-evident when examining the crimes of genocide and crimes against humanity (*Prosecutor v Kambanda* 1998). The individual circumstances of the accused were discussed since, at the time of crimes, Jean Kambanda was the Prime Minister of Rwanda and, in that capacity was criminally liable under Article 6(1) and 6(3) of the ICTR Statute. Of great interest and consequence was the consideration of the mitigating factors in this case: 'Defence Counsel has proffered three factors in mitigation: Plea of guilty, remorse; which he claims is evident from the act of pleading guilty; and cooperation with the Prosecutor's office' (*Prosecutor v Kambanda* 1998: para 46). The prosecutor affirmed that they, too, accepted the mitigating factors as put forward by the defence counsel and supported their request for sentencing consideration based on those factors. In their written judgment, the Trial Chamber did not accept the mitigating factor of remorse, stating:

> The Chamber notes, however, that Jean Kambanda has offered no explanation for his voluntary participation in the genocide; nor has he expressed contrition, regret, or sympathy for the victims in Rwanda, even when given the opportunity to do so by Chambers, during the hearing of 3 September 1998.
>
> (*Prosecutor v Kambanda* 1998: para 51)

The chamber continued to explore the relationship between the guilty plea and the idea of remorse as it is often applied in national jurisdictions. Having established the relevant factors for arriving at a sentence, the chamber concluded that:

> A sentence must reflect the predominant standard of proportionality between the gravity of the offence and the degree of responsibility of the offender. Just sentences contribute to respect for the law and the maintenance of a just, peaceful, and safe society.
>
> (*Prosecutor v Kambanda* 1998: para 58)

Given the gravity of the offences with which Kambanda was charged and pled guilty as well as the tribunal's mandate to effectively redress the violence that occurred and foster an environment conducive to the respect for the rule of law by eradicating the culture of impunity in Rwanda, the chamber's decision was that 'the aggravating circumstances surrounding the crimes ... negate the mitigating circumstances' (*Prosecutor v Kambanda* 1998: para 62). At the conclusion of the chamber's deliberations, it imposed a sentence of life imprisonment. As there are no provisions for parole or release from prison under UN law, the host country's laws take precedence in this regard once the transfer of the prisoner has been made.

Much discussion of the sentence, the conditions under which Kambanda finally agreed to plead guilty, and the consequences of the decisions made by the Trial Chamber have ensued following the Kambanda verdict. According to one defence attorney, the conditions of Kambanda's pre-trial detention and the way in which the plea was finally attained by the investigators were, in and of themselves, a miscarriage of justice. An accusation was tendered that the death threats towards both Kambanda himself and his family played a key role in obtaining his confession. The attorney stated that the investigators allegedly told Kambanda, 'If you are not going to talk with us, we can't protect your family. We can't help you' (HH 2005).[23] Furthermore, the attorney asserted that the chamber's assessment of the plea agreement did not fully disclose the true nature of the bargain that Kambanda was expecting to receive from the court with regard to the length of his sentence:

> For nine months, he refused. He said, 'I'm not guilty. I didn't do any of this.' Finally, he agreed to say, 'Ok, I will take limited responsibility for

what happened.' He was promised a deal – he's going to get 12 years, so he signs it and he pleads guilty. They give him life, so he tries to retract his plea. I saw him testify on the day that he tried to retract his appeal: 'This is what happened to me. They had me *in communicado* for nine months. It was psychological pressure. I didn't know where I was. I never saw a lawyer, never saw anybody. They finally wore me down.' 'Did you sign this saying this was a genocide?' 'No, I didn't say that. You read carefully and this is what I said: "As Prime Minister, I take full political responsibility to whatever happened, because I must as part of the position. But there was no plan for genocide. There were killings and if my government is involved, then I take full responsibility." That's as far as it goes.' 'Oh, but you signed.' 'Yes, I signed, but you guys promised me 12 years and gave me life and I'm telling you there was no planned genocide.' And they kept telling him, 'But you signed.'

(HH 2005)

Another interesting argument that came to light was made by another defence attorney on Kambanda's behalf:

It would have been nice if he were brought to trial. I think that was an absolute travesty. In the course of the investigation of my client's case, I discovered a huge amount of information relating to Kambanda, which was never mentioned at his trial.

(BB 2005)

In discussing the case further, BB noted that a vast volume of the radio broadcasts made by Radio Télévision Libre des Mitte Collines (RTLM). had never been transcribed and that they may contain information that could either convict or acquit a number of those standing trial at the ICTR, including his own client. Specifically referring to Kambanda's case and part of the indictment against him – that he never took steps to quell the violence – BB implied that in his research this so-called *fact* may actually be debated. As cause for opening this debate, he referred to a particular meeting involving Kambanda that was simultaneously broadcast over the RTLM radio network:

He affirms the government's support for the Arusha Accords. He suggests that the RPF, in the truce. He asks the Minister of Justice to punish the people who are responsible for the acts of violence, bearing in mind that this is a meeting of the [prefects], that he has gathered them together to give them messages, and she says that he doesn't give them any messages. He asked the [prefects] to transmit the government's message to the people that order must be restored. He tells the [prefects] to explain to the population that there must be no violence on the basis of ethnicity. He tells them that unauthorized roadblocks must be dismantled. He tells the [prefects] to instruct the people not to take the law into their own hands, and that the renewal of the offensive by the RPF must not be a pretext for the population to be attacking each other.

(BB 2005)

Further disappointment regarding the outcome has also been expressed in terms of the impact that the case has had on the ICTR itself. According to some:

> One of the grave disappointments of his trial was the missed opportunity to have him [Kambanda] divulge everything he knew about the events leading up to and during the genocide. According to the Tribunal's rules, a guilty plea automatically does away with the need for presentation of evidence by defence counsel and the court moves directly to sentencing. But in the process, the opportunity to learn the full story is sacrificed.
>
> (Caplan *et al* 2000: 181)

The use of the guilty plea in this case has severely impeded the potential for expediting subsequent trials by virtually closing the door on those prosecutors attempting to negotiate guilty pleas.[24] Despite its precedent-setting findings in the *Kambanda* case, the result of Kambanda having recanted his sworn testimony and appealed the court's ruling has been to leave open the question of the ICTR's success in dealing with the crimes committed during the Rwandan conflict: 'The ICTR record would be easier to evaluate were it not for the disturbing and inconclusive case of Jean Kambanda' (Caplan *et al* 2000: 180).

Prosecutor v Nahimana (Ferdinand), Barayagwiza (Jean-Bosco) and Ngeze (Hassan) *(Case No ICTR-99-52-T): the Media Case*

The final case relevant to the ICTR international legal precedents is the Media Case. According to the *Harvard Law Review*, the Media Case 'produced international law's first re-examination of the link between mass media and mass slaughter, convicting three media executives for the role of their newspaper and radio station in Rwanda's 1994 genocide (*Harvard Law Review* 2004: 2769). The importance of this re-examination is found in the decision of the Trial Chamber to find these accused guilty of the crime of genocide, conspiracy to commit genocide, and direct and public incitement to commit genocide, as well as two counts of crimes against humanity (murder and extermination), and sentencing each of them to life imprisonment.[25] The significance of the finding is that the conviction 'signal[ed] that hate speech can constitute international law's most heinous crimes' (*Harvard Law Review* 2004: 2769). The Trial Chamber, composed of Judges Navanethem Pillay (presiding), Erik Møse, and Asoka de Zoysa Gunawardana, state the fundamental issues of the trial:

> This case raises important principles concerning the role of the media, which have not been addressed at the level of international criminal

justice since Nuremburg. The power of the media to create and destroy fundamental human values comes with great responsibility. Those who control such media are accountable for its consequences.

(*Prosecutor v Nahimana* 2002: para 8)

The two media sources with which the accused was directly affiliated and of which they were determined to be in control are the RTLM radio station and *Kangura*, a newspaper.[26] In the course of the trial, the use of mass media was determined to be a key element in the production of an environment that both encouraged and facilitated the genocide. Numerous examples of the use of both media outlets in this regard were presented at trial. One such example presented was *Kangura*'s publication in December 1990 of the Hutu-power propaganda, *The Ten Commandments*:[27]

> *The Ten Commandments* were published in *Kangura* No.6, in December 1990, within the article entitled *Appeal to the Conscience of the Hutu.* The introduction of the article warned readers:
> The enemy is still there, among us, and is biding his time to try again, at a more propitious moment, to decimate us.
> Therefore, Hutu, wherever you may be, wake up! Be firm and vigilant. Take all necessary measures to deter the enemy from launching a fresh attack.
> (*Prosecutor v Nahimana* 2002: para 12)

Regarding the RTLM broadcasts made during the genocide, the chamber reported that ethnic stereotyping was extensively broadcast over the radio in such a way as to create an ethnic divide and incite the general population of Hutus against the Tutsi: 'After 6 April 1994, the virulence and the intensity of RTLM broadcasts propagating ethnic hatred and calling for violence increased. These broadcasts called explicitly for the extermination of the Tutsi ethnic group' (*Prosecutor v Nahimana* 2002: para 26).

In a similar manner to the *Akayesu* case, the trial chamber found that the statements broadcast and written in the two media outlets provided, by inference, the requisite element of *dolus specialis*. The chamber also recognized, with regard to the charge of conspiracy to commit genocide, that the three accused were acting in unison, 'that Nahimana, Barayagwiza and Ngeze consciously interacted with each other, using the organizations they controlled to promote a joint agenda, which was the targeting of the Tutsi population for destruction' (*Prosecutor v Nahimana* 2002: para 110). They further observed that the significant aspect of this case was the role of the media in the promulgation of genocide and the accountability of those who had the power to control such institutions the chamber provided an exhaustive review of the history of international precedents in this regard and discussed at length the application of the Article 3(C) of the ICTR Statute. Some of the factors that were given great consideration in this matter included the actual language used, the importance of protecting political expression and the causal link between the media statements and the outcomes said to result from them. In their summation of the issues surrounding hate speech, the chamber stated:

> [It] considers that speech constituting ethnic hatred results from stereo-typing of ethnicity combined with its denigration. In the Chamber's view, the accuracy of a generalization is only one factor to be considered in the determination of whether it is intended to provoke rather than educate those who receive it. ... The Chamber also considers the context in which the statement is made to be important. A statement of ethnic general-ization provoking resentment against members of that ethnicity would have a heightened impact in the context of a genocidal environment. It would be more likely to lead to violence.
>
> (*Prosecutor v Nahimana* 2002: para 94)

To reflect their grave concern for the accountability of those charged with the operation of the institutions of mass media, the chamber specifically addres-sed each of the defendants at sentencing. In addressing Ferdinand Nahimana, the chamber stated 'Without firearm, machete or any physical weapon, you caused the death of thousands of innocent civilians' (*Prosecutor v Nahimana* 2002); to Hassan Ngeze, 'Instead of using the media to promote human rights, you used it to attack and destroy human rights' (*Prosecutor v Nahi-mana* 2002); with regard to Jean-Bosco Barayagwiza, 'He is a lawyer by training and in his book professes a commitment to international human rights standards. Yet he deviated from these standards and violated the most fundamental human right, the right to life' (*Prosecutor v Nahimana* 2002).

The impact of these cases

While it will remain to be seen whether the impact of these cases will indeed provide international law with a functional body of jurisprudence, the cases described in this chapter can be argued to have provided a foundation upon which the future of international criminal law can further operate. According to the *Harvard Law Review*, 'though its elaboration of media causation is not perfect – particularly with respect to its broad inclusion of print media and its practical exclusion of sexual violence – the Tribunal nevertheless established a workable foundation for future development' (*Harvard Law Review* 2004: 2769). The ICTR has clarified the jurisprudence of genocide in the *Akayesu* case, including the act of rape as both a constituent element of genocide as well as a crime against humanity. It has also produced the first ever convic-tion of a former head of state for genocide in the Kambanda trial. Finally, it has reaffirmed and extended the recognition of hate speech and the role of the media in the inciting of a population to the crime of genocide.

Keeping in mind the evolving ICTR jurisprudence, various issues and concerns that have impacted the work of both the ICTR and the judiciary in Rwanda are explored in the next chapter. Each issue raises serious questions about the potential effectiveness of the role that the three realms of judicial response can have in achieving justice for the victims of the Rwandan genocide.

Notes

1 In the process of the interviews at the ICTR, it was noted by a number of interviewees that as a result of the ICTR's *ad hoc* nature, the jurisprudence that is created at the tribunal is technically not binding on the ICC However, as was noted in Chapter 5 of this work, with the shared appeals chamber operating in conjunction for both the ICTR and ICTY, there is a more consistent set of jurisprudence being formulated and, as such, there is a great likelihood that the jurisprudence will be, at minimum, referenced in any ICC cases.
2 Full names of the various sources are:

1. The London Charter of the International Military Tribunal: In pursuance of the Agreement signed on the 8th day of August 1945 by the Government of the United States of America, the Provisional Government of the French Republic, the Government of the United Kingdom of Great Britain and Northern Ireland and the Government of the Union of Soviet Socialist Republics
2. Convention on the Prevention and Punishment of the Crime of Genocide, Approved and proposed for signature and ratification or accession by General assembly resolution 260A, December 1948, entry into force: 12 January 1951, in accordance with Article XII.
3. Geneva Convention relative to the Treatment of Prisoners of War, Adopted on 12 August 1949 by the Diplomatic Conference for the Establishment of International Convention the Protection of Victims of War, held in Geneva from 21 April to 12 August 1949, entry into force: 21 October, 1950.
4. Protocol Additional to the Geneva Conventions of 12 August 1949, and relating to the Protection of Victims of Non-International Armed Conflicts (Protocol II), Adopted on 8 June 1977 by the Diplomatic Conference on the Reaffirmation and the Development of International Humanitarian Law applicable to Armed Conflicts, entry into force: 7 December 1978, in accordance with Article 23.

3 Article 2: Genocide:

1. The International Criminal Tribunal for Rwanda shall have the power to prosecute persons committing genocide as defined in paragraph 2 of this Article or of committing any of the other crimes enumerated in paragraph 3 of this Article.
2. Genocide means any of the following acts committed with the intent to destroy, in whole or in part, a national, ethnic, racial or religious group, as such:

   (a) Killing members of the group;
   (b) Causing serious bodily harm to members of the group;
   (c) Deliberately inflicting on the group conditions of life calculated to bring about its physical destruction in whole or in part;
   (d) Imposing measures intended to prevent births within the group;
   (e) Forcibly transferring children of the group to another group.

3. The following acts shall be punishable:

   (a) Genocide;

(b) Conspiracy to commit genocide;
(c) Direct and public incitement to commit genocide;
(d) Attempt to commit genocide;
(e) Complicity in genocide.

(ICTR 2007)

4 It is of interest here that the notion of 'judicial notice' within the context of the ICTR has not been made with regard to genocide. According to Obote-Odora, Special Advisor to the Prosecutor:

> On judicial notice, you recognize that in common law jurisdictions they tend to accept judicial notice only in civil cases, not in criminal trials. So, while here we can use it in criminal cases, the judges are pretty strict on that; so that there is not any appearance that the burden of proof is shifting. Based on that they have been reluctant to take judicial notice on even genocide itself, although, of course, over time, there have been convictions on genocide.
>
> (Obote-Odora 2005)

Additionally, if the tribunal did take notice that the crimes of genocide in 1994 constituted genocide, many accused would be deemed guilty simply as a result of command authority. Judicial notice of genocide would *inter alia* constitute a judgment of criminal liability. For a more detailed legal analysis of judicial notice and its relevance within the ICTR, see Stewart (2003).

5 Schiessl (2002) discusses these conventions with particular regard to the history of the crime of rape as a crime against humanity.

6 This should not be taken to suggest that the ICTR (as the focus of this work is the Rwandan context) has not indicted individuals for war crimes; indeed they have been successful in obtaining convictions as such.

7 Trial Chamber 1, composed of Judges Laïty Kama (Presiding), Lennart Aspergren, and Navanethem Pillay, rendered the decision.

8 The initial indictment against Akayesu was submitted to the chambers on 13 February 1996 contained 15 charges (later amended to include the crimes involving sexual violence on 17 June 1999) (*Prosecutor v Akayesu* 1998).

9 For each of the counts for which Akayesu was convicted, an individual sentence was proposed by prosecutor Pierre Jean Prosper, and handed down by the chamber. They included the following:

> For Count 1: life imprisonment for the crime of genocide.
> Count 3 of the indictment, life imprisonment for the crime – crime against humanity, extermination.
> Count 4, life imprisonment for direct and public incitement to genocide.
> Count 5, 15 years of imprisonment for crimes against humanity, murder.
> Count 7, 15 years of imprisonment for crimes against humanity, murder.
> Count 9, 15 years of imprisonment for crimes against humanity, murder.
> Count 11, 10 years of imprisonment for crimes against humanity, torture.
> Count 13, 15 years of imprisonment for crimes against humanity, rape.
> Count 14, 10 years of imprisonment for crimes against humanity, other inhuman acts.
> The chamber decides that the above sentences shall be served concurrently and therefore sentences Akayesu to a single sentence of life imprisonment.
>
> (*Prosecutor v Akayesu* 1998)

10 Dr Zachariah was a doctor working with the NGO 'Médecins Sans Frontières' in the Butare Prefecture of Rwanda, but had also traveled extensively throughout Rwanda during the genocide. In his testimony before the court:

He described in great deal the heaps of bodies which he saw everywhere, on the roads, on the footpaths and in rivers and, in particular, the manner in which all these people had been killed. At the church in Butare, at the Gahidi mission, he saw many wounded persons in the hospital who according to him, were all Tutsi and who, apparently, had sustained wounds inflicted with machetes to the face, the neck, and also the ankle, at the Achilles' tendon, to prevent them from fleeing.

(*Prosecutor v Akayesu* 1998: para 115)

11 Dallaire was the Commander of the UNAMIR forces in Rwanda during the genocide. He recorded the events that transpired during the fateful months of 1994 and was called as an expert witness in the *Akayesu* case:

Other testimonies heard, especially that of Major-General Dallaire, also show that there was an intention to wipe out the Tutsi population in its entirety, since even new born babies were not spared. Even pregnant women, including those of Hutu origin, were killed on the grounds that the foetuses in their wombs were fathered by Tutsi men, for in a patrilineal society like Rwanda, the child belongs to the father's group of origin.

(*Prosecutor v Akayesu* 1998: para 121)

12 Des Forges is a historian working in conjunction with the NGO Human Rights Watch. She has written extensively on the Rwandan genocide, including the book *Leave none to tell the story: genocide in Rwanda*:

Alison Des Forges, an expert witness, in her testimony before this Chamber on 25 February 1997, stated as follows, 'on the basis of the statements made by certain political leaders, on the basis of songs and slogans popular among the Interahamwe, I believe that there people had the intention of completely wiping out the Tutsi from Rwanda so that – as they said on certain occasions – their children, later on, would not know what a Tutsi looked like, unless they referred to history books.

(*Prosecutor v Akayesu* 1998: para 118)

Dr Alison Des Forges testified that many Tutsi bodies were often systematically thrown into the Nyabarongo river, a tributary of the Nile. Indeed, this has been corroborated by several images shown to the Chamber throughout the trial. She explained that the underlying intention of this act was to 'send the Tutsi back to their place of origin', to 'make them return to Abyssinia', in keeping with the allegation that the Tutsi are foreigners in Rwanda, where they are supposed to have settled following their arrival from the Nilotic region.

(*Prosecutor v Akayesu* 1998: para 120)

13 'He mentioned identity cards strewn on the ground, all of which were marked "Tutsi"' (*Prosecutor v Akayesu* 1998: para 116).
14 In the factual findings of the case, the chamber also referred to Rwanda's constitution, in place at the time that required every Rwandan citizen to carry an identity card, as well as the Civil Code (Article 118) that requires each birth certificate to identify the ethnicity of the newborn infant (*Prosecutor v Akayesu* 1998: para 170).
15 Based on the work of Dr Ruzindana, the ICTR provided in trial the definition of the Kinyarwanda word 'Inkotanyi':

The origin of the term Inkotanyi can be traced back to the 19th Century, at which time it was the name of one of the warrior groups of a Rwandese king,

King Rwaburgiris. There is no evidence to suggest that this warrior group was monoethnic. Dr. Ruzindana suggested that the name Inkotanyi was borne with pride by these warriors. At the start of the war between the RPF and the Government of Rwanda, the RPF army wing was called Inkotanyi. As such, it should be assumed that the basic meaning of the term is the RPF army. Based on the analysis of a number of Rwandan newspapers and RTLM cassettes, as well as his personal experiences during the conflict, Dr. Ruzindana believed the term Inkotanyi had a number of extended meanings, including RPF sympathizer or supporter, and, in some instances, it even seemed to make reference to Tutsi as an ethnic group.

(*Prosecutor v Akayesu* 1998: para 147)

16 See *Prosecutor v Akayesu* 1998: para 1.4.2 for a more detailed examination of the 'Accused's line of defense'.
17 See Sharlach (2000) for a more detailed description of the prevalence and intent of the use of rape during an armed conflict.
18 In addition to being convicted of rape as a constituent element of genocide, Akayesu was convicted of rape as a crime against humanity.
19 Charges 12A and 12B of the indictment read as follows:

12A. Between April 7 and the end of June, 1994, hundreds of civilians (hereinafter 'displaced civilians') sought refuge at the bureau communal. The majority of these displaced civilians were Tutsi. While seeking refuge at the bureau communal, female displaced civilians were regularly taken by armed local militia and/or communal police and subjected to sexual violence, and/or beaten on or near the bureau communal premises. Displaced civilians were also murdered frequently on or near the bureau communal premises. Many women were forced to endure multiple acts of sexual violence which were at times committed by more than one assailant. These acts of sexual violence were generally accompanied by explicit threats of death or bodily harm. The female displaced civilians lived in constant fear and their physical and psychological health deteriorated as a result of the sexual violence and beatings and killings.
12B. **Jean Paul AKAYESU** knew that the acts of sexual violence, beatings and murders were being committed and was at times present during their commission. **Jean Paul AKAYESU** facilitated the commission of the sexual violence, beatings and murders by allowing the sexual violence and beatings and murders to occur on or near the bureau communal premises. By virtue of his presence during the commission of the sexual violence, beatings and murders and by failing to prevent the sexual violence, beatings and murders, **Jean Paul AKAYESU** encouraged these activities.

(*Prosecutor v Akayesu* 1998: Indictment)

20 *Prosecutor v Akayesu* (2008):

731. With regard, particularly, to the acts described in paragraphs 12(A) and 12(B) of the Indictment, that is, rape and sexual violence, the chamber wishes to underscore the fact that in its opinion, they constitute genocide in the same way as any other act as long as they were committed with the specific intent to destroy, in whole or in part, a particular group, targeted as such. Indeed, rape and sexual violence certainly constitute infliction of serious bodily and mental harm on the victims and are even, according to the Chamber, one of the worst ways of [inflicting] harm on the victim as he or she suffers both bodily and mental harm. ... These rapes resulted in physical and psychological destruction

of Tutsi women, their families and their communities. Sexual violence was an integral part of the process of destruction, specifically targeting Tutsi women and specifically contributing to their destruction and to the destruction of the Tutsi group as a whole.

732. The rape of Tutsi women was systematic and was perpetrated against all Tutsi women and solely against them. ... This sexualized representation of ethnic identity graphically illustrates that Tutsi women were subjected to sexual violence because they were Tutsi. Sexual violence was a step in the process of destruction of the Tutsi group-destruction of the spirit, of the will to live, and of life itself.

733. On the basis of the substantial testimonies brought before it, the Chamber finds that in most cases, the rapes of Tutsi women in Taba, were accompanied with the intent to kill those women. ... Following an act of gang rape, a witness heard Akayesu say 'tomorrow they will be killed' and they were actually killed. In this respect, it appears clearly to the Chamber that the acts of rape and sexual violence, as other acts of serious bodily and mental harm committed against the Tutsi, reflected the determination to make Tutsi women suffer and to mutilate them even before killing them, the intent being to destroy the Tutsi group while inflicting acute suffering on its members in the process.

734. In light of the foregoing, the Chamber finds firstly that the acts described *supra* are indeed acts as enumerated in Article 2 (2) of the Statute, which constitute the factual elements of the crime of genocide, namely the killings of Tutsi or the serious bodily and mental harm inflicted on the Tutsi. The Chamber is further satisfied beyond reasonable doubt that these various acts were committed by Akayesu with the specific intent to destroy the Tutsi group, as such. Consequently, the Chamber is of the opinion that the acts alleged in paragraphs 12, 12A, 12B, 16, 18, 19, 20, 22 and 23 of the Indictment and proven above, constitute the crime of genocide, but not the crime of complicity; hence, the Chamber finds Akayesu individually criminally responsible for genocide.

(*Prosecutor v Akayesu* 1998)

21 For a more detailed examination of the concept of the gendered nature of the conflict in Rwanda, see Jones (2002).
22 Jean Kambanda was charged with, and pled guilty to, genocide, conspiracy to commit genocide, direct and public incitement to commit genocide, complicity in genocide, crimes against humanity (murder and extermination).
23 The protection of Kambanda's family as part of the plea agreement has been confirmed by other sources such as Caplan *et al* 2000 (para 18.28).
24 This was believed to be deemed as evident especially given that Kambanda expressed the desire to plead guilty and to tell the truth even before his arrest in Kenya (*Prosecutor v Kambanda* 1998: para 50).
25 The Appeals Chamber, following the initial conviction of Jean-Bosco Barayagwiza to life imprisonment, reduced the sentence to 35 years as a result of a violation of his rights by the proceedings at the Tribunal: 'The Chamber considers that a term of years, being by its nature a reduced sentence from that of life imprisonment, is the only way in which it can implement the Appeals Chamber decision' (*Prosecutor v Nahimana* 2003: para 1107).
26 Hassan Ngeze was the founder and editor of *Kangura*; Ferdinand Nahimana was the founder and director of RTLM radio with Jean-Bosco Barayagwiza considered being his 'second in command'. The positions that were held by the accused during the time of the alleged crimes in Rwanda was a key factor in determining their individual criminal liability in accordance with Article 6(1) and Article 6(3) of the ICTR Statute.
27 The *Hutu Ten Commandments*, as published in *Kangura*, is available at www.trumanwebdesign.com/~catalina/commandments.htm.

7 Issues impacting the search for justice: witness protection, hearsay evidence, and plea bargaining

> It is better to do part of the job really well than try to do the whole thing really badly, because at the end of the day justice is a sense of mind and if the perception is going to exist that people have been tried unfairly, then you don't have justice. So it is a balancing act.
>
> (Morley 2005)

Having provided an initial exploration into each realm of the judicial response to the genocide in Rwanda individually, we now turn our attention to a number of issues that can be observed to impact all *three* realms and their combined pursuit for justice and reconciliation in Rwanda. It should be noted that these topics only represent some of the matters that must be addressed and overcome in order to move forward effectively in prosecuting those accused of the crimes committed in 1994. Despite representing only a subset of myriad concerns, however, each plays an instrumental role in the attempts to adjudicate the alleged perpetrators. Additionally, although these three realms can be seen to address factors that are concerns of any national jurisdiction, there are additional complexities that arise given the context of an international adjudication process. Furthermore, these issues do not exist in isolation, but are interrelated and resonate throughout the entire scope of the adjudication process. The three foci of this chapter are therefore: (1) witness protection and allegations of witness tampering; (2) the acceptance of hearsay evidence across all three levels of the judicial response; and (3) the role of plea bargaining, and, *inter alia*, the incarceration of the convicted.

Witness protection

As opposed to the situation observed at the International Criminal Tribunal for the former Yugoslavia (ICTY) wherein Cheriff Bassiouni presented the tribunal with a plethora of forensic evidence of the massacres that took place in the former Yugoslavia (Hagan 2003: 45), the ICTR did not have such a forensic database from which to draw. In the aftermath of the genocide in Rwanda, there were neither the resources nor the personnel available to facilitate such a wide-scale effort on behalf of the national government. The result of this apparent lack of specialized forensic data has resulted in both the ICTR and the national government of Rwanda being much more reliant on the testimony of witnesses to the alleged crimes than the ICTY was. The significance of witness testimony at the ICTR became self-evident when the dispute between the Rwandan government and the ICTR resulted in the supply of witnesses being cut off from the UN investigators for a brief period of time; a turn of events that nearly caused the daily functioning of the ICTR to cease. Additionally, Article 29 of the Organic Law of the Gacaca states that:

> Every Rwandan citizen has the duty to participate in the Gacaca courts activities.

> Any person who omits or refuses to testify on what he or she has seen or on what he or she knows, as well as the one who makes slanderous denunciation, shall be prosecuted by the Gacaca Court which makes the statement of it. He or she incurs a prison sentence from three (3) to six (6) months. In case of repeat offence, the defendant may incur a prison sentence from six (6) months to one (1) year.
>
> (Government of Rwanda 2004d)

The Law compelling witnesses to testify seems to signify to the effective functioning of the measures utilized in Rwanda.

Within a context of continued unrest and violence in not only Rwanda itself, but in the wider East African Great Lakes region, the protection of these witnesses seems imperative for the processes to move forward.

Twelve years after the genocide occurred, the tragedy is still having a deleterious impact on individuals who were directly affected as victims as well as on others who are called as witnesses to the crimes. For both of these groups, there exists a real sense of anxiety and fear for their safety based on their knowledge of those events and their vulnerability to intimidation. From within the borders of Rwanda and neighbouring countries within the larger Great Lakes Region of Africa as well as in other countries as far away as Europe, stories of the intimidation and even the murder of many witnesses have been widely reported (Caplan *et al* 2000: 184).

The Coalition for Women's Human Rights in Conflict Situations reported on the extent of the intimidation and killing of those thought or known to be ICTR witnesses:

> Others who have testified have suffered harassment and intimidation after returning to Rwanda. One woman, after having testified, was forced to flee her home in fear of her life. In an interview she said, 'When I returned from [testifying in] Arusha, everyone knew I had testified. Everyone in my neighbourhood had nicknamed me, "Mrs. Arusha." Shortly after returning from Arusha, I was chased from the house I had been renting in Kigali.'
>
> (Coalition for Women's Human Rights in Conflict Situations 1997: 2)

Ibuka, a Rwandan organization that represents and assists the survivors of the genocide, further substantiated such claims: 'Ibuka ... said that one or two genocide survivors are killed every month but it says that three potential witnesses were killed recently in the south west province of Gikongoro' (AfricaBlog 2003). A further case was cited by Carroll: 'in the most recent case a man was killed and dismembered in front of his family as a warning to other potential witnesses' (AfricaBlog 2003: 2). The undertaking of the Gacaca may itself be a factor in the proliferation of the observed violence since it was observed that 'some of the suspects who remained free now feel threatened by the growing number of [Gacaca] courts, which are supposed to be swift and inexpensive, and want to kill or intimidate potential witnesses before being tried' (Carroll 2003: 2).

While attending a Gacaca court in the District of Kanombe in June of 2005, the author witnessed, first hand, a claim of intimidation by a potential witness at a Gacaca proceeding. As the court was drawing to a close, a woman sitting in the middle of the crowd arose from her seat and spoke to the court as a whole, but specifically addressed the Inyangamugayo. She pointed to another individual in the crowd and stated that she was being intimidated by this man who was pressuring her not to testify before the Gacaca. In accordance with the recent changes in the Gacaca law, the Inyangamugayo stated that this matter would be the first item on the agenda the next time (the following week) the Gacaca for that district met by which time they would have had an opportunity to investigate this allegation. Stories like these appear to be prevalent throughout the country. This situation has been potentially exacerbated by the release of a large number of prisoners previously held in Rwandan detention facilities:

> Threats against genocide witnesses also hampered the [G]acaca process; persons accused of genocide-related crimes, including some individuals who had been released by the government from [pre-trial] detention, reportedly made these threats. The government held local communities responsible for protecting witnesses, and relied on the LDF, local leaders, police, and community members to ensure the safety of witnesses. Despite these efforts, however, unidentified individuals killed approximately 15 genocide witnesses during the year. Although many fewer genocide witnesses were killed than in the previous year, many citizens still were too frightened to testify.
>
> (US Department of State 2006)

There is an additional source from outside of the country's borders that threatens not only potential witnesses, but also others who are viewed to be sympathetic to the current Rwandan government. According to a United Nations situation report for Rwanda, 'In September, the four western prefectures continued to be the site of attacks by insurgents and infiltrators, particularly against local officials and genocide survivors' (United Nations

1996b: 11). This concern further highlights the fact that the issues surrounding the Rwandan genocide must be viewed within a context of the Great Lakes region of Africa. The report states that many of the killings in these areas have been 'attributable to insurgents including members of the former Forces [Armées] Rwandaises (ex-FAR) and the Interahamwe militia' (United Nations 1996b). The majority of these attackers were located initially across the border in the Democratic Republic of Congo from where they planned and perpetrated their attacks.

According to Caplan *et al*, although repulsed by the Rwandan armed forces on two separate occasions, the proliferation of these attacks has increased security activities along the borders with the Congo (Caplan *et al* 2000: 208). More recently, the security of the border continues to be a concern as many genocide suspects are fleeing the Gacaca courts into the neighbouring countries. For example, one source reports that 'the Burundian government says that at least 5000 have fled to its territory alone since mid-March this year. Media reports also indicate that over 1000 have fled to Uganda' (Hirondelle News Agency 2005a).[1] According to another report the reason behind the exodus is fear: '"The threats became so serious that we were forced to flee" said Gaspard Sibururema. "They tell us that we will pay dearly for members of their families who died during the genocide" adds Isaie Nshimiyimana' (Hirondelle News Agency 2005b).

One final example of the range of these concerns is provided by the suspicious death of Juvenal Uwilingiyimana in Belgium in the fall of 2005.[2] A suicide letter was found some time after his body was discovered. The existence of this letter was argued as providing evidentiary proof that Uwilingiyimana had taken his own life. However, accusations have since come to light claiming that the letter is a forgery and that his death should be investigated for foul play. According to Hassan Bubacar Jallow, Chief ICTR Prosecutor, although a suspect under indictment by the ICTR, Uwilingiyimana had 'voluntarily agreed to cooperate [with the ICTR] in the search for truth and justice for the Rwandan genocide of 1994' (ICTR 2005/2006: 7). Furthermore, Jallow noted in the same press release that 'by cooperating with the Prosecutor such individuals mark themselves forever as traitors in some parts of their community and run the risk that vengeance will be undertaken against them or their families' (ICTR 2005/2006: 8).

Another source states that 'Alloys Mutabingwa, Rwandan envoy to the ICTR echoed Muyco's [Prosecutor General for Rwanda] assertions, saying Uwilingiyimana might have been assassinated by those who feared he would mention their names to the Tribunal' (Kimenyi and Baguma 2005: 1). The nature of the arrangement between Uwilingiyimana and the Office of the Prosecutor at the ICTR as well as his position in the former Rwandan government prior to and during the genocide suggests that he would be considered an insider witness of great value to the prosecution. Despite the extreme importance of this witness and the extraordinary measures taken to facilitate the meetings in Belgium between Uwilingiyimana and the ICTR investigators, as well as to protect him and his family from the perceived threat, his personal security remains a serious question: 'If it is determined that he was the victim of a homicide it will be clear that the protective measures were inadequate' (Kimenyi and Baguma 2005: 1).

The Rwandan government and the ICTR take a variety of measures into consideration in their attempt to ensure the safety of those who may find themselves victims of intimidation and possible violence. In 2004, after the process of reviewing the Gacaca courts, the Rwandan government recognized the need to address the concerns for the protection of witnesses. In the new Organic Law (No 16/2004 of 19/6/2004), they added Article 30 that states:

> Anyone who exercises pressures, attempts to exercise pressures or threatens the witnesses or the Seat members of the Gacaca shall incur a prison sentence from three (3) months to one (1) year. In the case of repeat offence, the defendant risks a prison penalty from six (6) months to two (2) years.
>
> Is regarded as an act of exercising pressures on a Court, anything aiming at coercing the Seat into doing against its will, translated into actions, words or a behaviour threatening the Seat, and clearly meaning that if the latter fails to comply with, some of its members or the entire Seat may face dangerous consequences. However, when the pressure is performed, provisions of the penal code of criminal procedure are applied by ordinary courts.
>
> Is considering as an attempt to exercise pressures on a Court, any behaviour translated into words or acts, showing that there has been an attempt to coerce a Court into taking a decision in a way or another.
>
> (Government of Rwanda 2004d)

This law clearly defines the act of interfering with witnesses and stipulated penalties that may result if one engages in such behaviour.

During an earlier visit to a Gacaca court in Kigali, in spring of 2004, a case was heard before the court concerning a woman who had allegedly coerced a witness to change his testimony before the court (although there was no evidence of an actual threat). The Gacaca process and deliberations resulted in the woman receiving a 2-year term of imprisonment for her actions. Although this current example does not quite fit precisely within the realm of protection for witnesses as discussed in this section, it does show that the government of Rwanda is nonetheless addressing the issue – especially when considering that the man whom this woman had persuaded to change testimony had himself previously received a term of imprisonment for perjury! The realm of protection extended in this type of instance not only prevents any form of persuasion of witnesses from occurring, but also speaks to a desire to ensure the overall integrity of the Gacaca proceedings.

Additional measures that are addressed within the context of the Gacaca courts are those that deal specifically with the crime of rape. In order to protect the victims from both coercion and the ordeal of testifying in public about their victimization, they may submit their complaints in writing to either a member of the Gacaca Seat or the Office of the Public Prosecutor. Furthermore, when the proceeding against the accused begins within the ordinary courts – as rape is a Category One offence and would end up in the Prosecutor's jurisdiction – there is a provision within Article 38 of the Gacaca Law that 'the formalities of the proceedings of the offence shall be conducted *in camera*' (Government of Rwanda 2004d)

The ICTR witness protection strategy

At the ICTR, a number of safeguards have been introduced to protect witnesses from the threat of violence and/or violence itself. Unlike what is observed in the Gacaca, which is entirely a public proceeding that does not afford any individuals the cloak of anonymity, the ICTR has introduced procedures that attempt to provide the witnesses with this safeguard:

> The ICTR has four categories of witnesses: expert (normally unprotected), protected witnesses, detainee witnesses (people detained in Rwandan jails, who also have their identities concealed) and lay witnesses who renounce their protected status. According to the ICTR section in charges of prosecution witnesses, about 95% of their witnesses are protected.
>
> (Crawford 2001: 1)

The clarification of these protective measures is found within the ICTR's Rules of Procedures in Articles 69, 70, and 75. In accordance with these rules, there are a number of strategies that can be used to try to provide anonymity and, hence, some degree of protection for the witnesses. These include:

(1) non-disclosure of the identity of witnesses;
(2) not compelling witnesses to answer questions that might compromise the witnesses' or other sources' identities;
(3) *in camera* proceedings; expunging names and other identifying features from public records; image- or voice-enhancing technology;
(4) the assignment of pseudonyms; closed sessions;
(5) and the use of one-way closed circuit television.

> (ICTR 2008)

Despite these provisions, there nevertheless remains no fool-proof way to protect a witness's identity. As a part of their investigation, for example, investigators can inadvertently 'out' (or identify) the witnesses by simply trying to contact a witness, arriving in a small village in UN vehicles, and being observed talking to an individual. The same point is made in a report presented by the International Federation of Defence Leagues:

> It is very difficult to maintain confidentiality on the identity of witnesses who leave their homes for weeks, more so as survivors – and hence the potential

witnesses – are quite well known by their neighbours ... Confidentiality is therefore only a theoretical notion, which only gives limited protection.

(Fondation Hirondelle 2003b: 5–6)

According to the same report, even greater concern is that the protections offered to the witnesses may not necessarily extend back to Rwanda once they have testified before the tribunal.

It was also noted by a source at the ICTR that the potential for identification and intimidation of witnesses was present due to the structure of the Witness and Victims Services Section. This section dealt with both defence and prosecution witnesses:

Last year [2004] for budgetary reasons, as I understand it, they [the separate programs for the prosecution and the defence] were amalgamated and so all of the staff ... could work with any kind of witness [both prosecution and defence]; and I can tell you that these allegations of tampering with witnesses may be a result of some of that.

(AA 2005)

Regarding the intimidation and/or threats and violence towards witnesses one must also take into consideration that there are, in fact, witnesses for both the prosecution and the defence. Despite the previous examples, that have described prosecution witnesses, examples do exist whereby similar tactics have allegedly been used towards defence witnesses. One such example came to light during the media trial presented in the previous chapter:

Mr. Martel [defence counsel for Hassan Ngeze] indicated that when RM 117 [protected witness] went to collect her travel documents, 'she was stopped from doing so by a group of Tutsis who abducted her and locked her up for more than 24 hours.' ... The witness only managed to escape because of a 'lull in her abductors' vigilance but she left the document behind. ... We fear for the security of the other three witnesses whose names were on the document.'

(Fondation Hirondelle 2003b)

A second and potentially more serious example, as it suggests that the Rwandan Government was the party responsible for the intimidation, surrounds the use of prosecution witnesses who are currently incarcerated in Rwanda either in custody awaiting trial or already incarcerated in Rwandan courts for their role in the 1994 genocide. According to one defence council, there remains an 'underlying suspicion, continuing suspicion of the defence, which in some cases is well-founded, but in others exaggerated, that witnesses are coached, prepared, taught to lie, told what lies to tell' (BB 2005). This concern and its prevalence amongst Rwandan prisoners were further discussed by another defence attorney working on a different case:

The problem with the witnesses that come, 90% of them are Hutus prisoners in jail who have been held. We had a guy last week, eleven years, no charges, no trials, and then suddenly they're released. Obviously, they testify here and they get released.

(HH 2005)

The promise of release, or the continued detention/incarceration within an overcrowded, unsanitary prison in Rwanda could easily be construed as an incentive, inducement, or threat towards individuals in exchange for their cooperation at the ICTR.[3]

The argument was also put forward by some defence attorneys that the Rwandan Government is also having a negative impact on the attorneys' attempts to mount a full defence by virtue of their scepticism regarding the genocide and the liability of representing accused who are well known in the public due to their political or military seniority. Potential witnesses for the defence are dissuaded from testifying for the simple fact that they will become known to the government since it must issue all travel documents to Arusha, and, thus, they may become viewed as sympathizers to the genocidaires. As a result, there is a great reluctance for witnesses to cooperate with the defence investigators and lawyers (GG 2005). This sentiment was also echoed for the cases taking place in the Rwandan courts: 'Defence counsel and witnesses continued to be intimidated causing the former to withdraw from trials and the latter to refuse to testify, aware that the prosecutorial staff would use their testimonies to implicate them in the crimes committed by defendants' (Amnesty International 2004: 7).

As a final comment on the issue of witness protection, there are some additional constraints present within the Rwandan context that are not legal in nature, but are cultural and geographical. Rwandan society, except perhaps in the capital city of Kigali, consists of small tight-knit communities, many of which have existed on a single hill for many generations. Within these communities, it is evident that there is a great deal of familiarity and awareness of all that transpires within each community and that communities are often linked through kinship ties throughout the entire country. There is an individual referred to as a *responsible* whose duty it is to be aware of all the activity that goes on within a grouping of approximately 10 houses (called 'the cell'). Above the cell is another individual who receives information from approximately 10 *responsibles* and so on and so forth. Based on this hierarchical and close-knit system of community in Rwanda, witness relocation would prove to be very difficult, especially given the small geographic size of the entire country.

As was noted previously, when people are absent from the community for a relatively small amount of time, their absence is recognized. Likewise, it may prove very difficult for individual witnesses to relocate into a new area for their own protection (due to their status as a witnesses), to relocate into a new area without their arrival being noticed and the reason for their move being discovered. With such an intricate system of social control existing in

Rwanda, it is very likely that any process of attempting to protect the identity of witnesses by relocating them would be difficult, if not futile.

These examples certainly raise serious concerns regarding the ability of both the Rwandan government and the ICTR, despite their best efforts, to provide adequate protection to witnesses of the 1994 genocide. According to a defence attorney at the ICTR 'There is, as a practical matter ... no way that this tribunal can protect you' (FF 2005).

Hearsay evidence

Despite the potential for controversy that may arise from the admission of hearsay evidence into a trial, it is readily apparent that its inclusion, albeit monitored to some degree, is present in the trials of the alleged perpetrators in Rwanda: 'Hearsay is defined as a statement that is made by someone other than the person testifying at the hearing and offered to prove the truth of the matter stated' (Strong and Dries 2005: 302). One possible reason for the judiciary to permit hearsay in these trials was put forward by a prosecutor at the ICTR:

> One must understand that a lot of the eye witnesses who might otherwise testify to what happened are dead. Those who survived hid and they might not have seen what was taking place at the roadblock because, if they had, they would have been killed. So, when they came back from where they hid, people talked about what happened and there's been information passed down from person to person. Hearsay evidence is a species of evidence which, in this imperfect world created by the slaughter, the tribunal admits in order to have more material upon which to consider the events; and if you get the same story being repeated by five or six different sources who say – 'this is what being said happened' – then it begins to look as if that might be what happened.
>
> (KK 2005)

Based on this observation, it appears that there has been a degree of latitude provided to hearsay testimony given the particular context in which the suspected crimes were observed to have taken place. Although the prosecutor was speaking directly to the circumstances of the ICTR, its inclusion it may be potentially extended to the situation of the judicial context within Rwanda as well. Investigations and prosecutions within Rwanda will most likely face the same challenges of finding individuals who survived the genocide, and actually witnessed the crimes, since they are employing similar tactics to evade becoming a witness as they employed to avoid the killings of 1994.

Additionally, according to Strong and Dries, hearsay is a contentious form of evidence, especially when the two competing systems of civil and common law come together in the tribunals (Strong and Dries 2005). Hearsay is 'an evidentiary issue that is well known in the common law tradition but which is virtually absent in the civil law tradition due to the non-adversarial nature of civilian judicial proceedings' (Strong and Dries 2005: 302). The melding of the two traditions of law within ICTR may provide an additional framework for the inclusion of hearsay evidence within the testimony at the tribunal. In attempting to merge the two traditions, there may have been an attempt to find a compromise in terms of how this potentially valuable, yet dangerous, testimony may be introduced and then dealt with in an acceptable manner. Furthermore, in achieving a contextual framework for the crimes that took place in Rwanda, Stewart stated that the approach taken by the ICTR incorporates:

> a method that [relies] on a more flexible reception of evidence. It's very important in these tribunals that you have essentially the continental approach to the reception of evidence. In Rule 89(c) which is one of the critical rules ... the ability of the trial chamber to receive any evidence that it inclines to be relevant and has probative value [is allowed], and that has opened the way to the use of hearsay evidence.
>
> (Stewart 2005)

For those attorneys coming from the common law background in their national jurisdictions, the inclusion of hearsay evidence appears to present a considerable challenge:

> The standard of evidence here, for the admissibility of evidence, is so broad, that anyone from a national jurisdiction in the common law system would feel that it's, they've fallen down a rabbit hole and things just get [more and more curious]; because basically, 99.5% of everything goes in. There's almost nothing that stays out [of evidence], and then everything that stays in, is then said to be considered for weight later on.
>
> (AA 2005)

With regard to the admission of hearsay statements into evidence at the ICTR, the chamber's comments in the *Akayesu* case provides some insight into the process. Evidence will be assessed by future chambers on an individual basis wherein an individual's testimony can be allowed to be entered into evidence on the basis of its probative value and then will be judged by the chamber 'according to its credibility and relevance to the allegations at issue' (*Prosecutor v Akayesu* 1998: para 131). One of the standards that is then applied by the chamber with regard to credibility of the individual testimony is founded in the civil law tradition, *unus tesits, nullus testis* (one witness is no witness), which, by extension, is argued that for an individual witness's testimony to be considered credible, it must be corroborated.[4] Even with the attempts to address credibility, there remains frustration and uncertainty on the part of some attorneys as to how and when this assessment should take place:

> Before deciding anything, you have to wait until all the evidence is in. Then with all the evidence in, we will assess issues of credibility. Here we know that what they probably do is look at one witness and they pretty well decide on that witness' credibility then and there. ... They really should wait until the end to assess the credibility.
>
> (GG 2005)

This defence attorney stated that the necessity for a preliminary assessment may be the result of the high numbers of witnesses that any given trial may call, the lengthy period of time over which a trial takes place, and the possible turn-over among judges. However, this initial assessment is not official and should be considered repeatedly in light of future witnesses who may verify or nullify a previous witness' testimony.

Another source of concerns raised by the attorneys is tied to both the witness protection concerns raised previously and the greater familiarity for some attorneys with the adversarial process because of their common law background. The protection of a witness's identity by allowing witnesses on the stand to keep their source of information confidential can be seen to conflict with the attorney's ability to cross-examine witnesses based on what they are claiming to be the facts in the case. An example of such a situation was presented in an interview with another defence attorney BB. In the process of cross-examining expert witness Alison Des Forges, there was reference made to a witness who had provided Des Forges with evidence that was under scrutiny in the trial:

> Eventually it came down to mentioning somebody's name that she is not prepared to give; [*presumably for fear of drying up her source as she needs to maintain the confidentiality of her sources for fear of their safety and continued provision of information*] which I have to say that I regard with some concern as a lawyer. Certainly in my country and within the jurisdiction of European connection of human rights, evidence from anonymous sources is frowned upon and not really permitted.
>
> (BB 2005, emphasis added)

The ability of the tribunal to balance legal protection of the rights of the accused in this case with the safety of the protected source appears to remain a delicate situation that will undoubtedly continue to arise over the course of the remaining trials. Provided that the chambers are able to succeed in the process of attaching appropriate weight to a given statement made by a witness, the inclusion of hearsay evidence is likely to be a persistent feature of the tribunal.

Hearsay evidence within the Rwandan courts and the Gacaca occurs, in part, because of the oral tradition that is dominant throughout Rwandan culture. A linguist and an expert witness at the ICTR, Mathais Ruzindana, addressed the existence of such a tradition in the *Akayesu* trial. In referencing some of the cultural elements that were perceived to have an effect on the statements made by witnesses, Ruzindana stated that 'most Rwandans live in an oral tradition in which facts are reported as they are perceived by the witness, often irrespective of whether the facts were personally witnessed or recounted by someone else' (*Prosecutor v Akayesu* 1998). Amnesty International reports that 'witnesses for the prosecution frequently give no evidence at all or evidence that is hearsay or circumstantial' (Amnesty International 2004: 4).

It was not uncommon at those Gacaca courts that were visited to have individuals report that they had information for the court that had been told to them by another person. It was not completely clear, in large part due to using a translator (as the cases are all presented in Kinyarwanda), whether the judges were stating any concerns or objections with regard to the introduction of hearsay evidence. Unlike the ICTR, there were no specific guidelines in Gacaca law to address the remedies that might be taken if the Inyangamugayos were presented with such a situation. In fact, it appears that the use of hearsay evidence is granted allowance. Under Article 29, which mandates the duty of all Rwandans to participate, there is a distinction made between what someone has seen and what they know, but the law requires that both be presented to the Gacaca.[5]

Both the ICTR and the courts in Rwanda (both the Gacaca and the regular judiciary) are facing a continuing dilemma regarding the allowance of hearsay evidence into the court proceedings. The amalgamation of the common law tradition (that typically finds hearsay as unreliable and therefore excludes it) and the civil law tradition (which is more sympathetic to hearsay evidence due its reliance upon judicial fact-finding) presents those involved in these discussions with an interesting and challenging dynamic that remains to be fully clarified and integrated into a single working model.

Given that all three realms were observed to be very dependent on the use of eyewitness testimony, there has been a great deal of latitude given to the admission of hearsay evidence as each judicial realm appeared to be very reluctant to censure their most significant source of facts. More specifically relating to the Gacaca, recognition of the collective nature of traditional Rwandan culture and its oral tradition was evident in the failure of the law to differentiate between knowledge based on individual experience and that based on what an individual was told by others and its probative value. So, while it has become relatively clear *how* the issue of hearsay is incorporated into the judicial realms, it is not clear how each is able to address the issue while avoiding the possibility of making erroneous deductions based on this form of questionable evidence.

Plea bargaining: negating a judicial outcome

The use of a negotiated guilty plea is a common practice in many Western judiciaries. According to Brannigan, 'of all the charges laid by police in criminal matters, only a small fraction ever go to a higher court to be tried by a judge and jury. The vast majority are disposed of in the lower courts by a magistrate' (Brannigan 1984: 135). The process of plea bargaining is utilized by both the prosecution and defence based on a number of motivating factors. Concerning the motivation on the part of the defendant:

> most criminologists argue that ... no matter what he or she might have originally done, [the motive] is to get away with the smallest penalty and/ or least serious police record as possible; in other words, the accused is rewarded for cooperation by facing a less severe penalty.
>
> (Brannigan 1984: 136)

An additional motivating factor for a given defendant is that, especially in a case in a which there is a recognition or understanding of the accused that they are in fact guilty, is that to proceed in a trial, 'one has to make a defence against the charge, something that is difficult if the evidence is clear cut' (Brannigan 1984).

Finally, the expediency argument may effect a decision to avoid trial by utilizing a negotiated plea agreement. According to this argument, which has not fully been supported in the research but does nevertheless represent a commonplace understanding of the process, the use of pleas is a means for avoiding the time, effort, and expense that going to trial would incur: 'If everyone facing criminal charges elected to have his or her case heard at a trial, the already crowded court calendar would face mayhem. Delays would be interminable' (Brannigan 1984). Given these motivations, it is not surprising that plea bargaining has become a well-used tool in the context of Western judiciaries. Within the context of Rwanda, it is equally not surprising that this judicial tool has been incorporated into the process for adjudicating the accused genocidaires. There are a number of issues, however, that have been raised with regard to the use of a negotiated plea within the trials taking place in Rwanda and at the ICTR.

The confession procedure within Rwanda

Not only has the use of plea bargaining simply been incorporated into the Rwandan judicial system, it has been referred to as 'the cornerstone of the Rwandan justice system' (Penal Reform International 2003).[6] In the years following the genocide, the Rwandan national judiciary has not been in a position to address the vast numbers of trials that were perceived to be required:

> Different strategies were used so as to speed up the court process for those accused of genocide: 'collective court-cases' of groups of people having committed the same crimes together, 'travelling' court where the courts would sit at the same location as the crimes committed, using a confession procedure and presenting the accused to the local population.
>
> (Penal Reform International 2003: 3)

These last two strategies, the creation of the Gacaca courts combined with the confession procedure, were viewed as essential by the Rwandan government as a way to expedite the trials of the genocide suspects and reduce the severely overcrowded prison system: '[t]he confession procedure seems to have taken inspiration from the Anglo-Saxon "plea bargaining" system whereby the defendant is allowed to plead guilty for a reduced sentence' (Penal Reform International 2003: 3). In the case of Rwanda, the motives behind the procedures for confessions and negotiated pleas were undoubtedly expediency, the avoidance of system capacity overload within the regular judiciary, and the attempt for a reduced sentence on the part of the defendant, which is congruent with the plea bargaining system in many Western countries.

The approach in the regular Rwandan judiciary to incorporate guilty pleas and confessions was then integrated in written form directly into the Gacaca Organic Law. Chapter II: Procedure of Confessions, Guilt Plea, Repentance and Apologies specifically outlines the government's adaptation of the negotiated guilty plea in the Gacaca proceedings,[7] Chapter III: Hearing and Judgement (Articles 64–67), and Chapter IV: Penalties (Articles 72–88). The motivating factor for the defendants accused of the various genocide crimes as articulated in the Organic Law is a significant reduction in their term of imprisonment. Another significant aspect in the reduction of penalties relates to *when* the defendant decides to take recourse of the confession procedure.[8] 'One may make a guilty plea at any time, but at the latest when the accused has been to court' (Penal Reform International 2003: 8). Depending on when they engaged in the confession procedure, those individuals whose crimes would have placed them in Category One of the Organic Law, could have had their sentence reduced from either the death penalty under the old law or life imprisonment to 25 to 30 years' imprisonment; defendants falling into Category Two, from 25 to 30 years' imprisonment to as low as 7 to 12 years. Those defendants, whose crimes place them in the second category of offences, and who use the guilty plea procedure, are granted an additional prison reprieve: half of their determined sentence is commuted into community service under an order of probation.

Although there is an apparent sentencing advantage for those defendants who use the confessions procedure, the sentence reduction is only applicable to the term of imprisonment and not for the additional penalties outlined in the Organic Law. There is no mention in the confessions procedure for any changes in sentencing with regard to the loss of civil liberties that an individual charged in Category One or point 1° of Category Two may incur. The strict prohibitions and limitations that accompany a conviction for those crimes appear to remain outside of the scope of sentence reduction in the confessions procedure. Unlike in some other national jurisdictions within which a reward for cooperation may include a reduction to the least serious police record, this does not present itself in the Rwandan confessions procedure.

Even after the accused has pleaded guilty to his or her crimes, the confession procedure states that the confession must be evaluated by the Gacaca

Seat as to its completeness. The requirements necessary to have one's plea accepted by the court are threefold as laid out in Article 54 of the Organic Law. In a Gacaca court that was attended in the district of Kanombe, after reading the requisite laws of the Gacaca, the Inyangamugayos read the statement of confession publicly to those in attendance. All of the aspects of the confession were investigated by the Inyangamugayos through the course of lengthy discussion that included anyone in attendance who professed to have information regarding the case. After a time of deliberation in private, the Inyangamugayos returned their verdict of acceptance of the confession and pronounced the requisite sentence in compliance with the Organic Law.

As of 2002, there was evidence that suggested that the confessions procedure was achieving positive results in the government's goal of reducing the caseload before the courts and reducing some of the prison population. Many of the prisoners have been incarcerated in Rwandan prisons since their arrests in 1994. A large number, given the sentence reductions, will have served much of the required time in jail. Another potential benefit as a result of the process is the provision of information these prisoners' confessions provided. The information provided first hand accounts of what happened in 1994 and assisted in establishing a record of what happened. They also provide victims with answers to questions previously unknown to them regarding missing family members, although there are noted regional differences. According to a Penal Reform International report, [I]n fact a third of the prisoners had confessed by the end of 2002' (Penal Reform International 2003: 5). During that year, two factors may have contributed to the noted rise in confessions in the second half of the year: the launching of the pilot courts of the Gacaca, and the Rwandan Government's efforts to provide information to the prisoners, educating them on the confessions procedure and its benefits (Penal Reform International 2003).

Despite these noted successes, there have been a number of criticisms and concerns levied against the confession procedure. One of the criticisms reported by Penal Reform International discusses the veracity of the pleas presented before the courts. According to the report:

> It is not unusual, as one would expect, that the inmates make partial confessions (when they know that proof exists of their guilt), or confess to minor misdemeanours. Certain inmates – but also those who are not in prison – try to present credible testimonies in order to save other inmates and to accuse individuals who are deceased, in exile or who are their enemies (false testimonies).
>
> (Penal Reform International 2003: 8)

Given that the Gacaca judges are not trained investigators and their voluntary status does not afford them the time that may be required to perform full investigations, and the potential for a massive number of defendants, the truthfulness of many confessions is likely never to be known. However, research into the confession records has shown that this concern may be somewhat, though not completely, overstated. In looking at the records, 'the table shows that more than 80% of the inmates are classed in Category n° 2, which corroborates the estimates we already have made. ... these confessions are surprising by the high number of serious crimes recorded' (Penal Reform International 2003: 9).

A further concern that becomes apparent in the search for justice is that the confession procedure has become a real concern for those who are currently incarcerated but who are, in fact, innocent. For individuals incarcerated in an overcrowded Rwandan prison for any significant length of time, there may be an incentive to plead guilty to a crime, even though innocent, as a means to end the time spent in jail:

> Encouragement to plead guilty ... and according benefit to those who do so could be detrimental to those prisoners who are innocent or who do not have a case and seems to go against the penal principle of the 'presumption of innocence' creating a 'presumption of guilt'.
>
> (Penal Reform International 2003: 4)

The idea that the *burden of proof*, a presumption of guilt rather than innocence, falls on the accused rather than on the court is disputed to a degree by Rwandan authorities. According to Prosecutor Mutangana, even though there is no prosecutor present in the Gacaca and it might appear that the burden of proof lies with the accused, the judges still operate with a file that has been investigated by the prosecution office. 'They will not take the burden of proof to lie on the accused first; it is based on what the prosecutor did' (Mutangana 2005). In the event that the individual decides to plead guilty to a crime, the consideration surrounding the burden of proof is that the accused is required to defend the authenticity of his or her confession.

A final concern that arises out of the confession procedure is that this procedure, which is the result of the adoption of part of an Anglo-Saxon model that is primarily adversarial in nature, conflicts with the cultural history of traditional law in Rwandan society.[9] More specifically, 'confessing in front of victims is considered an insult and [an] aggravating circumstance as it is considered to be a show of force' (Penal Reform International 2003: 3). This circumstance appears to have been confirmed in the Penal Reform International research, and suggests that the adoption of this process is in contradiction to what traditionally would have occurred in Rwanda. This may have an impact on the process of reconciliation, as there remain questions over the sincerity of the accused confessions and apologies.[10]

There will need to be, on the part of the officials in charge of the confessions procedure, a recognition of these potential difficulties if the system of confessions is to operate and achieve the stated goals.[11] Attempts to balance the need for expediency with the criticisms that have arisen from the process in action will present a challenge for the government. As discussed in Chapter

3, the government does appear to demonstrate a great deal of agency and the ability to make changes as issues arise.

The ICTR

The use of a negotiated plea agreement was observed to have been the exception rather than the rule at the ICTR. The lack of plea bargaining has been cited as one of the reasons for the slow progress attributed to the work at the ICTR.[12] Despite the fact that the President of the Tribunal, Judge Erik Møse, alluded to the possible increase in its use at the ICTR, compared with the ICTY, it has not been utilized to the same extent in prosecuting the accused. The operating rules and procedures of this judicial system do not explicitly negate the use of plea bargaining within its rules or procedures. The question remains, that given the restrictive time mandate under which the ICTR is operating and the observed length of some of the multi-accused trials, why it is that negotiated pleas have not been more utilized in an effort to achieve the expediency required to achieve its mandate?

The concept of inefficiency aside, there appears to be an additional significant motivation on the part of the prosecution when seeking a negotiated plea that has remained, for most part, under-recognized in the Office of the Prosecutor (ie the utility of a plea agreement in exchange for cooperation of the accused as an *insider witness* against other accused). In one interview, a senior investigator reiterated the difficulty of actually proving complicity in genocide, the organization and planning that occurred prior to the actual carrying out the *actus reus* of the plan (LL 2005). In order to obtain reliable information regarding meetings that took place and the plans developed at those meetings, it is imperative to have as a witness someone who was actually a participant in the meeting. Furthermore, one prosecutor additionally noted that the value of the insider witness is also seen in terms of reducing courtroom time:

> One of the associated problems with not having an incentive to plead guilty, there has also been a whole collection of people who have been targets that would have been excellent witnesses, the insiders, and we have not capitalized on the availability of insider witnesses that would allow the other trials that go forth to shorten up. So what we are faced with in the other trials is calling dozens of witnesses ... That one insider would have devastated [the defence].
>
> (AA 2005)

An initial factor that must be considered is the perception of justice that the ICTR is trying to achieve. Can anyone, in good conscience, engage in any kind of plea agreement with someone accused of committing genocide, the *crime of crimes*? There is also the fact that the international community is watching the cases being tried at the ICTR. One defence attorney interviewed at the ICTR stated:

These cases have international exposure. How would the international community see, in a case like my client, how could you give a bourgmestre life and give my guy fifteen years? They [the ICTR] are accountable before the United Nations. If they propose some type of deal like that they have to substantiate the reasons why.

(GG 2005)

The ICTR, in conjunction with the concept of concurrent jurisdiction with Rwanda and their continuing need for cooperation from the Rwandan Government, must also give consideration to any concerns regarding plea agreements stemming from within Rwanda. One example of a disagreement between the two jurisdictions is with regard to a plea agreement whereby the accused will plead guilty to a lesser charge such as crimes against humanity, which tend to carry a less punitive sanction than genocide. The inclusion of this method of plea bargaining was rejected outright by the Rwandan Government, which voiced its concerns to the ICTR: "'Agreeing to abandon the charge of genocide while plea bargaining is highly detrimental," said envoy Mutabingwa in a press release. "It could be construed as a new approach to negate genocide that undoubtedly occurred in Rwanda'" (Hirondelle News Agency 2006). Although disputed by the Deputy Prosecutor, Christopher Bongani Majola, in the same news item, he nevertheless stated that this process demonstrated a possible additional constraint faced by the prosecution in attempting to re-examine the use of plea bargaining at the ICTR.

If indeed there is, a decision to advance a plea agreement, the obstacle that then arises is what can the prosecutor offer to such an individual? The answer to at least one aspect of this question is that there is no agreement on the sentence that may be imposed upon the accused. This precedent has already been established in the *Kambanda* case and was likely one of the main reasons that further pleas were not negotiated until fairly recently. According to a defence attorney, the Kambanda ruling has essentially removed a key aspect for bargaining: 'How can anybody plead guilty to first degree murder, why would you plead guilty to first degree murder, sentenced to life, minimum 25 [years]. You might as well take your chances and go to trial' (GG 2005).

There may exist some latitude in future attempts to make plea bargains not involving the length of the sentence *per se* that might be utilized. The UN detention centre in an undisclosed location in the vicinity of Arusha is only used for pre-trial detention. Given the fact that the ICTR, and by extension, the United Nations, does not have a full-time dedicated prison, there possibly remains some options as to where in the world the sentence will be carried out. Provided that there is a list of potential host countries that have agreed to assist the United Nations in accommodating the convicted persons for the period of their incarceration, there may be some latitude for the prosecutor in arranging the sentence to be served in a more desirable location.[13] There is the related question as to whether an accused tried in a European location or transferred there might not benefit from the normal programmes of conditional release even with a nominally 'life' sentence.

The location of imprisonment also carries with it one substantial consideration: parole. The ICTR Statute does not specifically address in its statute or in the judgements handed down by the court, as of this date, any clarification of the specific nature of the sentence to life imprisonment. Some national jurisdictions, however, do provide for sentencing options that include eligibility for parole at various points in time. Others provide for alternatives to parole such as mandatory supervision. According to a senior investigator, for individuals convicted at the ICTR to serve their sentence in a jurisdiction that may allow for the possibility of parole, may be a significant bargaining chip for the prosecutor in future negotiations (LL 2005).

The final concern to an accused who is considering a plea agreement is the safety of his/her family. According to one senior investigator, this is the main reason why someone may agree to cooperate with the prosecution. However, he also stated that it is not without its challenges: 'For instance, we have to put security measures [in place] for the family [and have in place] an agreement with another country to change their identities. It is a very difficult issue to resolve' (LL 2005). Finding a country that is willing to accept the family of a convicted genocidaire is not an easy task.

There have only been a handful of guilty pleas tendered at the ICTR thus far. The *Kambanda* case appears to have set a precedent of mistrust on the part of the defendants and their attorneys as they were led to believe he would receive a sentence of only 12 years, but was subsequently sentenced to life imprisonment. Furthermore, given that the sentence is being served in Mali, it is imprisonment for life without the possibility of parole or other forms of supervised release. The case of Uwilingiyimana now appears to be the only case wherein it was reported that the defendant had planned to plead guilty of his own accord, in Belgium, and to testify against the other involved in the highest levels of the genocide planning. As noted above, Uwilingiyimana died under mysterious circumstances before the arrangement between himself and the ICTR was actually realized.

In this chapter, there has been a greater focus on the pragmatics of the application of law within the context of an *ad hoc* tribunal and a national judiciary operating in concurrent jurisdiction. The findings suggest that without a more clearly defined understanding of the process of finding, preparing, and protecting the witnesses, serious questions will continue to plague the various courts with regard to their efficiency in achieving justice while at the same time protecting their most essential element, the witnesses.

The policies regarding hearsay raise similar concerns. While the policies are observed to maximize the evidence that is admissible in court, they risk achieving convictions on the basis of potentially questionable evidence. While in the short term this may secure a conviction, it remains to be seen how it will stand up to appeal and the perception of achieving justice. Finally, there are misgivings evident in the plea bargaining process. Within the Gacaca, the process presents a situation whereby the innocent may actually plead guilty due to the perceived benefits associated with that plea. On the part of the ICTR, there remains a sense of ambiguity regarding plea bargaining. While not formally forbidden by the tribunal, this avenue, despite its potential usefulness in both efficiency as well as securing reliable evidence from co-conspirators of the genocide, remains surprisingly absent.

The issues discussed throughout this chapter, along with those of the previous chapter, highlight the conflict that can arise between the pragmatics of case completion and achieving justice, which then may then lead to setting valuable precedents for the future. This is crucial if justice is a perception as stated at the beginning of the chapter, then it is important to be sure that the job has been done well to ensure that the perception is that justice has been served. Finally, it should be stated that this chapter represents only a sample of the issues that have come to the foreground in the attempt to seek justice across the various realms of the judicial response. A more thorough examination needs to address such additional topics as: (1) the limited appeals process: (2) the transfer of cases from the ICTR to other jurisdictions: (3) the assistance of other countries (or their reluctance or outright refusal to assist) in the various aspects of the adjudication process: and (4) a more in-depth investigation into those crimes allegedly committed by RPF soldiers and the situation of their accountability.

Notes

1 It should be noted that, within the same article, the Rwandan government disputes the figure of 6,000 stating that 1,475 persons is a more accurate figure. Despite the 'dispute' over actual numbers, there is nevertheless an apparent trend, and therefore concern, with the number of people attempting to escape the Gacaca by fleeing Rwanda into neighbouring countries. Additionally, the government has created a commission to address this issue and has been involved in a process of sensitization as to the process and functioning of the Gacaca courts and, as such, has not only attempted to alleviate the fears of those considering the idea of fleeing the jurisdiction, but has also, although with limited success, achieved the repatriation of some who had previously fled.
2 There is an interesting controversy regarding the death of Juvenal Uwilingiyimana, particularly surrounding an alleged suicide note that surfaced only some time after his death. According to International Crimes Blog (a source that was forwarded to the researcher by Christopher Black, a defence attorney at the ICTR), the two sides of the controversy surrounding the letter include the following:

> The ICTR Prosecutor, Hassan Bubacar Jallow, stated in a December 23 press release that his office has never received a copy of the November 5 letter from Uwilingiyimana. Moreover, the Prosecutor identified 'powerful persons in the Rwandan exile community' as the source of Mr. Uwilingiyimana's fears in the weeks before his disappearance and ultimate death. Mr. Jallow stated that these fears were expressed orally in the context of interviews with I.C.T.R. investigators during November 2005.
> By contrast, the letter identifies Canadian investigators as the source of direct threats to the physical well-being of Mr. Uwilingiyimana. In it, the writer

[who it is claimed by the I.C.T.R. has not been identified] expresses a desire to cease cooperation with I.C.T.R. investigators based on these fears. This sentiment contradicts the Prosecutor's statement that the cooperation with the I.C.T.R. was ongoing and voluntary until the time of the accused former Rwandan Minister of Commerce's disappearance.
Mr. Black asserts that his client and other prisoners have confirmed the authenticity of the signature on the [suicide] letter.

(Black 2006)

With regard to the 'suspicious' circumstances of his death, see Black 2006.
3 It certainly appears that HH is referring to actions that are not ethical. However, it might be the case that, given the plea structure in Rwanda, the witnesses' cooperation at the ICTR may be part of their plea agreement within the Rwandan judicial system. That was not clarified by HH and, given other statements that were made by him during the interview, his intention was to suggest one of unethical behaviour.
4 There is an exception to this test for the cases of sexual assault whereby the *Tadic* decision at the ICTY dealt with the application of Rule 96(i) and declared that in this instance there was no need for corroboration:

Rule 96: Rules of Evidence in Cases of Sexual Assault
In cases of sexual assault:
(i) Notwithstanding Rule 90 (C), no corroboration of the victim's testimony shall be required;
(ii) Consent shall not be allowed as a defence if the victim:
(a) Has been subjected to or threatened with or has had reason to fear violence, duress, detention or psychological oppression; or
(b) Reasonably believed that if the victim did not submit, another might be so subjected, threatened or put in fear;
(iii) Before evidence of the victim's consent is admitted, the accused shall satisfy the Trial Chamber *in camera* that the evidence is relevant and credible;
(iv) Prior sexual conduct of the victim shall not be admitted in evidence or as defence.

(ICTR 2008)

5 Article 29 specifically states, 'Any person who refuses to testify on what he or she has seen or on what he or [she] knows ... [incurs liability]' (Government of Rwanda 2004d)
6 Since the inception of the Gacaca courts, penal reform has been involved in an ongoing research project that has been dedicated to providing, understanding, and discussing this system of justice and its benefits and concerns. They have generated numerous reports on the subject that were provided to the researcher over the course of the three research visits to Rwanda. The researcher met on numerous occasions with the first chief researcher Klaas De Jonge as well as the Chef du Mission Jean Charles Paras (both of whom have since moved on to other projects with Penal Reform International).
7 **Chapter II: Procedure of Confessions, Guilt Plea, repentance and Apologies**
Section One: Acceptance of Confessions, Guilt Plea, repentance and Apologies and Conditions Required
Article 54:
Any person who had committed offences aimed at in Article one of this organic law has the right to have recourse to the procedure of confession, guilt plea, repentance and apologies.

Apologies shall be made publicly to the victims in case they are still alive and to the Rwandan society.

To be accepted as confessions, guilt plea, repentance and apologies, the defendant must:
1° give detailed description of the confessed offence, how he or she carried it out and where, when he or she committed it, witnesses to the facts, persons victimized and where he or she threw their dead bodies and damage caused;
2° reveal the co-authors, accomplices and any other information useful to the exercise of the public action;
3° apologize for the offence that he or she has committed.

Article 55:

Genocide perpetrators coming under the first category who have recourse to the procedure of confessions, guilt plea, repentance and apologies for their offences before their names appear on the list drawn up by the Gacaca Court of the Cell, shall enjoy commutation of penalties in the way provided in this organic law.

Article 56:

Shall enjoy commutation of penalties in the way provided for in this organic law, persons in the 2nd category who:
1° confesses, pleads guilty, repents, apologizes before the Gacaca Court of the Cell draws up a list of authors of genocide;
2° already appearing on this list, have no recourse to the procedure of confessions, guilt plea, repentance and apologies after publication of the list of authors of genocide.

Article 57:

If it is found out subsequently offences that a person has not confessed, he or she is prosecuted, at any time, for these offences and shall be classified in the category in which the committed offence place him or her, and is punishable by the maximum penalty for this category.

Section Two: Procedure of confessions, guilt plea, repentance and apologies
Article 58:

The confessions, guilt plea, repentance and apologies are done before the Seat of the Gacaca Court, before the Officer for the criminal investigation or the Officer for the Public Prosecution in charge of investigating the case, in accordance with article 46 of this organic law.

The Seat for the Gacaca Court, the Officer for the criminal investigation or the Officer for the Public Prosecution in charge of investigating the case, must inform the defendant of his right and benefits from the confessions, guilt plea, repentance and apologies procedure.

Sub-section One: Procedure of confessions, guilt plea, repentance and apologies before the Officer for the criminal investigation or the Officer for the Public Prosecution
Article 59:

For files which are not yet forwarded to the Gacaca Courts of the Cells, the criminal investigations department or the public prosecutions receives the confessions, guilt pleas, repentance and apologies. The conclusion from confessions, guilt pleas, repentance and apologies shall be transcribed by an Officer of the criminal investigation or the Public Prosecutor. If confessions are forwarded in writing, the Officer of the criminal investigation or the Public Prosecution asks the petitioner to endorse it.

The petitioner signs or marks with a fingerprint the minute containing the confessions, guilt pleas, repentance and apologies and confirms what has been approved, as well as the minute containing confessions, if there is any, before the Officer of the criminal investigation or the Public Prosecutor who also endorses it.

Article 60:

If the Public Prosecutor finds that the confessions, guilt pleas, repentance and apologies are in conformity with the required conditions, he or she concludes the

file by establishing a note of investigation containing the petitioner's declarations
and forwards it to the competent Gacaca Court of the Cell.

If the Public Prosecutor finds that the confessions, guilt pleas, repentance and
apologies do note meet the required conditions or that the investigation has
revealed that the petitioner's confessions, guilt pleas, repentance and apologies are
false, he or she states in an explanatory note the elements missing, concludes the
file, and forwards it to the competent Gacaca Court of the Cell.

The Gacaca Court of the Cell, after checking if the confessions, guilt pleas,
repentance and apologies done before the Officer of criminal investigation or the
Public Prosecutor are complete, accepts or rejects them.

(Government of Rwanda 2004d)

8 According to Penal Reform International, the deadline for confessing to crimes
before the creation of the 'lists', and, as a result, benefit in the sentence reduction,
was 15 May 2003. On the Government of Rwanda website there are currently
approximately 2000 individuals who have been placed on the list of Category One
offenders (see www.gov.rw/government/category1.htm).

9 Penal Reform International makes reference in their report to the observations of
the traditional Rwandan law as discussed by Charles Ntampaka. He is quoted in
the report as saying:

When we talk of *gacaca*, two main characteristics can be pointed out: the
active role played by the population in determining the laws and the conciliatory nature of the decisions taken. The custom is that it is preferable to
come to an agreement than go to court. Taking someone to court should only
be a last resort.

(Penal Reform International 2003: 3)

10 According to Penal Reform International:

Some onlookers didn't show any emotion at all. Others listened seriously with
mixed feelings of anxiety, disbelief, shame and anger at what the detainees had
to tell. Not only because of the terrible crimes revealed and the naming of
accomplices who are still at large, but also owing to the often arrogant way
the confessions were made: standing in the middle of the grass field the men
(there were no women among the detainees) often spoke in a loud aggressive
voice, a stream of words expressed without any visible sign of feeling or
remorse, ending in vociferous attempts to pressure the victims to pardon them
immediately, on the spot. From the way some detainees acted, insisting on
being pardoned, it looked as if they didn't realize that although victims may
accept the apologies of the perpetrators, they also have the choice to refuse or
ignore them, and that the non-acceptance of the apology by the victim, does
not necessarily mean that a confession will not be accepted as sincere and
complete. This will be decided by the *Gacaca* judges after hearing the cases,
not by the victim.

(Penal Reform International 2002: 15)

11 See the various Penal Reform International reports for a more complete evaluation
of the confession procedure and the recommendations that have been proposed to
try and deal with the issues observed to be potentially undermining the process.

12 The lack of plea bargaining, albeit a repeated source of complaint with regard to
the tribunal's inefficiency, is observed to have seen improvements in 2004–5, which,
according to White, although perhaps not enough to save the whole process in
terms of efficiency, will show improvements (White 2005).

13 Although there are no specifics with regard to potential host countries for accommodating the sentences, there is likely little argument that prison conditions vary quite substantially over many different jurisdictions. This is substantiated by the observation that in order for Rwanda to house some of the convicted persons after the closing of the tribunal, it was necessary for a new and up-to-date facility to be constructed in Rwanda that would conform to at the least the minimum standards deemed acceptable by the United Nations for housing convicts.

8 Conclusions, predictions, and reflections

We're managing to work out some of those processes, some of them administrative, a few of them jurisprudential, that will hopefully assist the ICC in
carrying forth its mandate. Maybe it's not going to be in terms of the positive
things ... it's going to be in terms of what the negative things are ...
maybe its just in terms of those kinds of negative lessons that the whole process is going to work. ... I'm not sure that the actual jurisprudence is going to
survive so much as just the legacy of having done it, having gotten through it,
of having got past the first sort of the philosophical Nuremburg of 'it can be
done,' but, do we have the will to carry it forth administratively? How are we
going to do it? And what have we learned through the ICTR and ICTY?
Maybe that's it.

(White 2005)

Overall judgements

This book began with a description of observations made of the Gacaca court
operating in the district of Kanombe, a community just outside of the capital
city, Kigali. This particular court was part of the pilot-project of the National
Service of Gacaca Jurisdictions that was begun in 2002. Based on observations made following the launch of the pilot-project and research into the
effectiveness and feasibility of these courts, changes were made to the Organic
Law. In 2005, the Rwandan Government launched the revised Gacaca
nationally in each of the 9,100 cells throughout the entire country. While it
will take several years to determine how successful the Gacaca are in achieving their mandate, in the meantime it is possible to try and understand this
process and to draw some initial conclusions about the Gacaca, the national
judiciary, and the ICTR. Operating parallel to each other across different
realms of Rwandan society, these three separate judicial systems all share a
common search for *justice*. How they approach the achieving of that mandate
is different. Their prospects for success are related to the Rwandan definitions
of justice and methods for seeking it.

While at first glance, there appears to be a real sense of continuity existing between the three realms of the judicial response based on their increased cooperation and transfer of cases, there is an unfortunate discontinuity pervasive in the judicial responses to genocide in Rwanda. This discontinuity is greatest with regard to actual practice of justice. The distribution of both the numbers of cases and the resources allocated to each case is severely disproportionate given each realm's mandate. The Gacaca, on the one hand, is addressing the majority of the cases, and yet receives the least amount of funding and is forced to rely instead on the dedication of an enormous number of volunteers. On the other hand, the ICTR manages the fewest cases while absorbing the bulk of the resources expended in adjudicating accused genocidaires. What has been observed is that the annual budget for the ICTR, whatever one may say about its adequacy in the face of the demands on it, is approximately 200 times that of the entire Rwandan judiciary, a judiciary that must contend not only with the unprecedented caseload of genocide crimes but also the normal crimes that any national judiciary would face. Yet, the disparity in the cases that have been, or will be, processed in each realm is inversely disproportionate. By the end of its mandate, the ICTR is projected to have tried approximately 90 cases, the national courts in Rwanda, 77,000, and the Gacaca, 740,000 cases (not including the categorization of the approximately 77,000 transferred to the national courts).

Furthermore, there has been a distinctive lack of cohesiveness and cooperation between what is occurring within the borders of Rwanda and at the ICTR in Arusha. The *politics* of justice are interfering with the *administration* of justice. However, it should be noted that many of the instances of conflict, including witness protection, witness transportation, and the transfer of cases to Rwandan jurisdiction, have been or are being resolved at least to some degree. There nevertheless remains one significant aspect of the relationship that will continue to cause tension and hamper the realization of an overall achievement of justice for all the victims of the crimes committed during the armed conflict – the ICTR jurisdictional right to process the cases of war crimes and crimes against humanity allegedly perpetrated by members of the RPF. However, in recent days, this also appears to be in the early stages of garnering positive developments on the part of both the ICTR and, more impressively, the Rwandan Government. Trials of former RPF soldiers for crimes committed during the genocide have been handled in the military courts in Rwanda although information about these trials is sparse and has not been put into the public arena for consumption. However, recent events have brought these crimes to the forefront of discussion. A report from the *World News Journal* (13 June 2008) states that four members of the RPF were arrested in Kigali in conjunction with 'the 1994 assassination of 13 leaders of the Catholic Church in Kabgayi, including the archbishop of Rwanda' (Anonymous 2008). Although accusations of political placating are rampant within this news item, any progress toward seeking a more balanced docket at the ICTR should be seen as a positive step.

The Gacaca

The modernization and incorporation of the traditional Rwandan dispute resolution mechanism into a judicial process that is mandated to respond to a potential caseload estimated at over 800,000 accused represents a judicial experiment of a magnitude never before attempted. The policy of maximal accountability that was instituted by the Rwandan government in response to the high degree of complicity of the general population in the crimes committed in 1994, while perhaps understandable given the context in which it was developed, has resulted in the creation of a monumental task. The Gacaca would appear destined to fail in its original formulation if not for the flexibility and agency of those engaged in managing it.

The Rwandan national judiciary

Given the near total destruction of the judiciary in the aftermath of the genocide and the lack of resources, despite international donations of funds, the Rwandan national judiciary is not functioning in a manner that will permit it to address the cases of Category One offences transferred from the Gacaca. The efforts to rebuild a judiciary from virtually nothing, as well as the construction of one that operates at a standard greater than those observed throughout the majority of other African states, are huge tasks in and of themselves. These efforts should not only be applauded, but should also be recognized as contributing to the establishment of a system of justice worthy of its title. Given the historical antecedent of the current system, the newly-created system, guided in large part by a constitution built upon a firm foundation of judicial principles, may develop over time the respect and appreciation of the entire Rwandan society, reversing the negativity that was previously experienced.

However, within the context of the current enterprise, it appears to be overly optimistic that, in its current stage, the national judiciary will be in a position to address its standing mandate with regard to the genocide crimes it is designed to hear. The national courts do not have the operational capacity to process 77,000 serious criminal cases in a professional and timely manner, especially since they must address ongoing criminal activity at the same time. Recognizing this fact, judicial officials in Rwanda have discussed transferring Category One cases *back* to the Gacaca.[1] Although this remains a topic of discussion at this stage, there are serious concerns about such a policy. The idea of moving forward with formerly capital cases within the framework of the volunteer-run Gacaca is likely to garner a great deal of resistance from a variety of local as well as international sources.

A further observation concerning not only the national courts, but also the Gacaca, is the impracticality of the sentencing structure existing in both arenas of justice. The first question concerns the recent decision to abolish the death penalty. Without this reform some 76,000–100,000 people would have faced a possible death sentence. It is beyond the scope of reasonable thinking that the Rwandan Government would have been able to carry out such a massive number of executions, especially in light of the criticisms with which this fledgling judiciary is faced. Rwanda's international prestige improved significantly with this move but the prospect of unloading the most serious cases onto a volunteer system of justice is equally indefensible.

System capacity overload was already observed in the courts. Their attempt to deal with the expected influx of such a great volume of cases, destined to become a part of the prison system, presents a harrowing task. It has already been widely established that the current Rwandan prison system was over-extended in its operations when it attempted to accommodate 120,000 prisoners in the period immediately following the genocide. Human rights groups have recorded that prisoners were forced to live in atrocious conditions that violate international standards. The most recent numbers provided by the National Service of Gacaca Jurisdictions placed over 500,000 individuals in Categories One and Two; if convicted, these individuals face lengthy sentences of imprisonment. Even given the plea bargaining process and the reduction in jail time that may accompany a negotiated guilty plea, it is not possible for the Rwandan prisons to accommodate the increased volume of prisoners. According to Penal Reform International, 'the current methods of Community Service are unable to resolve the problem of prison overpopulation, as the TIG (community service sentence) is not a main penalty' (Penal Reform International 2007: 8). The system of community service attached to the sentence reduction in prison time will help alleviate some of the burden, but it is unknown at this time to what extent it will assist the prison overcrowding issue.

While the Rwandan Government has demonstrated great agency and ingenuity in the past, there will have to be further demonstrations of this in order for the judicial process to work. However, it is difficult to imagine a suitable alternative to imprisonment given the policy of maximal accountability. The situation is even more complicated since the Government has declared that without justice there can be no reconciliation. A formal declaration of amnesty provided to those who were involved in the crimes would be viewed as undermining the reform effort and would signal a return to the culture of impunity.[2] The use of selective prosecutions in cases of mass atrocity, particularly of Category One offences, might present a way to reduce the demands on a judicial system that does not have the capacity to proceed in its current course with even a modicum of real success. This would, however, leave a large number of perpetrators of very serious crimes outside of the process and, once again, undermine the government's goal of accountability and redress.

The need for justice, which is intricately tied to that of reconciliation, presents the Rwandan government with a very difficult situation. The impact of the current approach to justice on the process of national reconciliation remains unclear, and will only become apparent given time to move forward.

Faced with such a dire situation, the Government's demonstrated agency and flexibility, coupled with ongoing efforts to include the public in consultation, may yet provide another suitable alternative. Until that occurs, the process, out of necessity, will likely move forward haltingly. One prospect is to have convicted persons serve their time when facilities have *openings*; another is broadly-based annulments of sentences based on time already served.

The International Criminal Tribunal for Rwanda

The ICTR operates parallel to the judicial actions being undertaken by the Rwandan Government under a system of *concurrent jurisdiction*. Possibly representing the United Nations' recognition of the Rwandans' victimization both at the hands of the former regime and as a result of the international community's inaction despite their knowledge of the situation, the parallel arrangement is, in reality, a façade. The ICTR unquestionably has primary jurisdiction over those brought to trial for their crimes. Furthermore, it also has financial primacy with regard to appropriating the resources required to engage in the adjudication of those responsible for any mass atrocities.

Once again, despite the seeming similarities in the two processes, discontinuity is the reality. There is a discontinuity in the stated mandate of the ICTR and the actual practice of its operations. Although the mandate clearly indicates that the rebuilding of the Rwandan judicial system is one of the ICTR's goals, there is little or no concrete evidence that would suggest that this aspect of the mandate has been meaningfully addressed.

The ICTR has faced numerous criticisms stemming from a lack of qualified and competent personnel from the very beginning to allegations of mismanagement of funds and inefficiency. For a period in the 1990s, the registrar ran a cash payroll with suitcases full of bills from the United Nations in New York. We met several senior staff at the ICTR who worked the better part of a year before seeing their first pay cheque. In the Paschke Report, the United Nations addressed these concerns by way of an internal investigation into the issues. While the findings did not support accusations of intentional criminal activity, they did find that there had been significant mismanagement and poor execution of duties as well as in-fighting and power struggles between the different structural elements of the ICTR (ie the registry, the chambers, and the Office of the Prosecutor). These issues appear to have been more or less successfully addressed since 'In the second mandate (1999–2003), the judicial output has doubled' (Møse 2005: 920).[3]

Although the final number of cases to be tried at the ICTR is significantly smaller than the original estimates, the challenges and complexity that these unprecedented trials faced were unknown at the outset. The consequences of melding of two different judicial approaches and personnel with various legal backgrounds, language issues, transportation issues, and the use of a single prosecutor for both the ICTR and ICTY were not fully realized until the courts were in operation. Initially, the United Nations appointed judges and then decided on a prosecutor. However, this combination produced no cases due to the absence of competent police investigators. After 40 investigators were hired and warehoused in the Amohoro hotel, they were more or less house-bound until the United Nations realized that the use of Kinyarwanda translators was essential. It was only then that the evidentiary records were filled out and investigators engaged witnesses in the field.

Despite the criticisms and challenges faced, there may be many areas where the ICTR has achieved success. There has been substantial jurisprudence created by the decisions rendered over the ICTR's tenure including: (1) the first ever conviction for the crime of genocide; (2) the first ever conviction of a former head of state for genocide; (3) the recognition of rape and sexual violence as a crime of genocide; and (4) the re-visiting of the role of the mass media as an accomplice to genocide and, therefore, media accountability in the incitation of genocide. Although the successes of the ICTR are not well known within Rwanda, an aspect of its operations that requires further attention, the ICTR has contributed positively to the overall situation in Rwanda. The arrest, detention, and conviction of many of the key figures responsible for the genocide presents an application of the concept of *specific deterrence* in that key offenders are no longer in a position to attempt to continue working towards their previous goals. The legal process also presents an element of redress for the victims, while the counselling and health-care programmes for confirmed witnesses of the ICTR may also alleviate some of the suffering of those individuals resulting from the genocide. The work of the ICTR has additionally provided a modicum of justice for the Rwandan people as a whole by providing recognition of their victimization and a condemnation of the acts committed by the former regime.

Beyond the borders of Rwanda, the ICTR's operations have presented the International Criminal Court (ICC) with a number of valuable lessons upon which it can build. Despite the errors and problems that the ICTR has been forced to address, the lessons of the ICTR will be an asset for those involved in the operation of the ICC. The jurisprudence will provide the ICC with an incredibly valuable foundation from which to draw, even if formally it does not bind the permanent court. There may also be an element of *general deterrence* that comes from the creation of the ICTR. The international community has set a further precedent in the ICTR, namely that anyone found to have committed crimes of this nature may be held accountable in his or her personal capacity with no exceptions based on the accused's autonomy or activities in government.

The achievement of their *shared* mandate for Rwandans

The common search for justice among these realms has focused on two separate yet related components: eradicating impunity and facilitating reconciliation. Although these two concepts are unique, they are nonetheless interrelated. The eradication of impunity represents to some degree the desire to hold those responsible for their crimes accountable. The degree to which an offender accepts responsibility and displays contriteness for their actions can influence the process of reconciliation.

The combination of the trials in Rwanda and the prosecutions at the ICTR are significant in their attempt to address the culture of impunity that previously existed in Rwanda. Holding criminals accountable for their crimes sends a clear message that such behaviour will not be ignored, but will be dealt with in the future. Unfortunately, the majority of Rwandans are not aware of the events transpiring in Arusha since the system of justice that it employs is foreign to them in terms of both geography and the judicial process. Thus, despite their success in convicting many of the key individuals behind the genocide, the ICTR is likely to have less of an impact on culture of impunity *within* Rwanda's border than in the global arena. Likewise, despite the significant improvements made to the national judiciary over the past decade, average Rwandans are likely to remain sceptical of the courts, given the history of corruption and the limited time they have had to digest the changes and witness them functioning in a manner worthy of being called a justice system. Given its prominence in every community, its cultural relevance, and its participatory model, the Gacaca is likely to have the greatest impact in this area.

Reconciliation in Rwanda is crucial for the country to move forward in a state beyond that of simple peaceful co-existence. According to Staub, Pearlman, and Miller:

> [T]he essence of reconciliation is a changed psychological orientation toward the other. Reconciliation means that the victims and perpetrators do not see the past as defining the future, as simply a continuation of the past. It means that they come to accept each other and to see the humanity of one another and the possibility of a constructive relationship.
>
> (Staub, Pearlman, and Miller 2003: 288)

Although the process of reconciliation is a gradual one, the recent trials present one opportunity for this journey to begin. The impact that each judicial response has in facilitating reconciliation is a product of its approach to justice. As the ICTR and the national courts are engaged in adversarial trials, their impact is limited in this respect. The Gacaca, by engaging citizens in a dialogical approach to seeking justice, has provided a venue for discussion to take place thereby opening the door for the development of a shared understanding of the events that transpired in 1994.

However, for the culture of impunity to truly vanish in Rwanda and the process of reconciliation to begin, the crimes of the RPF must be publicly acknowledged and addressed with a transparency not yet observed within any of these three realms of justice. Additionally, the trials must move forward without political interference, maintaining their independence. Regardless of the claims that moral equivalence does not exist for these crimes, nevertheless

Figure 8.1 Photographs of genocide victims on a wall in Gisosyi (National Genocide Memorial).

they are crimes. The victims of these crimes must be acknowledged and given the same opportunity for redress and healing as those victimized by the genocidaires.

Reflections

Restorative and retributive justice

The overall judicial response to genocide in the Rwandan situation can be argued to incorporate an approach to criminal justice akin to Braithwaite's theory of *responsive regulation* (Braithwaite 2002). The central feature of the theory, the regulatory pyramid, suggests that the type of individual (virtuous, rational, and incompetent/irrational) with whom one must deal will determine the approach that is to be used. The theory suggests that, in directing the overall schematic for justice, the government should always begin with a restorative approach. Only when this proves unsuccessful should it then intervene, move the case up the regulatory pyramid, and apply increasingly restrictive sanctions. The pyramid is dynamic since not only can there be a progression up the pyramid with increasing sanctions, but also down the pyramid when there is an observed change in the offender.

The categorization of the offenders and the use of the plea bargaining procedures demonstrate an application of this theory in some respects. Those found to be in Category Three will not have to face the Gacaca proceedings if a resolution to their crimes can be found between the victim and the offender themselves. There is no intervention required if individuals within the community can resolve matters on their own accord. Allowing the individuals affected by the crime to engage in a dialogue among themselves and to seek an acceptable resolution on their own is central to a restorative justice approach and is the base of the regulatory pyramid. However, when there is an increase in the severity of the crime and offenders do not recognize their involvement or their responsibility to fix the damage caused, the theory requires the case be moved up the pyramid of regulation and seek more restrictive sanctions. Individuals in Category Two will be tried by the Gacaca courts and face lesser or greater penalties when consideration is given to their degree of acceptance of responsibility and their willingness to attempt to make things right through the process of plea bargaining. The accused, who demonstrates contrition by providing a full and complete confession, including a sincere apology, will see a reduction in his or her penalty as recognition. This same stepwise method can even be observed for those whose crimes would place them in Category One, provided they confess before their names appear on the official list.

The theory of responsive regulation, when applied to the judicial environment in Rwanda, contains elements of both restorative and retributive justice. As the crime increases in its severity and when the person refuses to acknowledge his or her accountability and refuses to display contriteness, the type of justice employed changes as does the location in which it will be addressed. The least severe crimes and the most contrite actors will be dealt with in the Gacaca courts. The national judiciary is then obligated to address Category One offenders, notwithstanding the previous discussion of the likely inability of the judiciary to address all such offenders.

Finally, the ICTR and use of its selective prosecution has attempted to engage in adjudicating the highest level of offenders: those most responsible for the genocide. However, there exists an apparent irony in the course of justice that is in complete contradiction with Braithwaite's (Braithwaite 2002) theory. It lies in the sentencing options that are available at the ICTR. In contradiction to the theory, those who are the most responsible and the least contrite (typically those tried at the ICTR) will face a maximum penalty of life imprisonment (with the possibility of parole depending on the venue for their incarceration); while others tried in Rwanda previously faced the death penalty and now life imprisonment without the possibility of parole. The incongruence in the sentences is not lost on the general populace in Rwanda.

The overall approach to adjudicating the perpetrators of the genocide demonstrates a combination of retributive and restorative justice approaches. The Gacaca provides a community-based response to the crimes that is somewhat congruent with the ideals of the restorative approach. The actual process of the Gacaca courts seeks to include active participation of all of the stakeholders in the crimes (the victim, the offender, and the community) within the process in an attempt to find a solution. The process of bringing all of these people into the discussion returns the conflict to those most affected by the crime. This presents the Gacaca courts with the potential to realize some of the strengths associated with the restorative approach to justice, including: (1) presenting opportunities for a process of norm-clarification within the community; (2) the avoidance of the segmenting effects observed in professional courts that come as a result of the depersonalization of both the individuals and the crime; and (3) the opportunity for the occurrence of repentance rituals whereby possibilities for forgiveness and a greater chance of reconciliation arise.

The community-based approach, under which the Gacaca functions, does not exclude a highly punitive aspect in its operations and, as such, is more likely to be considered a hybrid model. However, the legislative guidelines that govern the Gacaca courts, particularly those in which the sentences are pre-determined, limit the potential of the Gacaca to seek a truly restorative approach by restricting the ability of the stakeholders to arrive at their own solutions to the crimes. There has been a certain amount of independence granted to each Gacaca court on the part of the Government but, as the Gacaca was only recently launched nationally, it remains to be seen how much latitude will actually be accepted with regard to the sentencing decisions handed down by these courts.

The application of the liberal legalistic model's use of professional trials within the Rwandan national courts and the ICTR is not consistent with the restorative justice approach. The use of professionals in an adversarial environment that does not include the stakeholders – victims become peripheral to the process as they participate only as witnesses; offenders under the watchful eye of their attorneys remain silent and, unless convicted, do not accept responsibility or show remorse; and the community is completely absent for all intents and purposes. This approach does not embody the principles of restorative justice, but operates under the guise of the retributive model, seeking revenge and retribution for the crimes committed.

Regardless of the approach taken in the pursuit of justice, an additional element that is found in both forms of justice is that of individual accountability and responsibility. The genocide in Rwanda occurred under the auspices of mass participation. However, there were more individuals who did not engage in the crimes than those who did. By engaging in the judicial process and individualizing the perpetrators, the stigma that has been attached to all Hutus as genocidaires can be contested and possibly rejected.

The process of criminal justice represents only one available avenue to seek a more inclusive form of social justice. The individualization of the offences provides the possibility for those not involved in the criminal acts to move forward in a concerted front to address the effects of the genocide in the country. The Rwandan government has implemented a number of different strategies addressing the pre-conditions that may have precipitated the genocide. The key strategy in this struggle to achieve social justice is that of eliminating ethnicity as a source of social and political division. The recognition of equality for all within the newly constructed constitution and the establishment of the rule of law present significant progressive steps in this regard. Associated with this change is Mamdani's conceptualization of identity based on citizenship (Mamdani 2001b). The removal of ethnicity from Rwandan identity cards is another step in this process. There is no doubt that all Rwandans and their neighbours are still very aware of their ethnicity, but with continued efforts, this may become something that is treated of little consequence. According to Fiacre Birasa,[4] the hope for Rwanda lies in the observation that moving forward 'is not about Hutu and Tutsi, but about good people and bad people, and in Rwanda, there are more good people than there are bad' (Birasa 2004).

The biggest obstacle that lies in the path of justice is the remaining concern with the notion and practices of victor's justice. Despite the previously noted cases, as long as there is no serious attempt to address the crimes that were committed by the RPF, there remains a significant part of the population that is disenfranchised. The effective silencing of the victims of the RPF crimes marginalizes those individuals and may breed frustration and resentment rather than reconciliation. The Government of Rwanda needs to exercise transparency in the trials of former RPF members accused of crimes in 1994. While these trials have taken place in military courts that are *open* to the public (Bizimungu 2005), there remains little public knowledge of them in a situation similar to the cases at the ICTR. There is a fundamental discontinuity between the current practice and the establishment of the rule of law. Whether that means that those involved in reprisal crimes are brought before the Gacaca or before the criminal courts, something will have to be done.

Liberal-legalism

Bass discusses the triumph of liberal-legalism as the working model for adjudicating mass atrocity. He argues that this should serve as the conclusion of the debate between expedient show trials under totalitarian regimes and the cumbersome and demanding trial processes under Western democratic regimes (Bass 2000). The adoption of liberal-legalism is also argued to be a reflection of the foundational philosophy of the societies from which it emanates. Liberal-legalism offers an ideal toward which one may strive. In the context of the judicial response to genocide, it is manifested along this continuum of achievement. Within the Rwandan context, there remains the need to balance expediency while still applying the judicial principles associated with the liberal-legalistic model. In other words, liberal-legalism and expediency are not necessarily mutually exclusive.

The Gacaca is at one end of the continuum and demonstrates a modest degree of liberal-legalism in the application of trials that are organized within a legal framework combined with some of the procedural safeguards attributed to the liberal-legalistic model while demonstrating the greatest efficiency. The Rwandan national judiciary progresses further towards the ideal by attempting to incorporate as many additional facets of the model as are practical. Finally, the ICTR represents a continued move towards achieving a fully-integrated example of the model. As noted earlier, none of these realms of judicial response has achieved the sought after, albeit elusive, ideal of a truly liberal-legalistic approach to justice.

Ironically, the main criticisms of each of these levels of judicial response are tied to the debate between expediency and liberal legalism. The Gacaca and the Rwandan national judiciary are faced with the criticism of not meeting the standards of due process and fair trials that are central to the liberal-legalist approach. The Gacaca and the national courts are balancing the need for expediency in dealing with immense caseloads with the desire to involve the entire society within the process. It is ironic that this attempt to involve the populace is predicated on the desire to encourage and establish the *rule of law* in the face of a historical *culture of impunity* while the need for expediency and its related sacrifices may be seen to undermine that same goal. Furthermore, in the case of the Gacaca, the process may be seen as substantially more invasive in the lives of the Rwandan people, creating a sense of resentment for the process itself. At the same time, the embodiment of the liberal-legalistic model in the ICTR is ironically criticized for its lack of productivity given the time and effort required by the due process protections required by liberal-legalism.

Cosmopolitan law

Although not a concept that is widely incorporated into the vocabulary used at this juncture, cosmopolitan law presents yet another example of an ideal type of international justice that is attractive for those who dream of a law that transcends sovereign states and ensures protection from national laws. It is defined as an extension of international law since it challenges the concept of state sovereignty. Instead, cosmopolitan law searches for the protection of individual rights from a perspective of a global society of self-serving autonomous sovereigns. The concept of cosmopolitan law began within the context of the Nuremburg trials and has been extended further in the Rwandan context. Within the current discussion, cosmopolitan law presents a possible theoretical framework for understanding the combined adjudicatory enterprises at work in the Rwandan context and some of the benefits that they provide. Moreover, its proponents aspire towards the future transformation of international law into one of universal jurisdiction in future trans-national courts.

The combined efforts of all three realms of justice present an example of cosmopolitan law at work in that they are each focused on redressing the crimes committed by a genocidal regime that engaged in mass atrocities that undermine the fundamental philosophy of individual human rights. The fact that together they represent a concerted effort on the part of the international community is a further step towards the achievement of this ideal. The pre-cedent-setting trial and conviction of a former head of state in the Kambanda trial at the ICTR provided a concrete demonstration of a move by the inter-national community towards recognizing the fundamental nature of human rights and the need to protect them from their own government's abuses and crimes. The overall success of the judicial response to genocide in Rwanda may lie not in its achievement of individual convictions, but rather in its statement of recognition of the violation against the global community that these atrocities present. It also provides clarification and reiteration of the global norm that the kinds of atrocities adjudicated in Arusha are so shock-ing to civilization that their prosecution will not be overlooked for reasons of political expediency.

These are the lessons that should be drawn from this exploration of com-munity, national, and international judicial confrontation with some of the most heinous crimes imaginable. Cosmopolitan law is the space from which we seek hope for the future, a future that transcends the limits of national sectarianism, and ethnic and despotic frames of reference. While its progress is positive, borrowing a metaphor from one of the ICTR prosecutors, it nonetheless occurs as a rate that is *glacial*.

Notes

1 The notion of transferring back is italicized as in actuality this would mean that the cases would simply remain within the jurisdiction of the Gacaca. Other than cases currently emanating from the pilot phase of the Gacaca courts, which would involve a transfer back to the Gacaca, future cases would not move to the national court system.

2 Penal Reform International states that a further complication associated with the community service sentence is the perception on the part of some survivors that this sentence appears precariously close to a pardon-like provision and is an issue that needs to be addressed (Penal Reform International 2007: 3).

3 In the same paper, Judge Erik Møse explains how the first mandate of the ICTR was from 1995–9, the second from 1999–2003, and the third from 2003–7.

4 Fiacre Birasa is working on loan from the Canadian Department of Justice to help build the Rwandan High Courts.

References

AfricaBlog: exploring the policies that shape the continent (2003) *Hiding the truth* [online] available at: http://africa.ressurectionsong.com/archives/002101.html [accessed 26 May 2006].

African Rights (1995) *Rwanda: Death, Despair, and Defiance*, rev edn. London: African Rights.

Akhavan, P. (2001) 'Beyond impunity: can international criminal justice prevent future atrocities?' *The American Journal of International Law* [online] 95(1): 7–31 available at: www.jstor.org/ [accessed 21 January 2005].

Akhavan, P. (2005) 'The crime of genocide in the ICTR jurisprudence' *Journal of International Criminal Justice* [online] 3: 989–1006 available at: http://jicj.oxfordjournals.org/archive/ [accessed 18 May 2006].

Allen, J. (2001) 'Balancing justice and social unity: political theory and the idea of a truth and reconciliation commission' *University of Toronto Law Journal* [online] 49: 315–53 available at: www.jstor.org/action/showPublication?journalCode=univtorolawj [accessed 10 October 2005].

Amnesty International (2002) *Rwanda: Gacaca: a question of justice* AI Index: AFR 47 17 December 2002 [online] available at: www.amnesty.org/library/index/ENGAFR470072002 [accessed 18 August 2003].

Amnesty International (2004) *Rwanda: the enduring legacy of the genocide and war* AI Index AFR 47 6 April 2004 [online] available at: www.amnesty.org/library/pdf/AFR470082004ENGLISH/$File/AFR4700804.pdf [accessed 15 January 2006].

Amnesty International (2007) *Rwanda abolishes the death penalty* [online] available at: www.amnesty.org/en/news-and-updates/good-news/Rwanda-abolishes-death-penalty-20070802 [accessed 7 November 2008].

Anonymous (1990) *The Hutu Ten Commandments* [online] *Kangura* No 6, December, 1990, available at: www.trumanwebdesign.com/~catalina/commandments.htm [accessed 25 May 2006].

Anonymous (2008) 'Kigali arrests of R.P.F. suspects in 1994 priest killings' *World News Journal* [online] 13 June 2008, available at: http://africannewsanalysis.blogspot.com/2008/06/kigali-arrests-of-rpf-suspects-in-1994.html [accessed 23 November 2008].

Anonymous (2008) 'Spanish investigations into Rwanda put ICTR in awkward position' *World News Journal* [online], available at: http://africannewsanalysis.blogspot.com/2008/02/spanish-investigations-into-rwanda-put.html [accessed 20 February 2008].

Ayres, I. and Braithwaite, J. (1992) 'Responsive regulation: transcending the deregulation debate' *Oxford Socio-Legal Studies*, available at: www.myilibrary.com/Browse/open.asp?ID=44110&loc=ix [accessed 6 November 2008].

194   *References*

Bass, G. (2000) *Stay the hand of vengeance: the politics of war crimes tribunals*. Princeton, NJ: Princeton University Press.

Bassiouni, C. (2001) 'Universal jurisdiction for international crimes: historical perspectives and contemporary practice' *Virginia Journal of International Law Association* [online] 42: 81–62 available at: wwwheinonline.org/ [accessed 15 July 2005].

Bazemore, G. (1998) 'Restorative justice and earned redemption: communities, victims, and offender reintegration' *The American Behavioral Scientist* [online] 41(6): 768–813 available at: http://find.galegroup.com/itx/start.do?prodId=EAIM&userGroupName=ureginalib [accessed 13 December 2003].

Bazemore, G. (2001) 'Building community and nurturing justice: a review of the community justice ideal' *Contemporary Justice Review* 3(2): 225–32.

Bianchi, H. (1994) *Justice as sanctuary: toward a new system of crime control*. Bloomington, IN: Indiana University Press.

Birasa, F. G. (2004) [Interview] (personal communication, 2 June 2004).

Birasa, F. G. (2005) [Interview] (personal communication, May 2004, 2 June 2004, and January 2005). Rwanda.

Bizimungu, Captain C. (2005) [Interview] (personal communication, 31 May 2005). Republic of Rwanda.

Black, C. (2006) *ICTR-Uwilingiyimana letter controversy*. [International Crimes Blog 28 December 2005] (personal communication, 29 January 2006).

Boed, R. (2003) 'Current developments in the jurisprudence of the International Criminal Tribunal for Rwanda' *International Criminal Law Review* [online] 3: 169–81 available at: www.swetswise.com/FullTextProxy/swproxy?url=http%3A%2F%2Fopenurl.ingenta.com%2Fcontent%2Fswetsnet-4.1.ade081321aef32fa809faa7dcdb29d9b%3Fgenre%3Darticle%26issn%3D1567536X%26volume%3D3%26issue%3D2%26spage%3D169%26epage%3D181%26aulast%3DBoed&ts=1228504502719&cs=1883880044&userName=8900094.ipdirect&emCondId=8900094&articleID=27395264&yevoID=1690562&titleID=102924&referer=1&remoteAddr=142.3.152.21&hostType=PRO [accessed 2 February 2005].

Braithwaite, J. (1999) *Crime, shame, and reintegration*. Cambridge, MA: Cambridge University Press.

Braithwaite, J. (2002) *Restorative justice and responsive regulation*. New York: Oxford University Press.

Brannigan, A. (1984) *Crimes, courts and corrections: an introduction to crime and social control in Canada*. Toronto: Holt, Rinehart & Winston.

Brannigan, A. and Jones, N. A. (2008) *Genocide and the legal process in Rwanda before and after 1994: from amnesty to the new rule of law*. Paper for the Academy of Criminal Justice Sciences Annual Meeting, Cincinnati, OH, 13 March 2008.

Cain, M. and Hunt, A. (1979) *Marx and Engels on law*. London: Academic Press.

Caplan, G. (2005) *Genocide generation: remembrance and reconciliation or repetition*. Speech presented at Genocide generation: remembrance and reconciliation ... or repetition? University of Lethbridge, AB, October 2005.

Caplan, G. (2008) *The betrayal of Africa*. Toronto: Groundwork.

Caplan, G., Butra, A., Abebe, B. and Sangere, A. (2000) *The preventable genocide: international panel of eminent personalities*. [e-book] available at: www.grandslacs.net/doc/2764.pdf [accessed 16 May 2006].

Carroll, R. (2003) 'Genocide witnesses "killed to stop testimony"' *The Guardian* [online] 18 December 2003 available at: www.guardian.co.uk/international/story/0,3604,1109255,00.htm [accessed 26 May 2005].

Cayley, D. (1998) *The expanding prison: the crisis in crime and punishment and the search for alternatives*. Toronto: House of Anansi Press.

Chalk, F. and and Jonassohn, K. (1990) *The history and sociology of genocide: analyses and case studies*. Durham, NC: Yale University Press.

Chibundu, M. O. (2008) *Liberal internationalism, community and citizenship at the start of the twenty-first century* [online] available at: http://digitalcommons.law. umaryland.edu/cgi/viewcontent.cgi?article=1095&context=schmooze_papers [accessed 20 October 2008].

Christie, N. (1977) 'Conflicts as property' *The British Journal of Criminology* [online] 17(1): 1–14 available at: wwwheinonline.org/ [accessed 19 November 2003].

Coalition for Women's Human Rights in Conflict Situations (1997) *Letter to justice Louise Arbour: witness protection, gender and the ICTR* [online] available at: www. womensrightscoalition.org/advocacyDossiers/rwanda/witnessProtection/letterlouise arbour_en.php [accessed 26 May 2006].

Cole, D. H. (2001) 'An unqualified human good: E. P. Thompson and the rule of law' *Journal of Law and Society* 28(2): 177–203.

Collins, M. (2005) *The Uwilingiyimana Murder – is his letter a suicide note or an indictment of the illegal ICTR?* [online] available at: http://cirqueminime.blogcollective. com/blog/_archives/2005/12/27/1523635.html [accessed 29 January 2006].

Corey, A. and Joireman, S. F. (2004) 'Retributive justice: the Gacaca courts in Rwanda' *African Affairs* 103(410): 73–89.

Cosgrove, R. A. (1980) *The rule of law: Albert Venn Dicey, Victorian jurist*. Chapel Hill, NC: University of North Carolina Press.

Crawford, J. (2001) *Rwanda tribunal witnesses unhappy with their treatment* [online] Fondation Hirondelle: Media for Peace and Human Dignity, 29 May 2001 available at: www.hirondelle.org/hirondelle.nsf/0/925b4cfad00a68c0c1256820007a56b7?Open Document [accessed 26 May 2006].

Dallaire, R. (2003) *Shake hands with the devil: the failure of humanity in Rwanda*. Toronto: Random House.

Dallaire, R., Manocha, K., and Degnarain, N. (2005) 'The major powers on trial' *Journal of International Criminal Justice* 3(4): 861–978.

Daly, E. (2001–2) 'Between punitive and reconstructive justice: the Gacaca courts in Rwanda' *New York University Journal of International Law and Politics* 34: 355–96 [accessed 14 July 2005 from Hein Online database].

Daly, K. (2000) 'Revisiting the relationship between retributive and restorative justice' in J. Braithwaite and H. Strang (eds) *Restorative justice: from philosophy to practice*. Burlington, VT: Ashgate, pp 33–54.

Daly, K. (2002) 'Restorative justice: the real story' *Punishment and Society* 4(1): 55–79.

Degni-Ségui, R. (1994) 'Question of the violation of human rights and fundamental freedoms in any part of the world, with particular reference to colonial and other dependent countries and territories' *Report on the situation of human rights in Rwanda*, United Nations Economic and Social Council, Commission on Human Rights, 51st Session (Commission Resolution E/CN.4/S-3/1 of 25 May 1994).

Department of Peacekeeping Operations (2004) (adapted from *Locations of genocide massacres*, Mapping agency, Kigali, Republic of Rwanda, 1994). 1:750,000, Siemer, J., cartographer (University of Regina, Regina, SK, 2008) New York: United Nations.

Des Forges, A. (1999) 'Leave none to tell the story: genocide in Rwanda' *Human Rights Watch* [online], available at: www.hrw.org/reports/1999/Rwanda [accessed 29 July 2005].

Des Forges, A. and Longman, T. (2004) 'Legal responses to genocide in Rwanda' in E. Stover and H. M. Weinstein (eds) *My neighbor, my enemy: justice and community in the aftermath of mass atrocity.* Cambridge: Cambridge University Press, pp 49–69.

Dicker, R. and Keppler, E. (2004) 'Beyond The Hague: the challenges of international justice' *Human Rights Watch World Report 2004* [online], available at: www.hrw.org/wr2k.htm#_Toc58744959 [accessed day April 2004].

Dieng, A. (2004) 'The challenges of administration of international criminal tribunals with specific reference to ICTR' *Registrar of the International Criminal Tribunal for Rwanda, the prosecutors' colloquium on the challenges of international criminal justice* [online] Arusha, Tanzania 25–27 November 2004. ICTR available at: http://69.94.11.53/ENGLISH/colloquium04/index.htm [accessed 6 July 2005].

Drumbl, M. A. (1999) 'Sobriety in a post-genocidal society: good neighborliness among victims and aggressors in Rwanda?' *Journal of Genocide Research* [online] 1 (1):n 25–41, available at: www.informaworld.com/smpp/title~content=t713431069~db=all [accessed 5 July 2004].

Drumbl, M. A. (2000) 'Punishment, postgenocide: from guilt to shame to *civis* in Rwanda' *New York Law Review* [online] (75): 1221–326 available at: www.heinonline.org/ [accessed 5 July 2005].

Drumbl, M. A. (2005) 'Pluralizing international criminal justice' *Michigan Law Review* 103: 1295–328 [accessed 15 July 2005, from Academic Search Premier database].

Effange-Mbella, E. (2005) [Interview] (personal communication, 16 June 2005). Rwanda.

Fondation Hirondelle: Media for Peace and Human Dignity (2003a) *ICTR/Witness: issue of protection at the ICTR* [online] available at: www.hirondelle.org/hirondelle.nsf/0/925b4cfad00a68c0c1256820007a56b7?OpenDocument [accessed 26 May 2006].

Fondation Hirondelle: Media for Peace and Human Dignity (2003b) *Tribunal orders investigation into witnesses' security* [online] available at: www.hirondelle.org/hirondelle.nsf/0/925b4cfad00a68c0c1256820007a56b7?OpenDocument [accessed 26 May 2006].

Fyfe, N. and Sheptycki, J. (2006) 'International trends in the facilitation of witness co-operation in organized crime cases' *European Journal of Criminology* 3(3): 319–55.

Galaway, B. and Hudson, J. (1996) 'Introduction' in B. Galaway and J. Hudson (eds) *Restorative justice: International perspectives.* Monsey, NY: Criminal Justice, pp 1–16.

Garland, D. (1990) *Punishment and modern society.* Chicago, IL: University of Chicago Press.

Gourevitch, P. (1996) 'After genocide: a conversation with Paul Kagame' *Transition* [online] 72: 162–94 available at: www.jstor.org/ [accessed 15 July 2005].

Gourevitch, P. (1998) *We wish to inform you that tomorrow we will be killed with our families: stories from Rwanda.* New York: Picador.

Government of Rwanda (1963) *Law: general amnesty on political infraction made between 1 October 1959 and 1 July 1962.* 20 May 1963, JO 1963, p 299.

Government of Rwanda (1974) *Decree law 30 November 1974 for some political crimes.* JO, 1974, p 626.

Government of Rwanda (1991) *General amnesty law and refugees issues.* Law N° 60/91 13 December 1991. JO, 1991, p 1930.

Government of Rwanda (1995) *Recommendations of the conference held in Kigali from 1–5 November 1995 on Genocide, impunity and accountability: dialogue for a national and international response.* Office of the President: Kigali, Republic of Rwanda.

Government of Rwanda (1996) *Organic law on the organization of prosecutions for offences constituting the crime of genocide or crimes against humanity committed since October 1, 1990.* N° 08/96 of 30 August 1996. Kigali, Republic of Rwanda.

Government of Rwanda (2000) 'Rwanda: the troubled course of justice' (reply to Amnesty International's report May) [online] Kigali, Republic of Rwanda, available at: www.gov.rw/government/06_11_00news_ai.htm [accessed 11 July 2005].

Government of Rwanda (2001a) *Organic Law No 40 setting up 'GACACA Jurisdictions' and organizing prosecutions for offences constituting the crime of genocide or crimes against humanity committed between October 1, 1990 and December 31, 1994.* N° 40/2000 of 26/01/2001. Kigali, Republic of Rwanda.

Government of Rwanda (2001b) *Organic Law No 47.* Kigali, Republic of Rwanda.

Government of Rwanda (2003a) *Law representing the crime of genocide, crimes against humanity and war crimes.* N° 33 bis/2003 of 06/09/2003. Kigali, Republic of Rwanda.

Government of Rwanda (2003b) *Opinion survey on participation in Gacaca and national reconciliation.* National Unity and Reconciliation Commission. Kigali, Republic of Rwanda.

Government of Rwanda (2003c) *The Constitution of the Republic of Rwanda.* Adopted by the Supreme Court in its ruling N° 772/14.06/2003. 2 June 2003. Kigali, Republic of Rwanda.

Government of Rwanda (2004a) *Organic Law No 3.* Kigali, Republic of Rwanda.

Government of Rwanda (2004b) *The establishment, organization, duties and functioning of the national service in charge of follow-up, supervision and coordination of the activities of Gacaca jurisdictions.* Organic Law No 08/2004. Kigali, Republic of Rwanda available at: http://amategeko.net/display_rubrique.php?ActDo=all&Information_ID=1281&Parent_ID=30693047&type=public&Langue_ID=An&rubID=30693048 [accessed 21 November 2008].

Government of Rwanda (2004c) *Organic Law No 13.* Kigali, Republic of Rwanda.

Government of Rwanda (2004d) *Organic law establishing the organization, competence and functioning of Gacaca Courts charged with prosecuting and trying the perpetrators of the crime of genocide and other crimes against humanity, committed between October 1, 1990 and December 31, 1994.* No 16/2004 of 19/6/2004. Kigali, republic of Rwanda.

Government of Rwanda (2004e) *Organic Law on the statute of public prosecutors and personnel of the public prosecution service.* N° 22/2004 of 13/08/2004. Kigali, Republic of Rwanda.

Government of Rwanda (2005) *Court Statistics.* Supreme Court. Kigali, Republic of Rwanda. Author provided copies in Kigali, Rwanda.

Government of Rwanda (2007a) *Organic law modifying and complementing organic law n° 16/2004 of 19/6/2004 establishing the organization, competence and functioning of Gacaca Courts charged with prosecuting and trying the perpetrators of the crime of genocide and other crimes against humanity, committed between October 1, 1990 and December 31, 1994 as modified and complemented to date.* N° 10/2007 of 01/03/2007. Kigali, Republic of Rwanda.

Government of Rwanda (2007b) *Organic Law No 31.* Kigali, Republic of Rwanda.

Hagan, J. (2003) *Justice in the Balkans.* Chicago, IL: University of Chicago Press.

Harvard Law Review (2004) 'International law – Genocide – UN tribunal finds that mass media hate speech constitutes genocide, incitement to genocide, and crimes against humanity – Prosecutor v. Nahimana, Barayagwiza, and Ngeze (Media Case) Case No. ICTR-99-52-T (Dec. 2003)' *Harvard Law Review* [online] 117: 2769–76 available at: http://find.galegroup.com/itx/infomark.do?&serQuery=Locale%28en%

2CUS%2C%29%3AFQE%3D%28jx%2CNone%2C20%29%22Harvard+Law+Review
%22%24&type=pubIssues&queryType=PH&prodId=EAIM&userGroupName=
ureginalib&version=1.0 [accessed 15 July 2005].

Hatzfeld, J. (2005 [2003]) *Machete season: the killers in Rwanda speak* (trans from French) New York: Farrar, Straus & Giroux.

Hirondelle News Agency (2005a) *Rwanda disputes figures of Gacaca fugitives*, 2 May 2005 [online] Lausanne, available at: http://allafrica.com/stories/printable/200505050433.html [accessed 5 May 2005].

Hirondelle News Agency (2005b) *Rwandan refugees continue to stream into Burundi*, 5 May 2005 [online] Lausanne, available at: http://allafrica.com/stories/printable/200505050433.html [accessed 5 May 2005].

Hirondelle News Agency (2006) *ICTR and Rwanda dispute over plea bargains*, 22 April 2006 [online] Lausanne, available at: http://allafrica.com/stories/printable/200604240291.html [accessed 5 May 2005].

Hirondelle News Agency (2008) *Rwanda: president's aide formally indicted in France but out on bail*, 20 November 2008 [online] Lausanne, available at: http://allafrica.com/stories/200811210173.html [accessed 22 November 2008].

Hirsch, D. (2003) *Law against genocide: cosmopolitan trials.* Portland, OR: Glasshouse.

Honeyman, C., Judani, S., Tiruneh, A,, Hierta, J., Chirayath, L., Iliff, A., and Meierhenrichy, J. (2004) 'Establishing collective norms: potentials for participatory justice in Rwanda. Peace and conflict' *Journal of Peace Psychology* [online] 10(1): 1–24, available at: www.informaworld.com/smpp/title~content=t775653690~db=all [accessed 1 February 2006].

Human Rights Watch (1998) 'Human Rights Watch applauds Rwanda rape verdict: sets international precedent for punishing sexual violence as a war crime' *Human Rights Watch* [online] available at: www.hrw.org/english/docs/1998/09/02rwanda1311_txt. htm [accessed 21 May 2006].

Human Rights Watch (2001) 'Rwanda: observing the rules of war?' *Human Rights Watch* [online] 13(8), December, available at: www.hrw.org/reports/2001/rwanda2/ [accessed 1 August 2005].

Human Rights Watch (2008) 'Law and reality: progress in judicial reform in Rwanda' *Human Rights Watch* [online], 24 July, available at: www.hrw.org/en/reports/2008/07/24/law-and-reality-0 [accessed 20 October 2005].

International Criminal Tribunal for Rwanda (ICTR) (1996) *Report of the Office of Internal Oversight Services on the Audit and Investigation of the International Crime Tribunal for Rwanda* (UN Doc A/51/798), United Nations: New York [online] available at: www.un.org/Depts/oios/reports/a51789/ictrtit.htm [accessed 31 July 2005].

International Criminal Tribunal for Rwanda (ICTR) (2005/2006) 'Prosecutor's statement regarding the death of indictee Juvénal Uwilingiyimana' *ICTR Newlsletter*, available at: http://69.94.11.53/ENGLISH/newsletter/dec05-jan06/dec05-jan06.pdf [accessed 25 February 2009].

International Criminal Tribunal for Rwanda (ICTR) (2007) *Statute of the International Criminal Tribunal for Rwanda* United Nations: New York [online] available at: http://69.94.11.53/ENGLISH/basicdocs/statute.html [accessed 15 September 2008].

International Criminal Tribunal for Rwanda (ICTR) (2008) *Rules of Procedure and Evidence* United Nations: New York, 14 March 2008 [online] available at: http://69.94.11.53/default.htm [accessed 5 November 2008].

International Crisis Group (1999) *Five years after the genocide in Rwanda: justice in question*. ICG Report, Rwanda, 7 April 1999 [online] available at: www.crisisgroup.org/home/index.cfm?id=1412&l=1 [accessed 20 July 2005].

International Crisis Group (2003) *The International Criminal Tribunal for Rwanda: time for pragmatism. Executive summary* [online] available at: www.crisisgroup.org/home/index.cfm?id=2303&l=5 [accessed 8 May 2006].

Jacobs, S. L. (2002) 'Genesis of the concept of genocide according to its author from the original sources' *Human Rights Review* [online] 3(2): 98–103, available at: http://find.galegroup.com/itx/infomark.do?&serQuery=Locale%28en%2CUS%2C%29%3AFQE%3D%28jx%2CNone%2C21%29%22Human+Rights+Review%22%24&type=pubIssues&queryType=PH&prodId=EAIM&version=1.0 [accessed 16 August 2005].

Jallow, H. B. (2004) 'Challenges of international criminal justice: the ICTR experience' *ICTR, The prosecutors' colloquium on the challenges of international criminal justice* [online] Arusha, Tanzania, 25–27 November 2004, available at: http://69.94.11.53/ENGLISH/colloquium04/index.htm [accessed 6 July 2005].

Johnstone, G. (2002) *Restorative justice: ideas, values, debates*. Cullompton: Willan.

Jones, A. (2002) 'Gender and genocide in Rwanda' *Journal of Genocide Research* 4(1): 65–94.

Kagame, P. H. E. (2004) 'Preventing genocide: threats and responsibilities' *The Stockholm International Forum 2004* [online] Stockholm, Sweden, 26–28 January 2004, available at: www.dccam.org/Projects/Affinity/SIF/DATA/2004/page1399.html [accessed 28 December 2005].

Kaplan, G. (2008) *The betrayal of Africa*. Toronto: Groundwork.

Karekezi, U. A., Nshimiyimana, A., and Mutamba, B. (2004) 'Localizing justice: Gacaca courts in post-genocide Rwanda' in E. Stover and H. M. Weinstein (eds) *My neighbor, my enemy: justice and community in the aftermath of mass atrocity*. Cambridge: Cambridge University Press, pp 69–85.

Kayitana, C. (2006) [Interview] (personal communication, May 2004, 12 January 2005, 15 January 2005, June 2006). Republic of Rwanda.

Kigabo, P. (2005) [Interview] (personal communication, 7 June 2005). Republic of Rwanda.

Kimenyi, F. (2008) Rwanda: Quest to transfer genocide trials to Rwanda begin' *The New Times* [online] 24 April, available at www.afrika.no/Detailed/16574.html [accessed 26 February 2009].

Kimenyi, F. and Baguma, S. (2005) 'Genocide fugitives killed indicted suspect – Muyco' *The New Times* [online] 26 December, available at: http://allafrica.com/stories/200601030938.html [accessed 16 January 2005].

Kochavi, A. J. (1998) *Prelude to Nuremburg: allied war crimes policy and the question of punishment*. Chapel Hill, NC: University of North Carolina Press.

Lambourne, W. (2005) 'Reconciliation in Rwanda: applying Gacaca community justice to genocide' [draft notes] Seminar at COACS, University of Sydney, 12 September 2005 (personal communication, 3 October 2005).

LeBor, A. (2006) *Complicity with evil: the United Nations in the age of modern genocide*. New Haven, CT: Yale University Press.

Legal and Constitutional Commission (2002) *Towards a constitution for Rwanda: action plan 2003–2003* Legal and Constitutional Commission: Kigali, Republic of Rwanda, available at: www.cjcr.gov.rw [accessed 24 February 2006].

Lemarchand, R. (1998) 'Genocide in the Great Lakes: which genocide? whose genocide?' *African Studies Review* 41(1): 3–16.

Lemkin, R. (1945) 'Genocide: a modern crime' *Free World* [online] 4: 39–43 available at: www.preventgenocide.org/lemkin/freeworld1945.htm [accessed 16 August 2005].

Lemkin, R. (1946) 'Genocide' *American Scholar* [online] 15(2): 227–30 available at: www.preventgenocide.org/lemkin/americanscholar1946.htm [accessed 16 August 2005].

Llewellyn, J. J. and Howse, R. (1998) *Restorative justice: a conceptual framework* [online] Ottawa: Law Commission of Canada, available at: www.lcc.gc.ca/en/themes/sr/rj/howse/howse_main.asp [accessed 22 October 2004].

London Charter of the International Military Tribunal, The (1945) *In pursuance of the Agreement signed on the 8th day of August 1945 by the Government of the United States of America, the Provisional Government of the French Republic, the Government of the United Kingdom of Great Britain and Northern Ireland and the Government of the Union of Soviet Socialist Republics* [online] London: London Charter of the International Military Tribunal, available at: www.yale.edu/lawweb/avalon/imt/proc/imtconst.htm#art1 [accessed 29 September 2005].

London, R. D. (2006) 'Paradigms lost: repairing the harm of paradigm discourse in restorative justice' *Criminal Justice Studies* 19(4): 397–422.

Magnarella, P. J. (2000) *Justice in Africa: Rwanda's genocide, its courts, and the UN criminal tribunal*. Burlington, VT: Ashgate.

Magsam, D. (2004) [Interview] (personal communication, 17 June 2004).

Mamdami, M. (2001a) 'Reconciliation without justice', in Hent De Vries and Samuel Weber (eds) *Religion and media*. Stanford, CA: Stanford University Press, pp 376–88.

Mamdani, M. (2001b) *When victims become killers*. Princeton, NJ: Princeton University Press.

Manby, B. and Odinklalu, C. (2004) 'Peace and justice in Africa: where is the trade off?' *New Economy* [online] 11(3): 153–57, available at: www3.interscience.wiley.com/journal/120118379/issueyeargroup?year = 2004 [accessed 18 October 2005].

McCold, P. (1998) *Restorative policing experiment: the Bethlehem Pennsylvania Police Family Group Conferencing Project Report*. Pipersville, PA: Community Service Foundation.

Meltzer, B. D. (2002) 'The Nuremburg trial: a prosecutor's perspective' *Journal of Genocide Research* 4(4): 561–68.

Melvern, L. (2004) *Conspiracy to commit murder: the Rwandan genocide*. New York: Verso.

Miller, S. B. and Schacter, M. (2000) 'From restorative justice to restorative governance' *Canadian Journal of Criminology* 42(3): 405–21.

Mills, C. W. (1959/2000) *The sociological imagination*. New York: Oxford Publishing.

Moghalu, K. C. (2005) *Rwanda's genocide: the politics of global justice*. New York: Palgrave Macmillan.

Morley, I. (2005) [Interview] (personal communication, 21 June 2005). Arusha, Tanzania.

Møse, E. (2005a) *Address by Judge Erik Møse, President of the ICTR, To the United Nations Security Council* [online] 13 June 2005 available at: www.ictr.org/ENGLISH/speeches/mose130605.htm [accessed 13 July 2005].

Møse, E. (2005b) 'Main achievements of the ICTR' *Journal of International Criminal Justice* 3: 920–43.

Mugabo, D. (2005) [Interview] (personal communication, 10 June 2005, and following days). Republic of Rwanda.

Mukantaganzwa, D. (2004) *Gacaca jurisdictions: genesis, organization, functioning, achievements and future prospects*. Kigali: National Service of Gacaca Jurisdictions available at: www.inkiko-gacaca.gov.rw/PPT/Realisation%20and%20future%20persective. ppt#17 [accessed 22 November 2008].

Mukantaganzwa, D. (2005) [Interview] (personal communication, 30 May 2005). Republic of Rwanda.

Muramira, G. (2008) 'Rwanda: parliament to discuss ICTR concerns' *The New Times* [online] 4 November, available at http://allafrica.com/stories/200811040076.html [accessed 26 February 2009].

Mutangana, J. B. (2005) [Interview] (personal communication, 7 June 2005, and following days). Republic of Rwanda.

National Census Service (1991) *Census of Rwanda, 1991.* National Census Service: Kigali, Republic of Rwanda.

National Census Service (2005) *A synthesis of the analyses of the 2002 Census of Rwanda.* National Census Service: Kigali, Republic of Rwanda.

Netherlands Organization for International Development Cooperation (NOIDC) (1997) *Country assessment on Rwanda.* The Economist Intelligence Unit: The Hague, pp 1–31.

Newbury, C. (1998) 'Ethnicity and the politics of history in Rwanda' *Africa Today* 45 (1 January–March): 7–25.

Ngoga, M. (2004) 'Rwanda 10 years after the genocide: creating conditions for justice and reconciliation' Speech presented at the Prosecutor's Colloquium, 25–27 November 2004, Arusha, Tanzania, available at: http://69.94.11.53/ENGLISH/colloquium04/index.htm [accessed 6 July 2005].

Ngoga, M. (2005) [Interview] (personal communication, 24 May 2005, and following days). Republic of Rwanda.

Niang, M. (2005) [Interview] (personal communication, 16 June 2005). Arusha, Tanzania.

Ntampaka C. (2001) 'Rwandan gacaca, participative, repressive justice' RDO2001 in Penal Research International, *The Guilty Plea Procedure*, January 2003, p 3.

Obote-Odora, A. (2005) [Interview] (personal communication, 22 June 2005). Arusha, Tanzania

Penal Reform International (2002) *PRI research team on Gacaca: Report III: April – June 2002.* Penal Reform International: Republic of Rwanda.

Penal Reform International (2003) *PRI research on Gacaca report: Report IV: 'The guilty plea procedure, the cornerstone of the Rwandan justice system'.* Penal Reform International: Republic of Rwanda.

Penal Reform International (2007) *Monitoring and research report on the Gacaca: Community service (TIG) areas of reflection.* Penal Reform International: Republic of Rwanda.

Peskin, V. (2005) 'Courting Rwanda: the promises and pitfalls of the ICTR outreach programme' *Journal of International Criminal Justice* 3: 950–61.

Prosecutor v Akayesu (Jean-Paul) [1996] ICTR-96-4-I.

Prosecutor v Akayesu (Jean-Paul) [1998] ICTR-96-4-T.

Prosecutor v Kambanda (Jean) [1998] ICTR-97-23-A.

Prosecutor v Munyakazi (Yussuf) [2000] ICTR-97-36.

Prosecutor v Munyakazi (Yussuf) [2008] ICTR-97-36-R11*bis*, 28 May 2008.

Prosecutor v Nahimana (Ferdinand), Barayagwiza (Jean-Bosco) and Ngeze (Hassan) [2003] ICTR-99-52-T.

Prunier, G. (1995) *The Rwanda crisis.* New York: Columbia University Press.

Renaud, R. (2005) [Interview] (personal communication, June 2004, 12 January 2005, 8 June 2005, and following days). Republic of Rwanda.

Ritzer, G. (1992) *Classical sociological theory*, 2nd edn. Toronto: McGraw-Hill.

Rossouw, H. (2002) 'Rwanda's search for justice' *Chronicle of Higher Education* [online] 48(48): A41, available at: http://find.galegroup.com/itx/infomark.do?&ser Query=Locale%28en%2CUS%2C%29%3AFQE%3D%28jx%2CNone%2C31%29% 22Chronicle+of+Higher+Education%22%24&type=pubIssues&queryType=PH&prod Id=EAIM&userGroupName=ureginalib&version=1.0. [accessed 21 January 2006].

Rugege, S. (2005) [Interview] (personal communication, 25 May 2005). Republic of Rwanda.

Sarkin, J. (1999) 'The necessity and challenges of establishing a Truth and Reconciliation Commission in Rwanda' *Human Rights Quarterly* 21(3): 767–823.

Sarkin, J. (2000) 'Promoting justice, truth and reconciliation in transitional societies: evaluating Rwanda's approach in the new millennium of using community based Gacaca tribunals to deal with the past' *International Law Forum* 2: 112–21.

Schabas, W. A. (1996) 'Justice, democracy, and impunity in post-genocide Rwanda: searching for solutions to impossible problems' *Criminal Law Forum* [online] 7 (3): 523–60 available at: www.springerlink.com/home/main.mpx [accessed 6 March 2006].

Schabas, W. A. (1999) 'The genocide convention at fifty' *United States Institute of Peace (Special Report 41)* [online] Unites States Institute of Peace: Washington, DC, available at: www.usip.org/pubs/specialreports/sr/990107.html [accessed 30 September 2005].

Schabas, W. A. (2003) 'National courts finally begin to prosecute genocide, the 'crime of crimes' *Journal of International Criminal Justice* 1(1): 39–63.

Schabas, W. A. (2005) 'Genocide trails and the Gacaca courts' *Journal of International Criminal Justice* 3: 879–95.

Sharlach, L. (2000) 'Rape as genocide: Bangladesh, the former Yugoslavia, and Rwanda' *New Political Science* [online] 22(1): 89–102 available at: www.informaworld. com/smpp/title~content=t713439578~db=all [accessed 18 May 2006].

Schiessl, C. (2002) 'An element of genocide: rape, total war, and international law in the twentieth century' *Journal of Genocide Research* 4(2): 197–210.

Shklar, J. (1964) *Legalism*. Cambridge, MA: Harvard University Press.

Smith, J. M. (ed) (2004) *A time to remember: Rwanda ten years after genocide*. Kigali, Republic of Rwanda: The Aegis Trust.

Smith, K. Z., Longman, T., Kimonyo, J. P., and Rutagengwa, T. (2002) *Rwanda democracy and governance assessment*. Management Systems International, Washington DC.

Spitzer, S. (1983) 'Marxist perspectives in the sociology of law' *Annual Review of Sociology* 9: 103–24.

Sriram, C. L. (2002) 'Exercising universal jurisdiction: contemporary disparate practice' *The International Journal of Human Rights* 6(4): 49–76.

Staub, E., Pearlman, L. A. and Miller, V. (2003) 'Healing the roots of genocide in Rwanda' *Peace Review* 15(3): 287–94.

Stewart, J. (2003) 'Judicial notice in international criminal law: a reconciliation of potential, peril and precedent' *International Criminal Law Review* 3: 245–74.

Stewart, J. (2005) [Interview] (personal communication, 23 June 2005). Republic of Rwanda.

Strauss, S. (2004) 'How many perpetrators were there in the Rwandan genocide? An estimate' *Journal of Genocide Research* 6(1): 85–98.

Strong, S. I. and Dries, James, J. (2005) 'Witness statements under the IBA Rules of Evidence: what to do about hearsay?' *Arbitration International* 21(3): 301–31.

Taylor, C. C. (1999) *Sacrifice as terror: the Rwandan genocide of 1994*. New York: Oxford International Publishers.

Temple-Raston, D. (2005) *Justice on the grass: three Rwandan journalists, their trial for war crimes, and a nation's quest for redemption*. New York: Free Press.

Thompson, E. P. (1975) *Whigs and hunters: the origin of the Black Act*. London: Penguin Books.

Thompson, S. (2007) 'The unity-generating machine: state power and Gacaca trials in post-conflict Rwanda' Paper for Canadian Political Science Association Annual Meeting, Saskatoon, SK, 31 May 2007.

Tutorow, N. E. (1986) *War crimes, war criminals, and war crimes trials: an annotated bibliography and source book*. Westport, CT: Greenwood Press.

Twagilimana, A. (2003) *The debris of ham: ethnicity, regionalism, and the 1994 Rwandan genocide*. Lanham, MD: University Press of America.

United Nations (1948) *Convention on the prevention and punishment of the crime of genocide*. Adopted by Resolution 260 (III) A. 9 December 1948. Entry into force 12 January 1951. United Nations: New York, available at: www.preventgenocide.org/law/convention/text.htm [accessed 9 August 2005].

United Nations (1949) *Geneva convention relative to the treatment of prisoners of war*. Adopted by the Diplomatic Conference for the Establishment of International Convention the Protection of Victims of War, 12 August 1949, United Nations: New York.

United Nations (1977) *Protocol additional to the Geneva conventions of 12 August 1949, and relating to the protection of victims of non-international armed conflicts (protocol II)*. Adopted on 8 June 1977. The diplomatic conference on the reaffirmation and the development of international humanitarian law applicable to armed conflicts, entry into force: 7 December 1978, in accordance with Article 23. United Nations: New York.

United Nations (1993a) *Document S/RES/808*. UN Security Council 3175th Meeting, 22 February 1993. United Nations: New York.

United Nations (1993b) *Resolution 1503*. United Nations: New York.

United Nations (1994a) *Budget for the international criminal tribunal for the prosecution of persons responsible for the genocide and other serious violations of international humanitarian law committed in the territory of Rwanda and Rwandan citizens responsible for genocide and other such violations committed in the territory of neighbouring states between 1 January and 31 December 1994*. UN Doc A/56/497/Add.1. United Nations: New York.

United Nations (1994b) *Financing of the international criminal tribunal for the prosecution of persons responsible for the genocide and other serious violations of international humanitarian law committed in the territory of Rwanda and Rwandan citizens responsible for genocide and other such violations committed in the territory of neighbouring states between 1 January and 31 December 1994*. Draft resolution submitted by the Chairman following informal consultations. UN Doc A/C.5/56/L.26. United Nations: New York.

United Nations (1994c) *Human rights questions: human rights situations and reports of special rapporteurs and representatives: situation of human rights in Rwanda*. UN Doc A/49/508/Add.1,S/1994/1157/Add.1, 14 November 1994. United Nations: New York.

United Nations (1994d) *Letter from the permanent representative of Rwanda addressed to the president of the Security Council*, 28 September 1994. UN Document S/1994/1115. United Nations: New York.

United Nations (1994e) *Resolution 935.* Adopted by the Security Council at its 3400th meeting, 1 July 1994. United Nations: New York.

United Nations (1994f) *Resolution 955.* Adopted by the Security Council at its 3453rd meeting, 8 November 1994. United Nations: New York.

United Nations (1994g) *Security Council Report of the Secretary-General on the Situation in Rwanda,* S/1994/640. United Nations: New York.

United Nations (1994h) *Statute of the International Criminal Tribunal for Rwanda.* United Nations: New York, available at: http://69.94.11.53/ENGLISH/basicdocs/statute.html [accessed 25 July 2005].

United Nations (1994i) *Human Rights Questions: Human Rights Situations and Reports of Special Rapporteurs and Representatives: Situation of human rights in Rwanda.* UN Doc A/49/508/Add.1,S/1994/1157/Add.1, United Nations, General Assembly, Forty-ninth session, agenda item 100 (c), Security Council, Forty-ninth year, 14 November 1994. United Nations: New York.

United Nations (1996a) *Report of the Office of Internal Oversight Services on the audit and investigation of the International Criminal Tribunal for Rwanda,* UN Doc A/51/798. United Nations: New York, available at: www.un.org/Depts/oios/reports/a51789/ictrtit.htm [accessed 31 July 2005].

United Nations (1996b) *Rwanda: United Nations situation report* [online]. United Nations: New York, available at: www.grandslacs.net/doc/2241.pdf [accessed 26 May 2006].

United Nations (2003a) *Budget for the International Criminal Tribunal for the prosecutions of persons responsible for genocide and other serious violations of international humanitarian law committed in territory of Rwanda and Rwandan citizens responsible for genocide or other such violations committed in the territory of neighbouring states between 1 January and 31 December 1994 for the biennium 2004–2005.* UN doc A/58/269. United Nations: New York.

United Nations (2003b) *Resolution 808.* United Nations: New York.

United Nations (2003c) *Resolution 1503.* Adopted by the United Nations, Security Council 26 August 2003. United Nations: New York.

United Nations (2004) *Report of the Secretary-General on the situation in Rwanda UN Doc S/1994/640.* United Nations, Security Council. United Nations: New York.

United Nations (2007) United Nations Treaty Collection [As of 9 October 2001]. Convention on the Prevention and Punishment of Genocide, available at: www.unhchr.ch/html/menu3/b/treaty1gen.htm [accessed 26 February 2009].

US Department of State (2006) *Rwanda: country reports on human rights practices.* 8 March 2006, Bureau of Democracy, Human Rights, and Labor: Washington DC, available at: www.state.gov/g/drl/rls/hrrpt/2005/61587.htm [accessed 29 May 2006].

Uvin, P. (2001) 'Difficult choices in the new post-conflict agenda: the international community in Rwanda after the genocide' *Third World Quarterly* 22(2): 177–89.

Uvin, P. (2003) 'The Gacaca tribunals in Rwanda' in D. Bloomfield, T. Barnes and L. Huyse (eds) *Reconciliation after violent conflict: a handbook.* Stockholm, Sweden: International Institute for Democracy and Electoral Assistance.

Uvin, P. and Mironko, C. (2003) 'Western and local approaches to justice in Rwanda' *Global Governance* 9: 219–31, available at: http://find.galegroup.com/itx/infomark.do?&serQuery=Locale%28en%2CUS%2C%29%3AFQE%3D%28jx%2CNone%2C19%29%22Global+Governance%22%24&type=pubIssues&queryType=PH&prodId=EAIM&version=1.0 [accessed 5 July 2004].

Vandeginste, S. (1997) *Justice for Rwanda and international cooperation*, available at: http://129.194.252.80/catfiles/0814.pdf [accessed 1 August 2003].

Vandeginste, S. (1999) *Justice, reconciliation and reparation after genocide and crimes against humanity: the proposed establishment of popular Gacaca tribunals in Rwanda*. All-Africa Conference on African Principles of Conflict Resolution and Reconciliation. United Nations Conference Centre, Addis Ababa, 8–12 November 1999, available at: www.grandslacs.net/doc/3666.pdf [accessed 1 August 2003].

Van Ness, D., Morris, A., and Maxwell, G. (2001) 'Introducing restorative justice', in A. Morris and G. Maxwell (eds) *Restorative justice for juveniles: conferencing, mediation, and circles*. Oxford: Hart Publishing, pp 3–16.

White, D. (2005) [Interview] (personal communication, 27 June 2005, and following days). Arusha, Tanzania.

Wolters, S. (2005) *Situation report: the Gacaca process: eradicating the culture of impunity*. Institute for Security Services, available at: http://www.issafrica.org/AF/current/2005/050805rwanda.pdf [accessed 18 May 2006].

Yacoubian Jr., G. S. (1999) 'The efficacy of international criminal justice: Evaluating the aftermath of the Rwandan genocide' *World Affairs* 161(4): 186–92.

Yacoubian Jr., G. S. (2003) 'Evaluating the efficacy of the International Criminal tribunals for Rwanda and the former Yugoslavia: implications for criminology and international criminal law' *World Affairs* 165(3): 133–41.

Zehr, H. (1990) *Changing lenses: a new focus for crime and justice*. Scottsdale, AZ: Herald Press.

Appendix 1

Year 46 N° 5, 1st March 2007

Summary Law N° 10/2007 of 01/03/2007

Organic Law modifying and complementing Organic Law N°16/2004 of 19/6/ 2004 establishing the organisation, competence and functioning of Gacaca Courts charged with prosecuting and trying the perpetrators of the crime of genocide and other crimes against humanity, committed between October 1, 1990 and December 31, 1994 as modified and complemented to date.

CONTENTS

Article 19: Persons authorised to appeal in Gacaca Courts
Article 20: Reasons for the review of the judgement
Article 21: Repealing of inconsistent provisions
Article 22: Enforcement

ORGANIC LAW N° 10/2007 OF 01/03/2007 MODIFYING AND COMPLEMENTING ORGANIC LAW N°16/2004 OF 19/6/2004 ESTABLISHING THE ORGANISATION, COMPETENCE AND FUNCTIONING OF GACACA COURTS CHARGED WITH PROSECUTING AND TRYING THE PERPETRATORS OF THE CRIME OF GENOCIDE AND OTHER CRIMES AGAINST HUMANITY, COMMITTED BETWEEN OCTOBER 1, 1990 AND DECEMBER 31, 1994 AS MODIFIED AND COMPLEMENTED TO DATE

We, KAGAME Paul,

President of the Republic;

THE PARLIAMENT HAS ADOPTED AND WE SANCTION, PROMULGATE THE FOLLOWING ORGANIC LAW AND ORDER IT BE PUBLISHED IN THE OFFICIAL GAZETTE OF THE REPUBLIC OF RWANDA. **THE PARLIAMENT:**

The Chamber of Deputies, in its session of February 26, 2007;
  The Senate, in its session of February 13, 2007;
  Given the Constitution of the Republic of Rwanda of 04 June 2003, as amended to date, especially in its Articles 9, 61, 62, 66, 67, 88, 90, 92, 93, 94, 95, 108, 118, 152 and 201;
  Revisited Organic Law N° 16/2004 of 19/6/2004 establishing the organisation, competence and functioning of Gacaca Courts charged with prosecuting and trying the perpetrators of the crime of genocide and other crimes against humanity, committed between October 1, 1990 and December 31, 1994, as modified and complemented to date especially in its articles 8, 13, 14, 16, 23, 31, 41, 42, 43, 44, 51, 58, 72, 73, 76, 78, 80, 81, 90 and 93;

ADOPTS:

Article 1: Establishment of the benches of Gacaca Courts

Article 8 of Organic Law N° 16/2004 of 19/6/2004 establishing the organisation, competence and functioning of Gacaca Courts charged with prosecuting and trying the perpetrators of the crime of genocide and other crimes against humanity, committed between October 1, 1990 and December 31, 1994 is hereby modified and complemented as follows:

'Each Bench of the Gacaca Court is made up of seven (7) persons of integrity and two (2) substitutes.

A Gacaca Court may have more than one Bench where necessary.

The new Bench shall elect from its members an executive committee and shall be given cases to be tried.

The National Service of Gacaca Courts draws up the modalities for the establishment of the Benches of Gacaca Courts and their collaboration modalities.'

Article 2: The elections of members of the organs of Gacaca Courts

Article 13 of Organic Law N° 16/2004 of 19/6/2004 establishing the organisation, competence and functioning of Gacaca Courts charged with prosecuting and trying the perpetrators of the crime of genocide and other crimes against humanity, committed between October 1, 1990 and December 31, 1994 is hereby modified and complemented as follows:

'The General Assembly for Gacaca Court of Cell shall elect, within its members, seven (7) persons of integrity constituting the Bench and two (2) substitutes.

The General Assembly for the Sector shall elect, within its members, seven (7) persons of integrity and two (2) substitutes to make up the Bench of the Gacaca Court of Appeal and seven (7) persons of integrity with two (2) substitutes making up the Bench of the Gacaca Court of the Sector

Subject to provisions of Article 102 of Organic Law N° 16/2004 of 19/6/2004 establishing the organisation, competence and functioning of Gacaca Courts charged with prosecuting and trying the perpetrators of the crime of genocide and other crimes against humanity, committed between October 1, 1990 and December 31, general elections of persons of integrity for Gacaca Courts shall be organised and conducted by the National Electoral Commission.

A Presidential Order shall determine the modalities for the organisation of the elections of members of the organs of Gacaca Courts.'

Article 3: Conditions for being a member of the bench of Gacaca Courts

Article 14 of Organic Law N° 16/2004 of 19/6/2004 establishing the organisation, competence and functioning of Gacaca Courts charged with prosecuting and trying the perpetrators of the crime of genocide and other crimes against humanity, committed between October 1, 1990 and December 31, 1994 is hereby modified and complemented as follows:

'Members of the Benches of Gacaca Courts are Rwandans of integrity elected by the General Assemblies of their Cells of residence.

A person of integrity is any Rwandan meeting the following conditions:
1° not to have participated in genocide;
2° to be free from the spirit of sectarianism;
3° not to have been definitively sentenced to a penalty of at least six (6) months of imprisonment;
4° to be of high morals and conduct;
5° to be truthful;
6° to be honest;
7° to be characterised by a spirit of speech sharing;
8° to be free from genocide ideology.

Ideology of genocide consists in behaviour, a way of speaking, written documents and any other actions meant to wipe out human beings on the basis of their ethnic group, origin, nationality, region, colour of skin, physical traits, sex, language, religion or political opinions.

Any person of integrity who is at least twenty-one (21) years old and meeting all the conditions required by this organic law, can be elected a member of an organ of a Gacaca Court without any discrimination whatsoever, such as that based on sex, origin, religion, opinion or social position.'

Article 4: Reasons and procedures for the replacement of a member of the organs for Gacaca Courts

Article 16 of Organic Law N° 16/2004 of 19/6/2004 establishing the organisation, competence and functioning of Gacaca Courts charged with prosecuting and trying the perpetrators of the crime of genocide and other crimes against humanity, committed between October 1, 1990 and December 31, 1994 is modified and complemented as follows:

'Any person elected as a member of the organs for Gacaca Courts shall be replaced for one of the following reasons:
1° to be absent from the meeting sessions of the organs of Gacaca Courts for three (3) consecutive times without giving any convincing reasons;
2° to be definitively convicted of a crime punishable by a sentence of at least six (6) months of imprisonment;
3° to prompt sectarianism;
4° to exercise one of the activities provided for in article 15 of Organic Law N° 16/2004 of 19/6/2004 establishing the organisation, competence and functioning of Gacaca Courts charged with prosecuting and trying the perpetrators of the crime of genocide and other crimes against humanity, committed between October 1, 1990 and December 31, 1994 or occupying a position that is likely to impede participation in the sessions of the organs of Gacaca Courts;
5° to have a disease likely to prevent him or her from participating in the activities of the organs of Gacaca Courts;

6° to do any act incompatible with the quality of a person of integrity;

7° resignation for personal reasons;

8° to be prompted by genocide ideology;

9° death.

The decision to dismiss a member of the organs of Gacaca Courts who has been absent from their activities for three (3) consecutive times without convincing reasons, has instigated sectarianism or has done an act incompatible with the quality of a person of integrity, shall be made in writing, by the members of the Bench of the Gacaca Court, after consultations with the General Assembly of his or her Cell of residence. The member so dismissed shall be subject to a public caution before the General Assembly and can no longer be elected as a person of integrity.

Other reasons for the replacement referred to in this article, are ascertained by the same organ of the Gacaca Court.'

Article 5: The quorum

Article 23 of Organic Law N° 16/2004 of 19/6/2004 establishing the organisation, competence and functioning of Gacaca Courts charged with prosecuting and trying the perpetrators of the crime of genocide and other crimes against humanity, committed between October 1, 1990 and December 31, 1994 is hereby modified and complemented as follows:

'The Bench of the Gacaca Court meets legitimately if at least five (5) of its members are present.

When the quorum is not reached due to the absence of some members, the meeting is postponed.

When the quorum is not reached due to an absolute unavailability of the members for various reasons, it is completed by substitutes.

If the quorum is not reached, following objection or competence disclaimer from some of the Bench members, it is completed by their substitutes until the last decision or the closure of hearings.

When all Bench members are objected to or disclaim competence, the assistance of persons of integrity from the nearest Gacaca Court having the same competence is sought until the decision is taken or the closure of hearings. This cannot withhold those persons of integrity from elsewhere to carry on their duties in their usual Court.

The objected Bench, disclaimed Bench or any other person interested in the case, shall immediately inform the National Service in charge of following up, supervising and coordinating the activities of Gacaca Courts to decide on the Gacaca Court from which the persons of integrity can be borrowed.'

Article 6: Opposition and appeal

Article 31 of Organic Law N° 16/2004 of 19/6/2004 establishing the organisation, competence and functioning of Gacaca Courts charged with prosecuting and trying the perpetrators of the crime of genocide and other crimes against humanity, committed between October 1, 1990 and December 31, 1994 is hereby modified and complemented as follows:

'Cases tried pursuant to Article 29 of Organic Law N° 16/2004 of 19/6/ 2004 establishing the organisation, competence and functioning of Gacaca Courts charged with prosecuting and trying the perpetrators of the crime of genocide and other crimes against humanity, committed between October 1, 1990 and December 31, 1994 may be opposed and appealed against in accordance with the procedure provided for by this Organic Law.

Nevertheless, cases tried by the Gacaca Court of Appeal at the first resort, are appealed against in the nearest Gacaca Court of Appeal or in another bench of the Gacaca Court of Appeal that tried the case if it is available.'

Article 7: Competence of the Gacaca Court of Cell

Article 41 of Organic Law N° 16/2004 of 19/6/2004 establishing the organisation, competence and functioning of Gacaca Courts charged with prosecuting and trying the perpetrators of the crime of genocide and other crimes against humanity, committed between October 1, 1990 and December 31, 1994 is hereby modified and complemented as follows:

'The Gacaca Court of Cell only deals, at the first and last resort, with offences relating to property. It also deals with the objection against the sentence it has pronounced in the absence of the parties.

Gacaca Court of Cell classifies into categories accused persons suspected of having committed offences provided for in articles one and 51 of Organic Law N° 16/2004 of 19/6/2004 establishing the organisation, competence and functioning of Gacaca courts charged with prosecuting and trying the perpetrators of the crime of genocide and other crimes against humanity, committed between October 1, 1990 and December 31, 1994, as modified and complemented to date.'

Article 8: Competence of the Gacaca Court of Sector

Article 42 of Organic Law N° 16/2004 of 19/6/2004 establishing the organisation, competence and functioning of Gacaca Courts charged with prosecuting and trying the perpetrators of the crime of genocide and other crimes against humanity, committed between October 1, 1990 and December 31, 1994 is hereby modified and complemented as follows:

'The Gacaca Court of Sector deals at first resort, with defendants whose offences classify them into the second category and opposition made against sentences pronounced in the absence of the parties.

It also deals with the appeal lodged against judgements pronounced for offences provided for in articles 29 and 30 of Organic Law N°16/2004 of 19/6/2004 establishing the organisation, competence and functioning of Gacaca courts charged with prosecuting and trying the perpetrators of the crime of genocide and other crimes against humanity, committed between October 1, 1990 and December 31, 1994 and other decisions taken by the Gacaca Court of Cell.'

Article 9: Competence of the Gacaca Court of Appeal

Article 43 of Organic Law N° 16/2004 of 19/6/2004 establishing the organisation, competence and functioning of Gacaca Courts charged with prosecuting and trying the perpetrators of the crime of genocide and other crimes against humanity, committed between October 1, 1990 and December 31, 1994 is hereby modified and complemented as follows:

'The Gacaca Court of Appeal deals with appeal lodged against sentences pronounced at first resort by the Gacaca Court of the Sector.
    In addition, it deals with objection lodged against sentences pronounced in the absence of the parties.'

Article 10: Competence of the Gacaca Court based on the territory

Article 44 of Organic Law N° 16/2004 of 19/6/2004 establishing the organisation, competence and functioning of Gacaca Courts charged with prosecuting and trying the perpetrators of the crime of genocide and other crimes against humanity, committed between October 1, 1990 and December 31, 1994 is hereby modified and complemented as follows:

'The Gacaca Court of the area where an offence was committed is the one that is competent to hear it.
    Persons who committed offences in different places are tried before competent Courts in accordance with provisions stated in the first paragraph of this article.
    However, if the author of the crime cannot be prosecuted by the Gacaca court of where the crime was committed or when it was committed beyond the borders of Rwanda, the Gacaca Court of the area of his/her residence or domicile may prosecute him/her.'

Article 11: Categories of the accused

Article 51 of Organic Law N° 16/2004 of 19/6/2004 establishing the organisation, competence and functioning of Gacaca Courts charged with prosecuting and trying the perpetrators of the crime of genocide and other crimes against humanity, committed between October 1, 1990 and December 31, 1994 is hereby modified and complemented as follows:

'Following acts of participation in offences referred to in Article 1 of Organic Law N° 16/2004 of 19/6/2004 establishing the organisation, competence and functioning of Gacaca Courts charged with prosecuting and trying the perpetrators of the crime of genocide and other crimes against humanity, committed between October 1, 1990 and December 31, 1994, the accused may be classified in one of the following categories:

First Category:

1. The person whose criminal acts or criminal participation place among planners, organisers, incitators, supervisors and ringleaders of the crime of genocide or crimes against humanity, together with his or her accomplices;

1° the person who, at that time, was in the organs of leadership, at national, prefecture, sub-prefecture and commune levels, leaders of political parties, members of the high command of the army and gendarmerie, of communal police, leaders of religious denominations, or illegal militia groups and who committed those offences or encouraged other people to commit them, together with his or her accomplices;

2° the person who committed acts of rape or sexual torture, together with his or her accomplices;

The Prosecutor General of the Republic shall publish, at least twice a year, the list of persons classified in the first category, forwarded to him or her by Gacaca Courts of the Cell.

Second Category:

1° the well-known murderer who distinguished himself or herself in the area where he or she lived or wherever he or she passed, because of the zeal which characterized him or her in the killings or excessive wickedness with which they were carried out, together with his or her accomplices;

2° the person who committed acts of torture against others, even though they did not result into death, together with his or her accomplices;

3° the person who committed dehumanising acts on the dead body, together with his or her accomplices;

4° the person whose criminal acts or criminal participation place among the killers or authors of serious attacks against others, causing death, together with his or her accomplices;

5° the person who injured or committed other acts of serious attacks, with intention to kill them, but who did not attain his or her objective, together with his or her accomplices;

6° the person who committed or participated in criminal acts against persons, without any intention of killing them, together with his or her accomplices.

Third Category:

The person who only committed offences against property. However, if the author of the offence and the victim have agreed on an amicable settlement on their own initiative, or before the public authority or witnesses, before this organic law came into force, he or she cannot be prosecuted.'

Article 12: Confessions, guilty plea, repentance and apologies

Article 58 of Organic Law N° 16/2004 of 19/6/2004 establishing the organisation, competence and functioning of Gacaca Courts charged with prosecuting and trying the perpetrators of the crime of genocide and other crimes against humanity, committed between October 1, 1990 and December 31, 1994 is hereby modified and complemented as follows:

> 'The confessions, guilt plea, repentance and apologies are done before the Bench of the Gacaca Court, before the Judicial Police Officer or the Public Prosecution Officer in charge of investigating the case, in accordance with article 46 of Organic Law N°16/2004 of 19/6/2004 establishing the organisation, competence and functioning of Gacaca courts charged with prosecuting and trying the perpetrators of the crime of genocide and other crimes against humanity, committed between October 1, 1990 and December 31, 1994.
>
> The Bench of the Gacaca Court, the Judicial Police Officer or the Public Prosecution Officer in charge of investigating the case, must inform the defendant of his or her right and benefits from the confessions, guilt plea, repentance and apologies procedure.
>
> However, the person who opts for the guilt plea procedure before the Gacaca Court of Appeal cannot have his or her sentence reduced because it is too late.'

Article 13: Penalties to defendants falling within the first category

Article 72 of Organic Law N° 16/2004 of 19/6/2004 establishing the organisation, competence and functioning of Gacaca Courts charged with prosecuting and trying the perpetrators of the crime of genocide and other crimes against humanity, committed between October 1, 1990 and December 31, 1994 is hereby modified and complemented as follows:

> 'Defendants falling within the first category who:
>
> 1° refused to confess, plead guilty, repent and apologise, or whose confessions, guilt plea, repentance and apologies have been rejected, incur a death sentence or life imprisonment;
>
> 2° confessed, pleaded guilty, repented and apologised after being included on the list of the accused incur a prison sentence ranging from twenty five (25) to thirty (30) years;
>
> 3° confessed, pleaded guilty, repented and apologised before being included on the list of the accused incur a prison sentence ranging from twenty (20) to twenty-four (24) years.'

Article 14: Penalties to defendants falling within the second category

Article 73 of Organic Law N° 16/2004 of 19/6/2004 establishing the organisation, competence and functioning of Gacaca Courts charged with prosecuting and trying the perpetrators of the crime of genocide and other crimes against humanity, committed between October 1, 1990 and December 31, 1994 is hereby modified and complemented as follows:

'Defendants falling within the second category referred to in the first, second and third paragraph of Article 11 of this organic law, who:

1° refused to confess, plead guilty, repent and apologise, or whose confessions, guilt plea, repentance and apologies have been rejected, incur a prison sentence of thirty (30) years or life imprisonment;

2° confessed, pleaded guilty, repented and apologised after being included on the list of the accused and whose confession, guilt plea, repentance and apologises have been accepted, incur a prison sentence ranging from twenty-five (25) to twenty-nine (29) years, but:

a) they serve a third (1/3) of the sentence in custody;

b) a sixth (1/6) of the sentence is suspended;

c) half (1/2) of the sentence is commuted into community service;

3° confessed, pleaded guilty, repented and apologised before being included on the list of the accused, incur a prison sentence ranging from twenty (20) to twenty-four (24) years, but:

a) they serve a sixth (1/6) of the sentence in custody;

b) a third (1/3) of the sentence is suspended;

c) half (1/2) of the sentence is commuted into community service.

Defendants falling within the second (2nd) category referred to in the fourth (4th) and fifth (5th) paragraph of article 11 of this organic law, who:

1° refused to confess, plead guilty, repent and apologise, or whose confessions, guilt plea, repentance and apologies have been rejected, incur a prison sentence ranging from fifteen (15) to nineteen (19) years;

2° confessed, pleaded guilty, repented and apologised after being included on the list of the accused and whose confession, guilt plea, repentance andapologises have been accepted, incur a prison sentence ranging from twelve (12) to fourteen (14) years, but:

a) they serve a third (1/3) of the sentence in custody;

b) a sixth (1/6) of the sentence is suspended;

c) half (1/2) of the sentence is commuted into community service.

3° confessed, pleaded guilty, repented and apologised before being included on the list of the accused and whose confessions, guilt plea, repentance and apologises have been accepted, incur a prison sentence ranging from eight (8) to eleven (11) years, but:

a) they serve a sixth (1/6) of the sentence in custody;

b) a third (1/3) of the sentence is suspended;

c) half (1/2) of the sentence is commuted into community service;

Defendants falling within the second category referred to in the sixth (6th) paragraph, who:

1° refused to confess, plead guilty, repent andapologise, or whose confessions, guilt plea, repentance and apologies have been rejected, incur a prison sentence ranging from five (5) to seven (7) years, but:

a) they serve a third (1/3) of the sentence in custody;

b) a sixth (1/6) of the sentence is suspended;

c) half (1/2) of the sentence is commuted into community service;

2° confessed, pleaded guilty, repented and apologised after being included on the list of the accused and whose confession, guilt plea, repentance and apologises have been accepted, incur a prison sentence ranging from three (3) to four (4) years, but:

a) they serve a third (1/3) of the sentence in custody;

b) a sixth (1/6) of the sentence is suspended;

c) half of the sentence is commuted into community service;

3° confessed, pleaded guilty, repented and apologised before being included on the list of the accused and whose confessions, guilt plea, repentance and apologises have been accepted, incur a prison sentence ranging from one (1) to two (2) years, but;

a) a sixth (1/6) of the sentence in custody;

b) a (1/3) of the sentence is suspended;

c) half (1/2) of the sentence is commuted into community service.'

Article 15: Withdrawal of civic rights for persons convicted of the crime of genocide or crimes against humanity

Article 76 of Organic Law N° 16/2004 of 19/6/2004 establishing the organisation, competence and functioning of Gacaca Courts charged with prosecuting and trying the perpetrators of the crime of genocide and other crimes against humanity, committed between October 1, 1990 and December 31, 1994 is hereby modified and complemented as follows:

'Persons convicted of the crime of genocide or crimes against humanity are liable to deprivation of their civil rights in the following manner:

1° persons falling within the 1st and 2nd category are liable to deprivation of the right:

a. to be elected;

b. to become leaders, to serve in the armed forces, to serve in the National Police and other security organs, to be a teacher, a medical staff, magistrates, public prosecutors and judicial counsels;

2° persons in the first category are liable to permanent deprivation of rights prescribed in item 1° of this article;

3° persons in the second category, items 1°, 2° and 3° who refused to confess or whose confessions have been rejected, are liable to permanent deprivation of rights prescribed in item 1° of this article;

4° persons in the second category items 1°, 2° and 3° whose confessions have been accepted and those in items 4°, 5° and 6° are deprived of those rights only for the duration of the sentence given by the competent court;

5° the names of the persons falling within the first and the second category, convicted of the crime of genocide, together with a short description of their identities and the crimes they committed, shall be posted in the history section of the genocide memorials. Those names shall also be posted at the offices of their Sectors, registered in their 'criminal record' and published on the Internet.'

Article 16: Mitigating circumstances for children

Article 78 of Organic Law N° 16/2004 of 19/6/2004 establishing the organisation, competence and functioning of Gacaca Courts charged with prosecuting and trying the perpetrators of the crime of genocide and other crimes against humanity, committed between October 1, 1990 and December 31, 1994 is hereby modified and complemented as follows:

'Persons convicted of the crime of genocide or crimes against humanity who, at the time of events, were fourteen (14) years or more but less than eighteen (18) years old, are sentenced:

Defendants falling within the first category who:

1° refused to confess, plead guilty, repent and apologise, or whose confessions, guilt plea, repentance and apologies have been rejected, incur a prison sentence ranging from ten (10) to twenty (20) years;

2° confessed, pleaded guilty, repented and apologised in accordance with Article 60 of Organic Law N° 16/2004 of 19/6/2004 establishing the organisation, competence and functioning of Gacaca courts charged with prosecuting and trying the perpetrators of the crime of genocide and other crimes against humanity, committed between October 1, 1990 and December 31, 1994, after the drawing up of the list of the persons who participated in the genocide and whose confessions, guilt plea, repentance and apologises have been accepted, incur a prison sentence ranging from eight (8) to nine (9) years;

3° confessed, pleaded guilty, repented and apologised in accordance with Article 60 Organic Law N° 16/2004 of 19/6/2004 establishing the organisation, competence and functioning of Gacaca courts charged with prosecuting and trying the perpetrators of the crime of genocide and other crimes against humanity, committed between October 1, 1990 and December 31, 1994, before the drawing up of the list of the persons who participated in the genocide and whose confessions, guilt plea, repentance and apologises have been accepted, incur a prison sentence ranging from six (6) years and six (6) months to seven (7) years and six (6) months.

Defendants falling within the second category referred to in the first (1st), second (2nd) and third (3rd) paragraph of article 11 of this organic law, who:

1° refused to confess, plead guilty, repent and apologise, or whose confessions, guilt plea, repentance and apologies have been rejected, incur a prison sentence ranging from ten (10) to fifteen (15) years;

2° confessed, pleaded guilty, repented and apologised after being included on the list of the accused, incur a prison sentence ranging from six (6) years and six (6) months to seven (7) years and six (6) months, but:

a) they serve a third (1/3) of the sentence in custody;

b) a sixth (1/6) of the sentence is suspended;

c) half (1/2) of the sentence is commuted into community service;

3° confessed, pleaded guilty, repented and apologised before being included on the list of the accused, incur a prison sentence ranging from six (6) to seven (7) years, but:

a) they serve a sixth (1/6) of the sentence in custody;

b) a third (1/3) of the sentence is suspended;

c) half (1/2) of the sentence is commuted into community service.

Defendants falling within the second category referred to in the fourth (4th) and fifth (5th) paragraph of article 11 of this organic law, who:

1° refused to confess, plead guilty, repent and apologise, or whose confessions, guilt plea, repentance and apologies have been rejected, incur a prison sentence ranging from four (4) and six (6) months to five (5) years and six months;

2° confessed, pleaded guilty, repented and apologised after being included on the list of the accused, incur a prison sentence ranging from four (4) to five (5) years, but:

a) they serve a third (1/3) of the sentence in custody;

b) a sixth (1/6) of the sentence is suspended;

c) half (1/2) of the sentence is commuted into community service;

3° confessed, pleaded guilty, repented and apologised before being included on the list of the accused and whose confessions, guilt plea, repentance and apologises have been accepted, incur a prison sentence ranging from two (2) years and six (6) months to three (3) years and six (6) months, but:

a) they serve a sixth (1/6) of the sentence in custody;

b) a third (1/3) of the sentence is suspended;

c) half (1/2) of the sentence is commuted into community service.

Defendants falling within the second category referred to in the sixth (6th) paragraph of article 11 of this organic law, who:

1° refused to confess, plead guilty, repent and apologise, or whose confessions, guilt plea, repentance and apologies have been rejected, incur a prison sentence ranging from two (2) years and six (6) months to three (3) years and six (6) months but half (1/2) of the sentence is served in prison and another half commuted into community service;

2° confessed, pleaded guilty, repented and apologised after being included on the list of the accused, incur a prison sentence ranging from one (1) year and six (6) months to two (2) years and six (6) months, but:

a) they serve a third (1/3) of the sentence in custody;

b) a sixth (1/6) of the sentence is suspended;

c) half (1/2) of the sentence is commuted into community service;

3° confessed, pleaded guilty, repented and apologised before being included on the list of the accused, incur a prison sentence ranging from six (6) months to one (1) year and six (6) months, but:

a) they serve a sixth (1/6) of the sentence in custody;

b) a third (1/3) of the sentence is suspended;

c) half (1/2) of the sentence is commuted into community service.'

Article 17: Penalties in case of default by the convicted person to properly carry out community service

Article 80 of Organic Law N° 16/2004 of 19/6/2004 establishing the organisation, competence and functioning of Gacaca Courts charged with prosecuting and trying the perpetrators of the crime of genocide and other crimes against humanity, committed between October 1, 1990 and December 31, 1994 is hereby modified and complemented as follows:

'In case of default by the convicted person to properly carry out community service, the concerned person is taken back to prison to serve the remaining sentence in custody.

In that case, the Community Service Committee in the area where the convicted person is carrying out community service shall prepare an ad hoc report and submit it to the Gacaca Court of the Sector where community service is perlodged which will fill in the form to return the defaulting person to prison.

In case this is not possible, that report shall be submitted to the Gacaca Court that tried the person serving his or her community service.

A Presidential Order shall establish and determine modalities for carrying out community service.'

Article 18: Refusal of a sentence less than that provided for in the law

Article 81 of Organic Law N° 16/2004 of 19/6/2004 establishing the organisation, competence and functioning of Gacaca Courts charged with prosecuting and trying the perpetrators of the crime of genocide and other crimes against humanity, committed between October 1, 1990 and December 31, 1994 is hereby modified and complemented as follows:

'While determining penalties, the sentence less than that provided for in the law can not be applied under the pretext of mitigating circumstances. However, in case such mitigating circumstances exist, the minimal sentence provided for shall be applied.

The person convicted of the crime of genocide who commenced serving the sentence, shall not be released on bail.'

Article 19: Persons authorized to appeal in Gacaca Courts

Article 90 of Organic Law N° 16/2004 of 19/6/2004 establishing the organisation, competence and functioning of Gacaca Courts charged with prosecuting and trying the perpetrators of the crime of genocide and other crimes against humanity, committed between October 1, 1990 and December 31, 1994 is hereby modified and complemented as follows:

'The defendant, plaintiff or any other interested person may appeal against a judgment passed by a Gacaca Court, in the interest of justice.'

Article 20: Reasons for the review of the judgement

Article 93 of Organic Law N° 16/2004 of 19/6/2004 establishing the organisation, competence and functioning of Gacaca Courts charged with prosecuting and trying the perpetrators of the crime of genocide and other crimes against humanity, committed between October 1, 1990 and December 31, 1994 is hereby modified and complemented as follows:

'A judgement can be subject to review when:
  1° a person was acquitted in a judgement passed in the last resort by an ordinary court, but is thereafter found guilty by a Gacaca Court;
  2° a person was convicted in a judgement passed in the last resort by an ordinary court, but is thereafter found innocent by a Gacaca Court;
  3° a judgement was passed in the last resort by a Gacaca Court, and later on there are new evidence proving contrary to what the initial judgment of that Gacaca Court was grounded;
  4° a person was given a sentence that is contrary to legal provisions of the charges against him or her.
  Persons entitled to lodge a review of the judgement are the defendant, the plaintiff or any other person acting in the interest of justice.
  The Gacaca Court of Appeal is the only competent court to review judgements passed in the last resort.'

Article 21: Repealing of inconsistent provisions

All previous legal provisions contrary to this Organic Law are hereby repealed.

Article 22: Enforcement

This organic law shall come into force on the day of its publication in the Official Gazette of the Republic of Rwanda.
  Kigali, on 01/03/2007

The President of the Republic
KAGAME Paul
(sé)
The Prime Minister
MAKUZA Bernard
(sé)
The Minister of Justice

KARUGARAMA Tharcisse
(sé)
The Minister of Local Government, Good
Governance, Community Development
and Social Affairs
MUSONI Protais
(sé)
**Seen and sealed with the Seal of the
Republic:**
The Minister of Justice
KARUGARAMA Tharcisse
(sé)

Index

accountability, policy of maximal arrests 82–83; crimes against humanity 52; Gacaca courts 182; genocide 29, 52, 82; imprisonment 183; impunity, couture of 185–86; International Criminal Tribunal for Rwanda 126, 129; International Criminal Tribunal for the former Yugoslavia 7; mass arrests 82–83; mass participation 189; radio broadcasts 149–50; reconciliation 72, 183; restorative and retributive justice 126; rule of law 100, 123; Rwandan national judiciary 87; Rwandan Patriotic Front (RPF), soldiers of 10–11, 76, 100, 121–24, 127, 181, 186–87, 190

Akayesu, Jean Paul, trial of 115, 133–34, 138–43, 150, 165–67

Akhavan, P 121, 133, 134

amnesties 31–32, 51–52, 81, 183

anthropological considerations, Gacaca courts and 54–57

apologies 64–65, 66, 188

appeals; Gacaca courts 8, 59, 67, 92, 94; International Criminal Tribunal for Rwanda 107–8, 109; Rwandan national judiciary 92, 94

Arbour, Louise 112

arrests 82–83

Arusha Accords 1992 26–29, 147

Ayers, I 36–37

Banyarwandum people 17

Barayagwiza, Jean-Bosco, trial of 148–50

Bass, G 9–10, 39–41

Bazemore, G 69

Belgium and colonial era 20–24

Birasa, Fiacre 190

Bizimungu, Augustin 8, 51, 53, 54

Boed, R 108

Braithwaite, J 34–38, 72–73, 98–99, 187–88

Brannigan, A 167–68

burden of proof 94–95, 171

Caplan, G 159

Carroll, R 158

categorisation of crimes; confessions, plea bargaining and guilty pleas 169; Gacaca courts 57, 62–63, 66, 72–73, 169, 183, 188

Catholic Church 22, 23–24, 67

Chalk, F 3–5

Christie, N 71–72, 98

civil law 109, 110, 164–67

civil rights, loss of 66–67, 169

civil war 6–7, 25–27, 76

colonial era 20–25, 67

command responsibility 108

common law 110, 164–67

community sentences 66, 73, 183

conceptual framework 33–44; cosmopolitan law 33, 41–43; Gacaca courts 99; liberal-legalism 38–41, 74, 99–100, 127–28; responsive regulation 36–38, 72–74, 98–99, 127, 187–88; restorative and retributive justice 33–36, 68–72, 74, 98, 125–26; rule of law 33, 43–44, 74–77, 128–29

confessions, plea bargaining and guilty pleas 167–72; burden of proof 171; civil liberties, loss of 169; cultural issues 171; expediency argument 168, 171–72; family, safety of 174; Gacaca courts 2, 57, 63–66, 68–70, 72–73, 95, 168–71, 174–75, 188; information, provision of 170; International